TALL TREES, TOUGH MEN

TALL TREES, TOUGH MEN

By Robert E. Pike

W. W. NORTON & COMPANY

New York • London

First published as a Norton paperback 1984; reissued 1999
Copyright © 1967 W. W. Norton & Company, Inc.
"The Rivermen" appeared in *American Heritage*, February, 1967.

Library of Congress Cataloging-in-Publication Data

Pike, Robert Everding.
Tall trees, tough men, by Robert E. Pike. New York, W. W. Norton [1967]
288 p. map, plates (incl. ports.) 24 cm.
Bibliographical refernces included in "Foreword" (p. 11)
1. Lumbermen—New England.   I. Title.
HD8039.L92U57   331.7'63'49820974   67-11092
                                        MARC

ISBN 0-393-31917-2

W. W. Norton & Company, Inc.
500 Fifth Avenue, New York, N.Y. 10110
www.wwnorton.com

W. W. Norton & Company Ltd.
Castle House, 75/76 Wells Street, London W1T 3QT

4 5 6 7 8 9 0

To Frederick A. Noad, Esq.
In Memory of the Afternoon We Were Sluiced on Hurricane Ridge

Contents

ILLUSTRATIONS appear between pages 128 and 129.

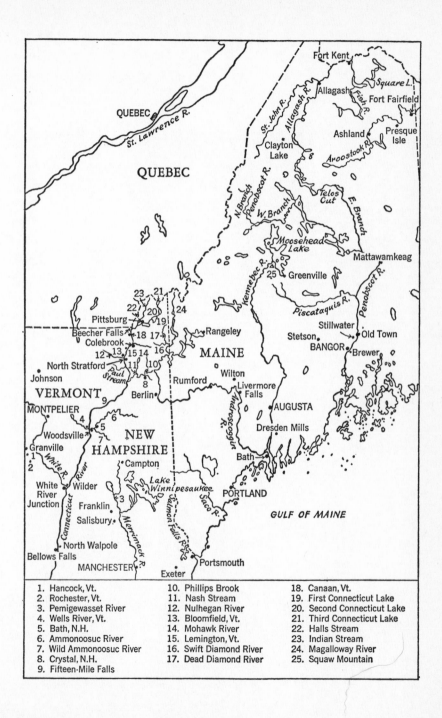

1. Hancock, Vt.	10. Phillips Brook	18. Canaan, Vt.
2. Rochester, Vt.	11. Nash Stream	19. First Connecticut Lake
3. Pemigewasset River	12. Nulhegan River	20. Second Connecticut Lake
4. Wells River, Vt.	13. Bloomfield, Vt.	21. Third Connecticut Lake
5. Bath, N.H.	14. Mohawk River	22. Halls Stream
6. Ammonoosuc River	15. Lemington, Vt.	23. Indian Stream
7. Wild Ammonoosuc River	16. Swift Diamond River	24. Magalloway River
8. Crystal, N.H.	17. Dead Diamond River	25. Squaw Mountain
9. Fifteen-Mile Falls		

Foreword

THIS BOOK has been a labor of love. To write it I have drawn freely from printed sources, oral reminiscences, and my own experience in the woods and on the river. I hope that the general reader will find the book interesting and that the expert will not find it inexact. Anyway, if it affords pleasure I shall have been amply rewarded.

It would be tedious to list all the printed sources I have utilized, though I cite most of them in the text, and all the people who have helped me in one way or another, but here are the principal ones:

Chief among the printed works are E. Francis Belcher, "Logging Railroads in the White Mountains" (a series in the magazine *Appalachia*); W. R. Brown, *Our Forest Heritage*; Perley W. Churchill, *Making and Driving Long Logs*; Philip T. Coolidge, *History of the Maine Woods*; Harold A. Davis, *An International Community on the St. Croix*; Fannie H. Eckstorm, *The Penobscot Man*; Alfred G. Hempstead, *The Penobscot Boom*; Richard G. Wood, *A History of Lumbering in Maine 1820–1861*; Austin H. Wilkins, *The Forests of Maine*, and two periodicals, *The Northern*, formerly published by the Great Northern Paper Company, and Felix Fernald's *Pittston Farm Weekly*.

Photographs, many of them extremely rare, and from many scattered sources, I give credit for as they appear in the book.

Among librarians I owe a great deal to Marjorie L. Marengo, Barbara L. Miller, Jean Stephenson, Robert Van Benthuysen, Margaret A. Whalen, Effie S. Willey, and Janet Bagonzi.

For oral reminiscences I am especially indebted to Will Andrews, Tom Cozzie, Herbert L. Cummings, Bill James, Dan Murray, Ludwig K. Moorehead, Frederick A. Noad, Harl Pike, Frank Porter, Omar Sawyer, and Ralph Sawyer, eleven men who are still very much alive on this tenth of May, 1966, although their combined ages total over a thousand years; and to dozens of good men now dead and gone whom I knew and worked with years ago: George Anderson, Will Bacon, Dan Bosse, Vern Davison, Jack Haley, Ed Hilliard, Bert Ingersoll, John Locke, Orton Newhall, 'Phonse Roby, Win Schoppe, *et al*.

And a special word for Katherine Henry Benedict.

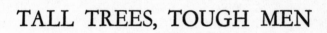

TALL TREES, TOUGH MEN

1

The Axe

A man was famous according as he had lifted up axes upon the thick trees. —PSALMS LXXIV.[5]

ONE OF the great dramas in the development of the United States is the history of lumbering. It is an epic story of courage, of great hazards and difficulties overcome, of success and failure in a struggle to provide some of the necessities of mankind. And the key to that history, to that drama, is the Axe.

Hand-hewn white pine built the houses for humans and the barns for their domestic animals, and a million hulks rotting in every port and on every sea-coast in the world today once took lumber and sea-power around the globe. It was the axe, even more than the rifle, that conquered the North American continent.

The axe is doubtless one of the oldest inventions of man. We have stone axes from the Stone Age, and bronze axes produced after metal was discovered. And axes have always been a symbol of power: in Crete, axes were worshiped; medieval knights used them as weapons; they figure on noble coats-of-arms; they beheaded kings and princes; they scalped American pioneers; and they denuded vast parts of Asia and other continents.

But is was in America that the axe reached its highest development. Nowhere else in the world was it used so much, did it undergo such change, was it adapted to so many uses. The first pioneers from England found the whole eastern seaboard covered with dark and "hideous" forests. "The rocking pines of the forest roared" to welcome the Pilgrims, and fearsome animals and fearful red men lived among those roaring pines. Untouched by an axe, those forests, especially in the Northeast, spread out for hundreds of miles, solid masses of giant trees that barely let through the sunlight. The old *coureurs-de-bois* grew sallow from lack of light.

To the early settlers, trees were a nuisance except when used for lumber. They had to cut them down in order to make farms. Indian-fashion, the white men girdled the trees in order to kill them and let in the sun. The deep mold, formed of aeons of fallen leaves and rotten tree-trunks, could be scratched with a wooden stick and produce more wheat to the acre than men in Europe had ever dreamed possible. Grass for the animals grew shoulder-high as the hardy settlers pushed ever back along the river intervals onto the hardwood ridges.

It was the axe that permitted them to do so. Every man and boy could handle one, just as today every man and boy handles the steering wheel of an automobile. And almost immediately there sprang up a special breed of man, the logger, or woodsman, or, as he was later called, the lumberjack. He reached his apogee in the late nineteenth century, and now he has almost disappeared.

Most farmers had little to do in the winter, and most of them went to work in the woods, as teamsters, axemen, log-drivers, in order to earn a little extra money. But they were primarily farmers. They handled an axe competently, but they were not experts.

The experts were men who worked in the woods all the time. The difference in their performance was as conspicuous as that of an expert in any line—they demonstrated ease and perfection and skill brought about by long, hard hours of trying to become perfect. They were Axemen, men who cherished their axe, who shaved down the handle until it sprang like whalebone, who carried an oilstone to keep the edge of their weapon always keen enough to shave with—though very few of them ever used it for that purpose. They knew exactly how to "hang" an axe—that is, to insert the handle, or helve, into the axe-head at the proper angle so it fitted the owner, and no other man. The importance of this primary mark of an axeman was magnificently demonstrated by Big Dan Murray (in 1966, ninety-five years old) of the Androscoggin, who was once accused of stealing an axe. He showed his complete disgust with the charge when he said, "Why in hell should I steal his axe? It wouldn't be hung right for me!"

The skill of these men was phenomenal, whether in cutting down trees or in making small, decorative furniture. Saws are a comparatively recent invention. Eighty years ago woodsmen went into the woods armed only with axes and built their camps and horse-hovels, their sinks and chairs, their doors and bunks, all with an axe. Such men would have been ashamed not to leave a smooth scarf on a tree, and in their hands the broad-axe squared both hardwood and softwood timbers as evenly as would a saw.

Your genuine woodsman, like all true artists, took pride in his work. This pride was expressed in the way he took care of his axe. An old-timer considered it a disgrace to have a nick in his axe. He never dropped it when he got through work, but put it where it was safe, carefully standing it in a corner, the blade often protected by a rude wooden sheath. He did *not* leave his axe sticking into a tree or a stump overnight, for he believed that to do so would bring bad luck. You could always tell a good axeman by examining his axe. If the toe, the outer corner, was well rounded, or the blade too thick, he had been striking rocks and hadn't kept the bit ground down.

Holding the handle close to the head of his axe, always kept sharp as a razor, a woodsman could shave a dozen slivers off an ordinary match. Or, grasping the head in both hands, and using short strokes, he could do as smooth a planing job as a carpenter with his plane. Indeed, holding a sharp axe by the head, one can often do more delicate work than with a knife, for the weight of the axe helps to regulate the stroke.

There were three kinds of axes used in the woods—the single-bitted, or pole-axe; the double-bitted axe; and the broad-axe.

The first two were made in various weights of from three to five pounds. Probably a three-and-a-half pound axe was favored by the majority of woodsmen.

The double-bitted axe was unknown in the New England woods before 1900. The choppers used a light pole-axe for chopping down trees and for "limbing out," that is, going along the fallen tree and slicing off the limbs, a couple of inches or so from the trunk. But if they felt like giving the sled-tender a hand and "knotting" the log, that is, smoothing off those branch-stubs close to the trunk, they did not use their precious falling axe. Oh no! They had a second one handy, another pole-axe to be sure, but heavier and with a different bevel, considered more suitable for that kind of work.

The only advantages of the pole-axe were that it could be used for driving splitting-wedges (seldom needed by a chopper) and that if you were carrying it on your shoulder in the brush you weren't so likely to gash the back of your neck.

But the double-bitted axe could be used to drive falling-wedges quite as well if not better than the pole-axe, and it had the great advantage of having two bits, or edges. You could keep one ground down for cutting purposes and keep the bevel on the other in a shape more suitable for other work, like splitting. A thicker blade split chunks apart more easily. Or a chopper could keep both edges fit for cutting, and if by mischance something happened to one, he had the other all ready for business.

All three kinds of axe had an "eye" right through the middle, into which was inserted the handle, or helve; into the end of this, to spread it and make it immovable, a small wedge was commonly driven.

The broad-axe might weigh as much as thirteen pounds, some even more, though most of them less. Its blade, or cutting edge, was much wider than that of a pole-axe. It was used for hewing and squaring, and in order to keep the axeman from barking his knuckles on the logs its handle was curved so that it was "set off" from the axe about four inches. The curve, made by steaming the wood and bending it when the handle was made, was toward the upper end of the helve, which was about two feet long, considerably shorter than that of the other two axes. It is interesting to note that a left-handed axeman could take that curved handle out of the eye and turn it around to suit his peculiarity.

An expert could take a broad-axe, and standing beside a log that had previously been scored to loosen the wood for the broad-axe (by sinking the blade of an ordinary axe into the side of the log, at an angle), he would start his swing from behind his head and hew out squared beams on which only the faintest axe marks showed that they had not been sawed.

It is true that some broad-axe men stood on top of the log, swinging an axe provided with a straight, long handle, like an ordinary axe, but unless you were used to such a tool you would invariably cut your feet and shins if you tried it.

The first step, of course, was to get the log up at the right height above the ground, on skids or blocks as easy to stand and work on as were available. Small stuff, for dam gates and the like, was yarded out and hewed on the yard. Much of the gate-timber consisted of pieces 2, 4, or 6 inches by 6, 8, or 10 inches.

In the early days of lumbering in this country, when much "ton" timber was cut and square-hewn in the woods (or even squared after it reached tidewater), a cutting crew consisted of three men—a liner, a scorer, and a hewer. The liner would remove a strip or bark from each side of the log and draw his line along it by pressing a chalked string against it. As chalk was scarce in the woods, a charred stick was generally used. If there was a slight crook in the log, the men sprang the line (stretching the string taut and not making a mark where the crook was), using their best judgment as to the way to minimize the crook when the log was squared.

The next step was for a damn good axeman to score the timber ahead of the broad-axe. The scorer always stood *on* the log, and he faced it from the direction opposite to that of the broad-axe man. It took a good axeman to do proper scoring, for he had to cut very, very close to what would eventually be the finished face of the log without going too deep, especially if he was scoring for a first-class hewer who, if a man scored too deeply, would tell the boss to fire him, else he'd be spoiling every log they had.

Big logs had to be scored down half-way and then rolled over so that what had been the lower half could be scored. The scorer had to cut deep enough to suit the hewer, and at the same time keep the face of the stick (the already scored side that the broad-axe man was hewing) perpendicular to the ground. The scorer not only scored, but also split off the chips or slabs.

Then came the broad-axe man, often a true artist, who "hewed to the line." A plummet gave the broad-axe man his true face. It is said that an expert axeman would plumb by spitting and watching the fall of his spittle. A broad-axe man who was good and mad could keep six scorers sweating. This was done by Mike Bouffard from Chartierville, Quebec, when the dam at Depot Camp on Indian Stream in Pittsburg, New Hampshire, was raised in 1900. Old men talk of it to this day. Harry Foster, a noted broad-axe man from Nova Scotia who worked for the Brown Company, could take a broad-axe and hew a board 12 feet long by 1 inch by 8 inches. Men say that he could hew with the chalk-line (that is, the string) still in place on a twenty-foot log and never be an eighth of an inch off the line and never cut the string. It is true that any fair axe-man could do a passable job with a broad-axe, but only an expert with that tool, like old Harry, could hew straight down a cross-grained log. Here again the grace, the precision, the ease of the expert was wonderful to watch.

When the broad-axe man had done the first two sides, the log was canted over. ("Cant" is a nautical term meaning a sudden thrust resulting in a change of direction, and doubtless was brought into the woods by Yankees who had worked in shipyards. In the mill, a cant was a log whose four sides had been sawed off.) Then the other two sides were squared up. Three men could square about six pieces a day, or one raft a season.

Unless you need game for the larder, a light axe is a much more useful companion than a rifle to take along on a day's tramp in the woods. With it you can cut firewood, hang blazes on tree-trunks, drop a bridge over a brook too deep to wade, cut a path through dense brush, and if need be, scare wild animals.

The major improvements in the axe were made in America. Even today, in European countries the woodsmen still use straight-handled axes with no give or spring to them, that drive a shock clear through your shoulder every time you strike. At first, that same old style was used in the United States, but when logging became a big business, a hundred and fifty years ago, the demand for better tools resulted in changes.

The single-bitted axe, or pole-axe, was for a long time the most popular in the Northeast, but the straight handle made it awkward to use. So someone invented the curved helve—almost inevitable in those days, when every man hung his own axe—and it quickly became universal. Its popularity was largely due to the use of good American hickory, a tough and elastic wood that permitted a more slender helve. Your true axeman puts most of his force at the end of his stroke, with almost no shock to his arms and shoulders. The first machine-made axe-handles appeared in 1853, but they were sold separately from the axe. No woodsman would ever have bought a factory-hung tool.

In different areas, different styles in axe-handles were favored. In the Northeast, helves from 28 to 32 inches were the most common, while out West they ranged from 36 to 41 inches. Probably the greater size of western timber accounted for this difference. In the southern states, where bare hands were used, a thicker handle was preferred to the slender helve prevalent in the North, where mittens were worn.

A grindstone, by the way, was used not to sharpen an axe, but to grind down the area behind the bit, to make it thin. Sharpening was done with an oilstone. Before about 1897, cross-cut saws were not used to cut down trees in the lumbering woods of New England. The head-chopper and the second chopper in a cutting crew did it all with axes. They used to keep one blade of their double-bitted axe for chopping, and the other for limbing out and for cutting off knots.

Such was the lumberjack in his prime, and such was his axe.

The following pages will deal with his picturesque calling in all its peculiar manifestations.

2

The Terrain and the Trees

TWENTY-FIVE thousand years ago, New England was covered by a glacier, a layer of ice ten thousand feet thick, that took its own good time—for after all, time means nothing to a glacier—in sliding southeastward into the Atlantic Ocean.

In New Hampshire, the "Granite State," the White Mountains stubbornly opposed the eroding force of the receding ice, and their great rocky summits still rise majestically above the rest of the scenery. The glacier, foiled at such points, took its revenge by squirming down into every possible spot that was softer, carving out the countless ravines and valleys that cut up the region and that indicate the meandering course of the glacier in its aeon-long journey toward the sea.

In Vermont the same conditions existed, save that the mountains were worn down to a greater extent. Eastward, in Maine, the granite upthrust continues in the northern part of the state. Many people do not realize that Maine has some very respectable mountains, Katahdin, the highest, being well over five-thousand feet tall, with a granite face that has won the respect of many a mountain-climber.

Massachusetts has its Berkshires, and even in northern Connecticut one finds some pretty good hills, but of course as one approaches the sea the landscape flattens out everywhere, even though, especially in Maine, a stretch of old granite is responsible for the beautiful "rocky" coast.

In southern New Hampshire and southeastern Maine the glacier left large areas of sand and gravel, extremely favorable for the growth of immense stands of great pine trees, while wherever in New England the basic rock was Silurian shale, softer than granite, the lofty mountains became rolling hills, often interspersed with swamps in hollow places where the glacier had blocked the drainage. This shale deteriorated into clay, common all over the region, but especially so in Maine. And, lastly, there are large areas in New England covered with glacial till—stony, ledgy, thin-soil areas ill adapted to farming.

Every bit of this great territory, save for the highest mountain peaks and an occasional old beaver-meadow, was covered with trees. The first explorers were unanimous in praising the quantity and quality and variety of timber, so abounding in strange beasts, birds, and ferocious insects.

James Rosier, writing in 1605 in his *Relation of Waymouths' Voyage to the Coast of Maine* tells of what he found along the coast of Maine:

... wood of sundry sorts, some very great and tall, as birch, ash, maple, spruce, cherry tree, yew, oak very great and good, fir tree, out of which issueth turpentine in so marvelous plenty, and so sweet. ...

We might call James the first timber-cruiser, for he goes on:

A brief note of what profits we saw the country yield in the small time of our stay there:

Trees. Oak of an excellent grain, straight and great timber: elm, beech; birch, very tall and great, of whose bark they make their canoes. Witchhazel, alder, cherry-tree, ash, maple, yew, spruce, aspen, fir, many fruit trees which we knew not.

Fowls, eagles, hernshaws, cranes, mews, turtle doves , ducks great, geese, swans, penguins, crows, shrikes, ravens; many birds of sundry colors; many other fowls in flocks unknown.

Beasts. Reindeer, stags, fallow-deer, bears, wolves, beaver, otter, hare, cony, hedge-hogs polecats wild great-cats, dogs some like wolves, some like spaniels.

Most famous and most useful of all these very great and tall trees was the white pine (*Pinus strobus*), which James refers to as "fir." The white pine has faded from New England as a commercial lumber tree, but it will endure for eternity in history and in men's imagination and memory.

Amply attesting its usefulness and fame is an entry in the diary of Samuel Pepys, then an under-secretary of the British Admiralty, for December 3, 1666. He had had a bad day at the office, "with everybody prophesying destruction to the nation," but he closed with this comforting item: "There is also the very good news come of four New England ships come home safe to Falmouth with masts for the King; which is a blessing mighty unexpected, and without which, if for nothing else, we must have failed next year. But God be praised for this good fortune, and send us a continuance of his favor in other things."

As for the solid place of the pine tree in American history, heraldry, and legend, we have only to remember that it adorns the seal and flag of the state of Maine, which is known as the "Pine Tree State." But not only in Maine was the pine tree famous. A hundred years before Maine became a state the colony of Massachusetts Bay established a mint and turned out the "pine-tree shilling," so called because a pine tree decorated one face of the coin. At the Battle of Bunker Hill the Americans fought under a flag that showed a pine tree in one corner. The earliest American navy, Washington's six cruisers, flew a flag that bore a green pine tree on a field of white. One of these ships, the *Lady Washington*, was captured by the British in 1775, and the pine-tree flag can be seen today in the Admiralty office in London. The next year Massachusetts had its own navy, the ensign of which was the pine-tree flag with the words "An appeal to God" over the pine, while beneath it was a coiled rattlesnake and the legend "Don't tread on me."

"White" pine was not the only kind that adorned the New England landscape. There were several others, each distinguished by its leaf clusters and its bark, and when sawed into boards, by the appearance and quality of its lumber.

The old white pine that grew so luxuriantly on the sandy plains and uplands of southern New England was called "punkin" because its wood was so soft and its grain so fine that it could be cut easily in any direction, like a pumpkin. Also, the boards were of a light golden color, again like a pumpkin. As it could be carved without difficulty, it was in great demand for making ship figureheads, as well as the carved mantels and doorways of those beautiful examples of Colonial architecture found in cities and towns along the sea-coast.

These tremendous trees grew to a height of over two hundred feet, and (says the *History of the Town of Dumbarton, N.H.*, 1860, by Caleb Stark, Jr.) were sometimes ten feet in diameter. They might reach the age of a thousand years or more and still look strong and sturdy, although not infrequently, when cut down, they could not be used because of a "hollow heart"; that is, they were rotten inside, a condition probably caused by the freezing of water between the annual rings. Occasionally they were so big that after they were felled and cut into logs the nearest stream did not have enough water to float them and they had to be left to rot.

Relentlessly hunted out and cut down by the lumbermen (indeed, my own great-grandfather cut down pine over three feet through and with oxen hauled the logs into piles and burned them, simply to clear the land, along the Fifteen-Mile Falls of the upper Connecticut), the old-growth punkin pine was already becoming scarce as early as 1860. A magnificent stand on the Connecticut River at Concord, Vermont, probably the last virgin pine in that state, was cut down in 1920, and a portable mill sawed it up. When I was a young fellow I used to wander through that grove of cathedral pine, many of which were from three to four feet in diameter, and to this day I remember the deep silence, broken only by a screeching bluejay, and always, in the tree-tops, a soft rustling, serious and solemn, a mysterious rhythm, like the breath of an eternal ruling power, and the hot, pungent odor rising from the thick brown layers of needles. And to this day I wonder that men could cut down such trees.

The Society for the Preservation of New Hampshire Forests used to have, perhaps still does, a grove of monstrous old-growth white pine in

Sutton, New Hampshire. The giants were even equipped with lightning-rods, to deflect thunderbolts. There is another considerable grove at Durham, New Hampshire, owned by the state university. One of the pines there, with a diameter of four feet, is quite a tree, but it does not approach the seven foot eight inch giant cut at Dunstable, Massachusetts, in 1736.

The last white-pine operation of any size in New England ended a couple of years ago at Pleasant Lake in Piscataquis County, Maine, where a great many trees three feet through were cut. There are still a good number of old-growth white pine on the north shore of Chesuncook Lake, in Maine, although they have been considerably thinned out in late years by the Atkinson-Davis firm of Claremont, New Hampshire, which specializes in making fine pine furniture, for this old punkin pine possesses a fine natural color and texture. Such old monsters require a special logging technique.

White-pine lumber was used for building structures of all sorts, including ships. Two hundred ships a year were launched on the Piscataqua River above Portsmouth, New Hampshire, and the small town of New-buryport, Massachusetts, once had seventy-two ships on the stocks at one time. In Colonial days white pine was especially valued for navy masts, a fascinating subject to which part of a later chapter is devoted.

Besides the white-pine blister rust—which must have currant or gooseberry bushes as an intermediate host before it attacks the pine, so that the remedy is to hunt out and destroy currant and gooseberry bushes—the greatest enemy of the white pine is the large wood-ant. These critters attack the tree either in its base or at some place in its branches where a case-knot, which is caused by the decay of some small branch, occurs. Wherever there is a crack or a crevice in the tree, the ants will work their way in. There are generally rift-shakes running through the heart of the very best punkin pines. These are the ants' great opportunity, and they avail themselves of it. They seldom attack any tree other than the punkin pine and the fir.

At certain seasons of the year the wood-ants, or probably only the males, are winged; these wings they lose, and old woodsmen say they have seen the ants carrying their wings in their mouths. The ants remain all winter in hollow or rotten places in the tree, in a torpid state. When the trees are being felled in the winter it often happens that bunches of these frozen ants fall out of the holes. The woodsman would gather such frozen ants in his hand and eat them. They taste much like cranberries.

My old friend Phil Coolidge asserts that another pest, the Black Hills beetle, so called, caused a poetical forester to compose a rhymed alphabet, one stanza of which goes:

> *B is the Black Hills beetle,*
> *Which lives in the bark of the pine,*
> *He lives on pitch, the son of a bitch,*
> *And is harder to kill than a lion.*

Inferior to *Pinus strobus* as lumber is the Norway pine, heavier than its white cousin, while its boards are of a pale red color. The only other valuable variety of New England pine is the "pitch" pine, which grows up to sixty feet high and the lumber of which, though resinous, can be used for box boards.

Next to pine in usefulness, in New England, is the spruce. It, too, comes in three principal varieties: red, white, and black. Very frequently mentioned in conversation are "cat," "skunk," "bull," "cow," and "pasture" spruce, but they are all names designating white spruce. All the varieties of spruce are used for pulp, but the red species, with its light, soft, close-grained wood, is also valuable for boards. Formerly it was much used in building airplanes.

The black spruce grows mostly in bogs, and in Colonial times it was much prized as the source of "spruce beer." The young twigs were boiled, and the resultant liquid, sweetened with molasses, "makes one of the most pleasant wholesome beverages which Nature affords," wrote New Hampshire's great historian Jeremy Belknap in 1792. In Quebec to this day black spruce is still called *épinette à la bière* ("beer spruce").

Sergeant (later General) William Chamberlin relates that at Crown Point, on Lake Champlain, after our terrible retreat from the abortive invasion of Canada in 1775 and 1776, when soldiers were dying of smallpox by the score, he, with true Yankee acumen, began the brewing of spruce beer, of which he sold all he could make at three dollars a barrel. His example was soon followed by others, and there is no doubt that the beer did much to restore the emaciated soldiers.*

Spruce is now the best source of paper, but the manufacture of paper from wood fiber was unknown a hundred years ago. That it was still considered a novelty in 1883 is shown by a curious news item in the Colebrook (New Hampshire), *Sentinel* on August 10 of that year which relates that

a stick of timber was placed against the barn of A. W. Drew in front of the doors for the purpose of driving into the barn with greater ease. At the time of the great hail storm on South Hill a week ago last Sunday, and the hail beating against the boards of the barn, fell down and covered it up to a considerable depth. After the hail had melted away, this stick of timber was found to be covered with a substance resembling paper pulp, which was peeled off in sheets

* See *Proceedings of the Massachusetts Historical Society*, 1896, X, 491 ff.

resembling coarse brown paper a foot or more square. It was full as tough as
ordinary brown paper and tore like it. It was of very even thickness and
formed by the hail beating the substance off of the sound spruce boards on the
side of the barn, and collected and beat together on the stick of timber. This
was a new process of paper making but as it was upon the whole rather expensive and the machinery of uncertain duration, we understand that Mr. Drew
does not expect to apply for a patent.

The spruce is essentially a North Country tree, and grows at high
altitudes. Red spruce may be three feet or more in diameter breast-high,
and grow over a hundred feet tall. In 1957 a ninety-foot white spruce was
cut near Island Pond, Vermont, and brought to Rockefeller Center in
New York City, where it served as a Christmas tree. Such a tree would
make a cord and a half of pulpwood.

In the days of white-pine supremacy, before 1850, eccentric lumbermen in Maine who started to cut spruce were regarded as little better
than crazy. As early as the 1830's however, a lot of spruce was cut in Victory, Vermont, and floated down to mills on the Connecticut. Spruce was
first cut on the Penobscot in 1845, and on the Kennebec five years later.
But the Maine pine was rapidly becoming exhausted, and by 1880 four-
fifths of the annual cut on the Kennebec was spruce.

Billions of board feet of spruce and more than a billion cords of
pulpwood have floated down the Androscoggin since 1860. But the last
long-log drive on the Androscoggin was in 1930, and 1964 saw the last of
the river-driven four-foot wood.

Years ago, every spring would see the river choked with long logs
for sixteen miles above Berlin, New Hampshire, where the Brown Company had its big sawmill and later its paper mills. After saw-logs vanished
from the Androscoggin a "holding ground" was established in the logans
above Pontook dam in Dummer, New Hampshire. From there fifteen to
twenty thousand cords of pulpwood would be sluiced through at a time,
to be caught in booms in Dummer and Milan, where the passing tourist
was bemused by the sight of a solid river of wood extending as far as he
could see.

Because it brings more money as four-foot pulpwood, not much
spruce is made into boards in New England these days, but millions of
cords of pulp are cut every year in Vermont, New Hampshire, and
Maine. In 1964 over two million cords were cut in Maine alone.

A once very important by-product of spruce that seems odd today
was spruce gum. Picking gum provided a living for hundreds of professional pickers, and for ten times as many part-timers. Hundreds of tons
were gathered every year. It is doubtful that one hundred pounds was
produced in 1965 in the whole of New England.

A good sound spruce tree will not yield gum. It is only through a wound that the resin, which in time forms into gum, exudes. These wounds are made by woodpeckers, squirrels, porcupines, frost cracks, snowbreak, windfalls, and especially by lightning and by logging operations that tear off or break branches on the trees left standing. Back around 1907 a spruce beetle of some kind made a great many holes in spruce trees in Essex County, Vermont, that exuded a superior gum. Experiments have been tried to force the resin to exude by cutting the tree with an axe, or by punching it with some small instrument, but they have never paid high dividends.

Spruce gum may occur anywhere on a tree, from the roots to the topmost branch. In the old days, gum was collected in abundance from the mature, old-growth spruce. Some of the nodules were as big as hens' eggs. But there isn't any more old-growth, and the gum collected today from younger, smaller trees is decidedly inferior in quality.

Harry Davis, of Monson, Maine, ninety-one years old in 1965, was long known as the "Spruce-Gum King." He was the largest resident refiner of spruce gum in the state and used twelve tons of the rough gum per year for forty years. But wages got so high and the market slowed down so that he closed his factory in 1948. When he was in business not only did he have pickers all over Maine, but he used quantities of gum sent from Nova Scotia.

As the spruce gum was gathered, the clear tit gum was separated out by the picker, for that was worth about five dollars per pound; you could buy it in all the drugstores in New England. This clear tit gum was all ready for chewing just as it came from the tree, but the rest, about 97 per cent of the whole, was put through a refining process and sold in penny sticks. Mr. Davis shipped gum as far as California and Texas. The rough gum, he tells me, was worth about twenty-five cents a pound to the picker. He says that even today a few stores in Maine carry a package of so-called spruce gum (at fifteen cents per package) but he doubts that there is much, if any, real spruce in it. He opines that not over two-hundred pounds of this mixture is sold in a year all over Maine.

The numerous old two-legged woodchucks that one used to meet between September and June out in the woods, armed with a hatchet, a tin pan, perhaps a long pole having a knife-like hook on one end, and a sack to lug the gum home in, have vanished. One such well-known character of my acquaintance was old George Willard, in Guildhall, Vermont. George used to collect spruce gum by the barrelful. Around 1885, the pure tit gum was worth a dollar a pound. Today it would be worth ten, if you could find any. Enthusiastic youngsters and other amateurs, lured by the rumor of many dollars a pound for spruce gum, have never been able to understand that gum is of many different qualities, and that the highest price is paid only for the best—which has always been comparatively rare and is now harder to find than ever. For there is no more old-growth spruce in Vermont, while the last stand of any size in New Hampshire, on the east side of Second Connecticut Lake, was cut in 1957. The St. Regis Paper Company, which owns the region, did leave a strip to rejoice nature-lovers and antiquarians. And there are still a few lots of virgin spruce far up on the Penobscot and Kennebec waters, and back of Lincoln, New Hampshire, which are too remote to log profitably.

Willard would take the gum home and steam it to remove all the bark, bits of dirt, and other impurities. It is a curious fact that spruce gum that has been steamed won't get hard when chewed. After he had steamed it, he would strain it through spruce boughs and it would come out clear as crystal. Much of it he used to make up into sticks about the size of his little finger; these he sold to a dealer in Portland for sixty cents a hundred. The dealer sold them for a penny apiece.

Spruce gum had other interesting commercial uses. A salve made from it was commonly employed sixty years ago to cure piles. It was also used in medicines such as cough syrup.

The Woodsville (New Hampshire) *News* of April 26, 1907, notes that "Joseph Boutin is building a spruce oil distillery on Stowe Hill, in Benton, where he is expecting to do a good business." Spruce oil is simply an extract of the resin from the needles. Its manufacture has been attempted quite recently down in Maine, but there isn't much demand for the product.

The spruce tree has suffered much over the years from the ravages of insects and epidemics. Notable inroads were made in 1916–17 by the spruce bud-worm, which killed perhaps half of the spruce and fir in New England. The dying went on for two or three years and then the epidemic, like most epidemics, passed. In 1938 the spruce saw-fly appeared, and away back in 1882 serious destruction was caused by the spruce bark beetle, a close relative of the son of a bitch who lives on pitch.

Besides pine and spruce, a notable softwood is hemlock. Although a handsome tree, attaining a height of up to a hundred feet and a diameter of from three to four feet, it is not a good lumber tree, being cross-grained and "shaky," i.e., marred by "shakes," or cracks caused by frosts. It sinks easily, like hardwood, and therefore could not be driven down the river to market, but it is used today for pulp, and for more than two hundred years it was the almost exclusive source of "tan-bark," necessary for tanning leather.

Unlike spruce, hemlock does not readily reproduce itself, and tanneries were generally built in the neighborhood of a big hemlock stand in order to avoid the cost of transporting bark. Tanneries were very common in all the New England states; in Maine alone there were 120 of them in 1880, but by 1935 they had dwindled to 3, all of which tanned only sheepskin, and the last of these closed in 1955. Depletion of the hemlock was a principal cause of their going out of business; another, of course, was the invention of chemically manufactured tanning agents that replaced hemlock bark.

All over New England—and in other states—the great tree-trunks were disdainfully left to rot after the bark had been stripped from them. Not until long after 1900 was hemlock used for pulp and, occasionally, for boards. The procurement of hemlock bark was different from any other kind of logging. A crew consisted of one chopper, one knotter, one ringer and splitter, and one spudder; there were also a swamper, who built roads, a teamster, whose horses hauled the bark, and a jumper tender, who helped load. "Barking" season was considered to last from the full moon in May till the full moon in August, at which time the sap ceases to flow and the bark consequently sticks to the tree. Midges, black flies, mosquitoes, and a couple of kinds of big flies made life miserable until mid-July. The only palliative was to mix lard with tar and slap it onto your face, but the no-see-ums would crawl up your nose, into your eyes and ears, down your neck, up your pants-legs. Decidedly, hemlock-bark cutting was no picnic.

The ringer cut the first ring at the base of the tree, and that ring of bark was taken off before the tree was felled; otherwise cutting at the stump would have spoiled that piece of bark. The chopper then would fall the tree and the knotter would trim off the branches. Ringing and splitting was done by one man, who cut a ring around the now fallen tree and split it along the top of the log. Then came the spudder, who removed the bark. A spud resembles a carpenter's chisel, though the neck between the socket and the blade is much longer than that of a chisel and the blade much shorter and not so thick. The blade is two and one-half inches wide, rounded somewhat on the edge and ground thin, and curved a little downward so as to follow the convex surface of the log when it is forced under the bark. Into the socket is fitted a wooden handle some two feet in length.

The bark was piled, inner side up, beside the stump, and was hauled on a sled called a "jumper" in loads of one-quarter to three-quarters of a cord, to a parallel road cut into the timber. Then it was loaded onto "two-sled" rigs, with an adjustable binding-pole on each side, about two cords to a load.

Besides serving as a source for tan-bark, the hemlock has had some other interesting uses. Since its topmost twig, if uninjured, invariably tips to the east, it is a helpful guide to men in the woods.

Hemlock wood makes a hot, crackling fire, and there exists a story, probably based on fact, that a dying woodsman expressed as his last wish, that his comrades bury him in a hemlock coffin so he'd go through hell acrackin'.

Another very extensive use of hemlock in New England in the middle of the nineteenth century was as planks to cover toll-roads (turnpikes). In 1849 the Vermont legislature passed an act incorporating the Lamoille County Plank Road Company for the purpose of building a plank road from Waterbury to Hyde Park. By 1851 a plank road using hemlock three inches thick had been built on timber foundations from Waterbury to Stowe. About two million board feet of lumber was used on that one stretch of road.

The tamarack, often called larch, hackmatack, or even, incorrectly, juniper, is unique among the conifers in that it is the only one that sheds its leaves, turning a golden-brown in the fall and making a beautiful addition to the scenery. Its light-green leaves, nearly an inch long, which grow in triangular clusters of ten, reappear early in the spring. A handsome old specimen on the lawn of Charles Adams at Waterford, Vermont, blew over in the Great Hurricane of 1938, which laid low a billion and a half board feet of trees in New England. It measured fifty-eight inches across the stump.

The tamarack is a swamp-loving tree, found all over New England, but never in large stands. It was formerly much sought after by boat-builders, who used the curved pieces cut from stumps and roots for ships' knees. The knees consisted of that portion of the tree which forms the angle between the trunk and the root, and were turned upside down to be used. Often these tamarack knees had to be dug out of the ground. Even today a few knees are still cut from time to time. In the winter of 1849–50, one Kelley cut 252 eight-inch, 63 seven-inch, and 63 six-inch knees.

Tamarack makes one hell of a hot fire, in a stove or anywhere else. Many a backwoods farmer learned this the hard way. He'd fire up his cooking stove in the morning with some dry tamarack and come back from his early chores expecting to have some nice pancakes for breakfast, but to his sorrow he would find his stove had warped itself into a permanent hump on which a frying pan could not stand.

And tamarack will never rot. I have seen more than one old driving dam built more than sixty years earlier, now worn down to just a rotten hair-line beneath the water, with the old tamarack pins still there, silent, sturdy, tough, just as on the day they were made. Tamarack is of such texture and grain that if kept wet it will never check. For that reason, before the day of cast-iron pumps, wooden ones were made of tamarack. It was also used for pump-logs, and I have read somewhere that in the state of Maine there is a whole village where even the water mains are of tamarack.

Common in the swamps of northern New England is the white

cedar, frequently the material for fenceposts, and formerly for railroad ties and paving-blocks. And always it is used for shingles. In Maine, cedar shingles once served as legal tender, with grocers and traders maintaining a shingle yard instead of a cash register. The shingles were tied in bundles, often with white-birch withes in lieu of spun yarn. The shingle maker first sawed his log, whether cedar or pine, into blocks, which he then "rived" (split into thin pieces) with a special tool called a froe. Then the shingle was placed in a vise and "shaved" (tapered) with a draw-knife. Then the shingles were bunched by an instrument known as a shingle mold, a standard-size frame duly tested by the authorities in which could be placed a quarter of a thousand shingles.

They used to say that an experienced shingle weaver, as the shingle workers were called, could keep one shingle in the air all the time. This professional boast must have been at least approximated back in 1856, when the Hallowell (Maine) *Gazette* on April 25 noted that two young men of Durham had sawed, shaved, and bunched 11,250 shingles in one day, "a little the smartest day's work, in the shingle line on record."

Last among the softwoods, is the balsam fir, tall as spruce, but not so big—it grows to a hundred feet in height but seldom as wide as two feet in diameter—which is slaughtered by the million every year for Christmas trees. It is a faster-growing tree than the spruce, but it is not a good lumber tree, being subject to early decay—one often finds fir trees in the woods broken off several feet above the ground. However, it is easily cut and handled, and makes good pulpwood. Also, its tips, stuffed into a casing, make a fragrant pillow. Formerly, when there was a demand for it, fir was much used to make packing boxes.

Harry Davis, Maine's spruce-gum king, did a big business during World War II collecting the fluid from balsam-fir blisters. This form of liquid pitch is worth fifty dollars a gallon today. It is formed under the outer bark of the fir in small blisters and the only way to gather it is to take a small, thin metal can, go to the tree, punch the blister, and press its contents out into the can. Each blister contains only a few drops. The pitch must not become warmer than 70 degrees, nor touch water in any form, and it is not found in any other tree.

Throughout the war, Harry gathered it for the War Department. It was used to fuse two pieces of glass, such as microscope slides, sights for big guns, and double-vision glasses, for it was the most transparent substance known at that time. He hired girls and took them out into the forest, where each one gathered about a pint in three hours.

New England has many kinds of hardwoods, some of the finest and best of which, such as the chestnut and the elm, have been practically wiped out by various imported diseases. No longer of much commercial value are hickory, beech, walnut, cherry, and even ash. But oak, maple, and birch are another story.

Birch comes in two principal kinds—white and yellow—besides two inferior species, gray and black. The yellow birch grows in the northern part of New England. Farther south grows the white birch. The bark of the white birch was used to make canoes, and is still used to make horns on which hunters imitate the mating call of the amorous moose. Every country child knows that the smooth inner side of the bark makes good writing paper. Back in 1913, when Joe Knowles went into the woods at Eustis, Maine, stark naked, to prove that a modern man can still live off the country, just like his primitive ancestors, he wrote a daily dispatch on birch bark and put it into a hollow tree, where it was picked up and relayed to the Boston *Post* for the delectation of city readers.

Shoe-pegs, spools, and clothespins are also made from white birch. One Maine mill alone consumes annually fifteen thousand cords of white birch to make spools. It is also used for ice-cream spoons and, curiously, hand grenades, and it makes good firewood.

White birch is employed commercially in the manufacture of toothpicks. Before an enterprising Yankee named Forster initiated the wooden-toothpick industry, in the 1850's, people had used a goose-quill, or the point of a sheath-knife. When Forster, who came from the town of Strong, in Maine, traveled in South America, he found the natives wielding the wooden toothpick. He whittled out the first Yankee toothpicks and sent a boxful home to his wife. By mistake, a hotel man received the package, and he ordered a box for himself.

More orders came, and soon Forster had people whittling them out for hotels all over the United States. Next to the spittoon, the toothpick was probably the greatest social invention of the century. So popular did toothpicks become that in 1860 he began to turn them out by machinery. The first year he sold sixty-five cases, containing 250,000 toothpicks. Today Maine uses thousands of cords of white birch a year in this industry, turning out a carload a day, sometimes two.

The yellow birch is highly prized for furniture, and its price has shot up amazingly of late. Twenty-five years ago it sold for $5 per thousand board feet. Today the price is $35. Of course it is steadily growing scarcer. Up until forty years ago, except for a rare logging railroad, water was the only means of transportation for logs, and the lumberjacks didn't touch hardwood because it won't float and there was no way of getting it out. But since we have learned how to make hardwood into paper pulp, and since logging trucks have been invented and gravel roads have penetrated the farthest corners of the primeval forests, yellow birch is rapidly becoming extinct.

Furthermore, prolonged droughts and an insect called the bronze birch borer killed off, between 1939 and 1952, nearly three-quarters of the white and yellow birch in New England, as well as in Canada. The industry definitely suffered as a result of the birch losses, and it still talks of the situation with concern. Five things resulted: many of the mills requiring veneer-size yellow birch closed; white-birch mills had to obtain wood from areas many times larger than those supplying them prior to birch losses; wood of smaller size and poorer quality was included in their mill receipts; other woods were substituted for white birch in some items; and the size of the cutting operations in the mills was reduced.

Beech is now used for clothespins and is actually at least as good as birch. Red maple is used more, and mills have convinced customers that some painted or inferior products can just as well be made of other species to conserve the valuable and attractive birch for appropriate and necessary uses. But the industry is still keenly interested in methods of regenerating birch.

The old-growth yellow birch usually is festooned with long, curly streamers of old bark. Woodsmen will sometimes, after dark, touch a match to this highly inflammable material, and in an instant the fire runs up the trunk and out to the uppermost tip of every branch, making a huge and beautiful display of fireworks that lasts nearly half a minute. It is not, however, a trick to try in dry weather.

Gray birch isn't worth a damn, except as firewood, and while it may surprise the reader to learn that the principal use of trees in this world, even in 1966, is as plain firewood, he may be even more surprised to know that in northern New England, which is largely covered with hardwood, wood is the most expensive kind of fuel available. Sixteen-inch dry maple or birch that used to sell for ten dollars a cord, delivered, can't be had today for less than forty dollars.

An intriguing news story in the Hanover (New Hampshire) *Gazette* for June 20, 1902, relates what happened when the irresistible force of Yankee ingenuity met an immovable body of gray birch in East Eddington, Maine. Mr. Asa Penny returned in 1897 from Boston, Massachusetts, to his ancestral farm in East Eddington, to find it grown up to a dense stand of gray birch trees, of which the largest were less than four inches in diameter.

Asa surveyed the scene with a jaundiced eye, but a gleam of inspiration soon replaced his dejection. City life had not made him forget how to handle an axe. He cut off thousands of those birch saplings, just about six inches above the point where two branches first formed a solid fork. He was in no hurry. He waited patiently for five years, and in 1902 he went to work to complete his Five-Year Plan. He cut down some of those forked saplings, which had continued to wax strong during the interval, and cut them off about two feet below the crotch. He took them home and whittled on them a little, nailed a nifty cross-piece below the fork of each, near its base, and shipped a carload of his brain-children to Chicago, where they were snapped up at twenty-two cents apiece. He shipped a second carload, but he had glutted the market and received only twenty cents apiece. Nothing daunted, he sent the next carload to Minneapolis— and got twenty-two cents again.

Other cities were eager to do business with him, and he figured on a market for all he could produce. "Two thousand trees to the acre," said he, "and the rest of the tree can be sold for firewood."

Any farmer will tell you that a yield of $440 to the acre is almighty remunerative.

Oh yes, I almost forgot to say what Asa's peculiar product was. Bootjacks! And much sturdier than the machine-turned variety. . . .

Of oak there are red and white. Years ago, both were much in demand for shipbuilding. A hundred ox-team loads a day passed through the village of Alfred, Maine, in 1854. All the New England states produced commercial oak in abundance.

In Colonial times, and much later, it was especially used to make clapboards, and staves for barrels and casks. It seems that about everything in those days was kept and transported in casks: molasses, rum, corpses, lime, meat, bread—even water. In rural New England people still say of a man who works quickly, "He jumps around like a cooper around a barrel."

In the early days, lime, which was made in huge quantities in Rockland and Thomaston, Maine, was shipped in bulk, and very often, because of green lumber, seams would open up in the wooden-bottomed ships, with disastrous results. The water turned the lime into a sticky mass, impossible to unload. Thus it became necessary to ship lime in casks.

Oak was used in the manufacture of furniture and in building, of course, and along with other kinds of wood was once consumed in immense quantities in the burning of pit-charcoal, and of lime. Seth Nason, the last pit-charcoal maker in New England, died in Kingston, New Hampshire, in 1940. He used to sell his product to restaurant-keepers in Boston. Pit-charcoal was also used in smelting bog iron, which was the only kind of iron produced in the United States before 1850. The cost of wood for charcoal was four cents per bushel, and about two-hundred bushels were required to smelt one ton of iron.

The primitive method of burning was to stack cordwood—four-foot lengths of wood—on end in a pit, several layers thick, around a flue or chimney. When the mound of wood was of sufficient size it was covered with alternate layers of wet clay and moss. A flammable liquid was poured down the chimney and the kiln was then ignited. A week or more of slow burning and careful observation were required to complete the process. Blue smoke appearing from holes bored in the clay sides indicated that the wood was done. Later, brick kilns of a bee-hive shape replaced the pit-burning.

Back in 1890, J. E. (Old Ave) Henry, a noted lumberman and a canny businessman, was pulling out of Zealand, New Hampshire, to go to Lincoln. He owned a whole mountainside, in fact, several mountainsides, covered with hardwood, facing the famous Bretton Woods Hotel near the foot of Mount Washington. Ave wanted to sell his hardwood to the hotel company, but they refused to pay his price.

"All right," said Ave. "Then I'll put up some charcoal kilns and burn every tree in sight!"

They didn't believe him, but when they saw a crew of men come in, with a lot of bricks, and the maples began to fall, they couldn't stand it. Mountains denuded of trees would have spoiled their hotel undertaking for fair. Reluctantly they paid Mr. Henry his price, and he, chuckling over his successful bluff—for he had no intention of going into the charcoal business—took the money and departed.

In the days of wood-burning locomotives in New England, vast amounts of hardwood were cut and stacked here and there along the tracks; when a locomotive's supply grew low the train stopped and everyone, including the passengers, pitched in and loaded her up.

The oak is not found in the northern part of New England, but it was plentiful all over the southern section. It has been decimated since 1900 by the gypsy-moth—another European importation.

The maple tree is found everywhere. There are red maple, silver maple, swamp maple, white (or soft) maple, rock (or hard) maple. The best maple sugar in the world comes from the Vermont rock maple, though many people are surprised to learn that more comes from New York than from any other state. In 1853 the United States produced more than two million tons of maple sugar. Today, sad to say, "Set up the maples!" means set up wooden pins, not dishes of delicious syrup, for the cost of sugar production, especially the cost of hired help, is so high, that very many farmers have sold off large and formerly profitable sugar-places to people who manufacture bowling pins. An "average" tree will produce about a pound and a half of hard sugar in a season, but the St. Johnsbury (Vermont) *Caledonian* of April 14, 1882, records a local tree that produced eight pounds in three days' run of sap!

Sawmill men handling old tapped sugar-maple logs make it a practice to cut off five feet from the butt. The sound of a circular saw biting into a nail can spoil a sawyer's whole day.

Like the price of birch, the price of maple for lumber to make into veneer and fine furniture has skyrocketed in proportion as the wood becomes scarcer and the number of young married couples increases. I read recently that new and ingenious methods now produce a veneer much less costly and "just as good" as the old more expensive kind. In a veneer mill there is usually a large amount of cull and low-grade veneer that cannot be used for commercial grades of plywood. Perhaps the new veneer is made by gluing this cull into good core stock which is finished with one lamination of the desired finish material on each side.

In Colonial times, and for many years thereafter, the maples, like all other trees, were cut down just to clear the land for farming. They did, however, bring in some ready cash, for the settlers converted them into potash, for which there was always a ready market. It was said that a "stout young man" could earn a shilling a day making potash. Potash-making, once widely practiced in every township in New England, is now a lost art, like making horse-collars, whetting scythes, and emasculating old tom-cats.

Every pioneer farmer had one or more potash kettles, great iron affairs which lasted a hundred years after potash ceased to be made, and which nowadays bring fancy prices from collectors of antiques. A big seven-hundred-pound kettle turned upside down on a flat rock served as a jail in the Indian Stream Republic, the smallest independent republic in North America, which for four turbulent years after 1832 held its own against Canada on the north and the United States on the south.

A writer in 1811 notes that "the appearances even of the best potash are so various that it is difficult to judge of its quality from that alone. It is considered impure if it has a honeycomb appearance or an acid taste. That which is white or cream-colored, and has crystallized in small round grains is esteemed the best."

And he adds this interesting paragraph: "Besides the innumerable uses to which this important article has been applied, as well in medicine as in various trades, it has been discovered to possess the remarkable property of extinguishing flame in the most speedy and effectual manner, and for this purpose has been successfully used in some parts of England to extinguish burning houses, a quantity of it being dissolved in the water with which the fire engines are charged."

The French Duc de la Rochefoucauld-Liancourt, a keen observer, traveled in the United States in 1795 and wrote a book about his travels. In it he gives a detailed account of how potash was made in New England. He tells us that "by a general estimate from five to six hundred bushels of ashes yield a ton of potash," and he gives many curious details. He goes on to tell how the more valuable pearlash was obtained, how it was barreled, and how it was sold. Both potash and pearlash were still being manufactured and still being inspected by a government inspector in Maine as late as 1856.

About that time chemical fertilizers were invented which replaced the old ashes. It was a good thing, or we wouldn't have a tree left in the country today.

3

The Genesis of the Lumberjack

THE first European in the future United States who was interested in anything except murdering the natives and stealing their goods was probably John Smith, the celebrated captain who knew Pocahontas when that dusky maiden was twelve years old and, "stark naked, used to turn cartwheels all through the fort," as a contemporary visitor noted in his diary.

Captain Smith was America's first lumberjack, for he put his people to cutting down trees and cutting them up to ship to England. "We wrought upon Clapborde for ye English," recorded one of Smith's sailors, in 1608. Another, Anas Todkill, who had never seen such logging operations in the old country, rather enjoyed them. The swish and crash of the great trees, the ever-present danger of being maimed or killed, all impressed him. He was also impressed by the fact that the men began to utter "Great Loude Othes" as the unaccustomed toil blistered their hands.

Captain Smith, however, had a "fair remedie of this sinne." He set a spy to listening to the pained woodsmen and counting their oaths, and at evening a "Canne of water" was poured down the upraised sleeve of every man for each profanity uttered. The remedie worked. "Within a week," says Todkill, "a man would scarce hear an Othe."

Captain Smith was the first and probably also the last woods boss to be thus interested in saving his men's souls. Many later travelers noted the profusion of cuss-words in the speech of the average logger, but the more thoughtful ones, entranced by the vigor and incongruity of the naughty words, realized that often nothing blasphemous was meant.

It is true that itinerant priests and preachers have occasionally wandered into logging camps on a Sunday and tried, more or less successfully, to hold divine services, but they have not come at the behest of the camp boss. On March 19, 1873, the Eastport (Maine) *Sentinel* reported a prayer meeting held in a camp on the St. Croix River. An old lady, anxious about her husband's state of grace, was called upon to pray. She said that she could not, but proceeded instead to regale the congregation with a song:

> *I love the Lord, indeed I do*
> *I wish my husband loved Him too,*
> *Hi galloping, ralloping, randy,*
> *Dandy, andy, O!*

Captain Smith's boatload of Clapborde was the first of many lumber exports from America. The Pilgrims in Massachusetts and the Cavaliers in Virginia hacked valiantly into the forest, swinging their solid, straight-helved pole-axes with many a grunt and great loud oath. Nor did they live in log cabins, but in frame houses.

To get the boards to build those houses they first dug holes in the ground and probably drew lots to see which unfortunate would have to go down into them. Such holes were called saw-pits. Although the large timbers for house building and shipbuilding were hewn out and squared with a broad-axe, the planks, boards, and boat sides were mostly made by pit-sawing. This was a common industry in England, where the settlers had come from, and its prevalence was one reason why England had no sawmills until after 1788, for the people always (as today) opposed labor-saving machinery and destroyed the first sawmills as fast as they were built, for fear that the pit-sawyers would be thrown out of work.

Pit-sawing was done by two men with a long saw that had cross-handles at each end. A stick of timber, hewn square, was placed over the pit, or elevated on trestles. One man stood on top of it and pulled the saw up, and one man stood in the pit below to pull the saw down. The work-man on top, who guided the saw along the chalk-line, and who was sup-posedly the better man, was called the top-sawyer. The one below was called the pitman. Itchy sawdust and sweat ran down his neck and into his eyes and ears, and his pious oaths must have spattered like raindrops.

When sawmills were first substituted for pit-sawing in this work, the saw was held taut on the upward stroke by a spring-pole overhead, and was worked up and down by a wooden beam attached to a crank on the mill wheel. This wooden beam was called the pitman, and is still known by that name in every sawmill in the country.

Pit-sawing, or whip-sawing as it is often called, was not entirely aban-doned with the introduction of sawmills. The old method was still useful in sawing long stuff, because in many mills the carriage was not long enough to saw planks of the desired length. As late as 1860 a writer noted at Painted Post, New York, a large, square stick of timber being sawed in the old fashion into long planks for the sides of a canal boat.

With a wealth of proper timber close at hand, shipbuilding speedily became a leading industry, especially in Massachusetts and New Hamp-shire. When the big trees close to the water became exhausted, gangs of shipwrights would march a mile or two into the woods. There, with

plenty of trees all around, they would build a ship of a hundred tons burden, mount it on immense sleds of strong timbers, hitch on a team of two
hundred oxen, and drag it in triumph over the snow until it rested on the
frozen surface of a navigable stream. There it stayed until the ice melted
in the spring and it could be floated down to its destination.

These monster teams of oxen were organized at first to bring the
great mast pines, needed for the Royal Navy, and often 120 feet long, out
of the forest to a river's brink. The first log drive in America was of such
pines, on the Piscataqua; they were brought down to Portsmouth by a
crew of pig-tailed, pantalooned Pilgrims.

An ox is not a lively beast, at best, and it was exceedingly difficult to
start so many inert creatures into a living, moving team. Doing so was
called raising them, and an expert raiser was honored by his peers. Once
started, such a team could not be permitted to stop. If an ox fell, he was
cut out and another forced into his place so no headway would be lost.

Winter was the time for hauling, although for rush orders the masts
were occasionally moved to the rivers before snow was on the ground, as
was noted by Judge Samuel Sewall of Boston on a visit to Salmon Falls
(New Hampshire) in 1687. He records in his *Diary:* "Rode into a swamp
to see a mast drawn of about 26 inches or 28; about two and 30 oxen before, and about four yoke by the side of the mast between the fore and
hinder wheels. 'Twas a notable sight."

And that was only a small pine. Many were three times as big and
required three times as many oxen. For such summer hauling two sets of
wheels were used—one pair at the front end of the log, one pair at the
rear end—and sometimes a third pair in the middle. The wheels were
eighteen feet high, to enable the big log, drawn up on chains beneath the
axles, to clear obstructions. This laborious arrangement was retained for a
hundred and fifty years, but "now," wrote Belknap, the New Hampshire
historian, in 1792, "they tip the wheels so one lies on the ground, they roll
the log onto it, and a pair of oxen pulling on a chain attached to the lower
wheel, jerk it erect."

When woodsmen left the settlements to go searching for suitable
trees, they were said to have gone a-masting. The men were known as
mast-men or masters, and the numerous workmen employed to dress and
hew the timbers in the long mast-houses at the mouth of the Piscataqua,
the Saco, and the Presumpscot, were called mast-wrights.

The giant white pines used for masts were the true monarchs of the
forest. They usually grew not in large stands, but in clumps, or even isolated, towering head and shoulders above all the other trees of the woods.
Many of the logs brought into the mills for lumber were so large that
they had to be slabbed down by the millmen before they could pass the
saw-gates.

A more majestic, graceful, even awe-inspiring tree never existed. One old Maine writer, G. T. Ridlon, in *Saco Valley Settlements and Families* (1895), has noted that he who sits far below the foliage of the old forest monarchs when they are touched by the passing winds will hear voices that sound like the distant ocean's roar; their music ranges through infinite variations in sweetness, compass, and power. There are swelling strains like the chorus of a mighty orchestra; sounds as solemn and awe-inspiring as the piteous music of the Miserere, or the wail of a lost soul. Again it floats in gentle undulations like the dying echoes of a vesper chime, or the symphonies of an angel's song."

Though not described under their particular names until later, the professions of the timber-cruiser, the lumberjack, the teamster, and the riverman had already become well developed as early as 1666, thanks to the masting trade. Experts were required to go out into the woods and not get lost, to locate the needed trees; and to fall a tree a couple of hundred feet tall and three or four feet thick without breaking it all to hell took more than a strong back, a solid axe-handle, and a few Great Loude Othes.

In short, lumbering had started in earnest. The mast-man took a pouch of parched corn, a wooden canister of rum, a blanket, and an axe, and departed from civilization. When he figured he was in a likely spot he clambered up the tallest tree available (if the one he chose didn't have any limbs for the first sixty feet or so he would fall another one against it to serve as a ladder), and from his perch he could easily pick out the lofty pines he was seeking. Then he shinnied down to the ground and headed for his first victim. At a glance he could tell whether its size and height were suitable for his purpose.

But that was not all. The pine had to be solid, and while many of those old giants might contain thousands of board feet of merchantable lumber, even if their hearts were hollow, such sticks were worthless as masts. Approaching the tree, the mast-man dealt it several hard blows with the head of his axe. If the tree was solid to the core, the axe-stroke produced a dull, hard sound; if decayed within, a hollow, reverberating echo. This test wasn't fool-proof, but it was pretty reliable. It worked better when a second master stood a few feet away and listened attentively to the strokes.

If the old pine passed muster, the next step was to lay out a road on which to balk it, as hauling the log was called in those days, to the nearest waterway, often miles away. First of all, the road had to be straight, for one doesn't turn corners with a log over a hundred feet long and a yard or two thick. So swampers cut down trees and underbrush, dug out rocks, cut off projecting roots, filled hollows, bridged streams and gullies, and "wharfed" side-hills with logs.

These necessary preliminaries having been completed, the axeman appeared on the scene. It took skill to fall such an immense tree, and only the most capable men were given the task. A nicety of judgment was required that could be found only in experts. Even a slight error by an axeman could ruin the tree for use as a mast by causing the trunk to split before it fell or to break as it fell. The loss would not be total if the tree was cut up for lumber, but it would be close to 50 per cent.

As such loss had to be borne by the contractor, the latter saw to it that few chances were taken. First of all, the mast pine had to fall in the direction opposite to that in which it would be removed from the forest. Winter was the favorite season for the cutting because then the deep snow leveled the inequalities of the ground and acted as a cushion to the falling tree. In fact, a bed was prepared to catch the giant, consisting of small trees and brush, with springy evergreen boughs on top, to soften and break the violence of the fall. The process was called bedding. Also, all bushes and obstructions were removed from about the base of the tree so that the choppers could avoid the danger of rebound by darting away when the old hero fell.

At last all was ready. Saws were unknown in the woods. Two brawny axemen stepped forward and threw their shining, keen-edged steel into the mellow wood. A two-faced notch was made in this kind of work, the lower one to facilitate cleavage. The angle on the stump side of the incision would descend but slightly toward the heart of the tree; the one above would intersect at an angle of 45 degrees where the heart was reached. By cutting in this way the skilled axeman wasted only a minimum of the valuable tree.

The strokes followed one another with the regularity of clock-work. The gleaming blades, "thrown" at the tree, disappeared half their width into the wood. An axeman took pride in leaving a scarf as smooth as marble, and chips half as big as a platter would fly a dozen feet through the air, to the discomfiture of curious spectators. But at last the sweaty choppers reached the heart of the tree. Now was the moment of truth. No matter how expert and careful he was, no woodsman could calculate correctly every time. The north woods are dotted with the graves of good men who made one little mistake.

For a moment the old monarch who had laughed at a thousand tempests and had shaken his enormous arms in defiance of the winds of hundreds of winters, would stand unmoved, as if determined never to descend from his lofty throne. Far above the surrounding forest a passing breeze might touch him, and a quiver, a shudder, would run all the way down his trunk. The axemen would give the tree a final push, and run like rabbits, shouting TIMBER-R-R! at the top of their lungs. With a dying groan, followed by a tremendous swish and an awful roar, the king of the forest would come down with a crash like a thunderbolt, making the earth quake; then, a last rebound like the death struggle of an expiring behemoth. All was over, the great tree lying prostrate. Even the most unimaginative of woodsmen found the death of such a forest patriarch sublimely impressive.

By this time the road had been packed as smooth as glass. The oxen had been brought up, and a trial run had been made. A bowsprit was usually used for the test, being much easier to haul than a mast because of its different shape. If all went well and the road held up without slumping, smaller masts or spar timber were hauled over it. Then the turn of the big mast came.

Laboriously they hoisted it into the air beneath the wagon wheels, or else rolled it onto a great mast-sled made for the purpose, fastening it securely with big chains and hawsers brought from the mast-house. The log was ready to move. Before, the axeman had been the cynosure of all eyes. Now came the "master-carter's" turn.

The woods seemed full of ox-teamsters, all shouting and yelling at once, but it was the master-carter who superintended the undertaking. His orders were arbitrary, and nobody disputed them. Others might offer suggestions, but the ruling of the chief was final. His place was at the seat of honor, standing upon the fore end of the mast-stick. From this position he could see all obstructions and observe the movements of the men and their teams. To keep his foothold while the great jolting mass moved forward was an accomplishment worthy of an expert, and but few were competent for the place.

Imagine the sight—a tree-trunk from three to seven feet through and perhaps 120 feet long being dragged through the primeval forest by a double string of long-horned, heaving oxen strung out over a furlong's distance, with "spare" steers switching their tails against the mosquitoes, or shivering with cold, stationed here and there in the brush beside the trail, ready to step into the traces of a fallen brother. Usually, on such a haul, four or five pair of oxen fell and had to be destroyed.

The drivers with their goads were assisted by men stationed along the line of oxen to keep them from getting down or from getting the chains crossed over their backs when crossing depressions or topping steep rises; should that happen, the animals' backs would be instantly cracked. Far in the rear a couple of pair of oxen were often hitched onto the tail end of the mast, to hold it back going down the hills. This practice was called tailing. But if the top of the hill was sharp, it often happened that the great length and weight of log would jerk these tongue oxen off their feet into the air, and they would choke to death.

Balking a big mast wasn't difficult on level ground, or even on ground with a slight down-hill cant, but it took a lot of profanity and tobacco-juice, and liberal applications of the goad-stick, to force the straining, slow-footed oxen up the steep hills.

Your old-fashioned Yankee bull-whacker was a great believer in noise. He talked to his team, he yelled at them, he blasphemed most hideously when anything went wrong. Merely his fantastic facial contortions as he spat tobacco-juice and swore were enough to scare Adam's off ox, and he did not hesitate to punish his cattle unmercifully with hickory and steel.

But every once in a while, usually at the broad top of a hill, the master-carter would call a halt, not so much to give the grateful oxen a rest, as to prudently look over the terrain ahead, to see that his bridle-chains were in order, or that a snub-rope several hundred feet long was attached to the end of the mast while a couple of men took a few turns with its running end around a sturdy oak. This rope, paid out slowly, would serve to hold back the load as it went down the steep hill.

Pleased at having come so far so well, the teamsters would gather round and swap stories of mast-hauling aforetime, and take a swig of rum, that necessary concomitant of every great Colonial undertaking. Then the master-carter, satisfied with conditions fore and aft, would give the signal, and with shouts from the teamsters and creaks and groans from the equipment, the whole vast machine would get under way again.

The patient oxen would crinkle their tails and snort and moan and lean into the yoke, and away they would lunge down the hill, every man wondering whether or not the bridge at the bottom would hold up, but pretty well satisfied that—since the master-carter had inspected it and found it all right—it would. And so, by good judgment, good management, and cautious driving, which some people would call good luck, the mast arrived at its destination.

We have now seen the "how" of masting, but its "why" merits our attention, since it is precisely the cutting of white-pine trees for masts that gave birth to the American lumberjack and to the American riverman.

The strength of England, the mother-country, depended on its navy, and the British Admiralty quickly appreciated the potentialities of the American Colonies as sources of supplies for ship construction, particularly spars and masts. The Royal Government took measures to conserve these resources for itself as early as 1691, in the Province of Massachusetts Bay, where it was forbidden to cut any pine over twenty-four inches in diameter, except on privately owned land. Successive acts, up to 1729, prohibited, under penalty of a fine of fifty pounds sterling per tree, the cutting of any kind of pine tree anywhere in New England and in New York, except on private land.

Half of the fine was to go to His Majesty and half to the informer.

Ingenious scofflaws sought out many inventions to evade the law, but the judges usually found them guilty. Thus in 1769 an operator named Dean, at Windsor, Vermont, on the Connecticut River, was fined eight hundred pounds for having cut sixteen pine trees fit for masts, despite his obviously mendacious defense that he was merely clearing a meadow in order to sow wheat. As a matter of fact, proof was shown that he had contracted to cut and raft half a million feet of lumber at a dollar per thousand. Dean, who had hidden all his personal property so that it would not be attached to pay his fine, had to stay in prison four months, where he suffered much contumely.

In 1691 the Government appointed a Surveyor-General and gave him four Deputies. These five men were supposed to cruise all the millions of acres of pathless forests in British North America, and with an axe place on every pine tree that was sound and straight and over twenty-four inches in diameter the mark of the King's "Broad Arrow"—three cuts through the bark, resembling the barbed head of an arrow or the track of a crow. This mark had been used on all Government stores, especially naval stores, since time immemorial. It was also branded onto criminals deported from England.

When leisure hung heavy on their ten hands, the Surveyor-General and his Deputies were supposed also to seize illegally cut timber, prosecute offenders, and instruct the colonists in the proper way of preparing pitch and tar for the use of the Royal Navy. Likewise, they were to encourage the raising of hemp.

One Surveyor-General of the King's Woods followed another after 1691. Some were good and some were better. One John Bridger held the office from 1706 to 1720, when he was recalled for having done his duty too vigorously. (His victims complained to Higher Authority, and they had some influence.) But despite his energy and zeal he realized that his task was well-nigh impossible. He reported that of seventy great pines marked at Exeter, New Hampshire, all but one had been illegally cut and hauled away, leaving no trace. No settler seemed to know anything about the matter. It was the same elsewhere. "These frontier people depend on the woods for their livelihood," Bridger wrote; "they say the King has no woods here, hence they will cut what and where they please." Yet, with his four Deputies, John marked 3,030 mast pines.

The center of the mast trade for many years—up to 1772, when Portland, Maine, then called Falmouth Neck, took the lead—was Portsmouth, New Hampshire, which from 1741 to 1767 was the seat of Governor Benning Wentworth. Benning was the prototype of our modern solons who arrive in Washington with an empty carpet-bag and leave a few years later with a full Saratoga trunk. First, he purchased from the current Surveyor-General the latter's title and office, paying him two thousand pounds, even though the post carried an annual stipend of only two hundred pounds.

His brother Mark had practically a monopoly of the American mast trade, for he stood in well with the British Navy Board, whose policy was to procure masts and other ship timber, such as spars and bowsprits, by a system of contracts for cutting and delivering at beach head the desired timber, for shipment across the Atlantic. Mark was a member of the Governor's Council, and at least one of Benning's four Deputies resided in Ireland and never saw America.

As governor, Benning had the right to sell new townships in the hinterland of New Hampshire and what today is Vermont—and to reserve the mast pines. Since brother Mark owned the mast trade, and brother Benning could sell off contracts to cut and deliver his cannily preserved pine, one can easily understand why the Broad Arrow passed into a quarter century of peaceful oblivion in North America.

Only once was the Wentworth monopoly of the mast trade challenged. In 1761 an enterprising Yankee named Jared Ingersoll, of Connecticut, persuaded the Navy Board to give him a contract to procure eighty "Mast Pines" (that is, two ship-loads) on the Connecticut River, the same to be cut anywhere between Deerfield, Massachusetts, and "ye Cohees" (i.e., Coos—pronounced "Cowoss") now Haverhill, New Hampshire.

The drive of those monstrous logs down the Connecticut, with its numerous bends, falls, gorges, islands, and rapids, was undoubtedly the outstanding one of its kind, and must have borne the same relation to the labor of driving long logs as the long-log drives bear to pulpwood drives. Eighty-nine white pines of mast size were felled, of which five were broken in the fall. There were also sixty-three "Defective Trees" cut. In all, 147 trees were balked to the river by oxen. Two of the logs broke "in rolling down the bank," and one thirty-inch mast "lying somewhat further than the rest," had to be abandoned when a five or six days' supply of hay for the oxen used in balking was carried away by a disgruntled citizen.

The drive was hampered by low water, so that twenty-one logs which jammed on a rapid were not gotten down until the next spring. One thirty-six-inch stick was broken in two going over Bellows Falls, and another was badly damaged in the rapids at Deerfield.

As fewer than the eighty masts contracted for reached the lower Connecticut, the drivers were forced to go back up river in low water to procure additional "Mast Pines." And while Ingersoll's logs were lying at Middletown, Connecticut, awaiting the arrival of a mast ship to take them to England, the shadow of the long arm of the Wentworth monopoly hovered over them. It manifested itself in the form of a visit from Wentworth's deputy, a Colonel Symmes, who threatened to seize all the logs under contract length which had been floated down with the mast pines. Ingersoll was ultimately successful in forestalling the seizure of his logs, which reached England in 1764, but he did not renew his attempt to transfer to the Connecticut the supremacy in the mast trade so securely enjoyed by the Piscataqua region and by the Wentworths.

But one would dearly have liked to see those hundred-foot masts boiling down through the passionate waters of Bellows Falls (which, assured Connecticut's veridical historian, the Reverend Samuel Peters, in 1787), are so powerful that an iron bar thrown into the gorge will not sink, but will be carried down the entire stretch on top of the water. Jared must have counted himself lucky that he lost only one stick in the passage.

That plenty of mast pine existed on the upper Connecticut is abundantly testified. In Lancaster, New Hampshire, as late as 1817, was recorded a white pine 264 feet tall, and in 1785, Henry Porter, of Northampton, Massachusetts, who ran a general store and conducted large timber operations up the river, offered to furnish each year one or more cargoes of masts from thirty-four to thirty-nine inches in diameter, to be floated down to Lyme, Connecticut.

John Wentworth, Benning's nephew, succeeded his uncle as both governor and Surveyor-General in 1767. He was the last occupant of both posts, for after him came the American Revolution. Unlike his uncle, John took his office seriously. His duties entailed long and arduous journeys into uncharted and unexplored wilderness, but he and his Deputies ranged from Lake Champlain to Moosehead Lake, undergoing physical hardships and some considerable danger, and marking the King's Broad Arrow on mast pines all over New England.

When an informer, anxious to earn his split of the fee, came to report monkey business on the distant Androscoggin, or on the even more distant Connecticut, John promptly betook himself to the spot. Such faith in himself did he have that he once stood up to a crew of tough, bewhiskered loggers on the upper Androscoggin who had threatened to throw him into the river, and not only read the riot act to them, but persuaded the owners to give up voluntarily their illegally cut logs.

Or take the Dean case, previously mentioned. Dean had relied on the remoteness of the spot and the winter season for immunity from the interference of the Surveyor-General. But Wentworth, having been informed, thought nothing of making the three-hundred-mile round trip over ice and snow, clear across New Hampshire, to surprise the lumberjacks in their logging camp. He found the sixteen mast pines a hundred feet long on the ground, and hundreds of logs already landed on the ice of the Connecticut.

In actual fact, although not given much space in the history books, the King's Broad Arrow policy did more to cause the American Revolution than the Stamp Act and the tea tax put together. The first and chief malcontents in Colonial days were New Englanders, and nowhere were they more malcontent than in New Hampshire, where the pine-tree law hit them hard and often. The backwoodsmen of the Granite State flouted the law openly, profanely, and perennially. As early as 1721 a Deputy Surveyor-General reported that he had found some twenty-five thousand logs in New Hampshire, all of mast diameter. He estimated that for every mast sent to England, five hundred were destroyed. The scofflaw backwoodsmen sawed them into boards. And since it was illegal to own boards over twenty-four inches wide, they made boards twenty-three inches wide and threw away the residue of the big logs. In 1736 a seizure by Surveyor-General Dunbar enraged the inhabitants at Exeter so mightily that they disguised themselves slightly as redskins and beat up Dunbar's party, sank their boat, and chased them into the woods, where they hid all night.

In William Little's *History of Weare, N.H., 1735–1888,* we read that

in 1772, when Sheriff Benjamin Whiting called on one Ebenezer Mudgett to arrest him for making free with the king's white pine, he was told that bail would be put up the next morning. After spending a busy evening with his friends and fellow-citizens, Mudgett went to the inn at dawn, woke up the sheriff, burst into the room and told him bail was ready. Whiting rose, chid Mudgett for coming so early, and began to dress. Then more than twenty men rushed in, faces blackened, switches in their hands, to give bail. Whiting seized his pistols and would have shot some of them, but they caught him, took away his small guns, held him by his arms and legs up from the floor, his face down, two men on each side, and with their rods beat him to their hearts' content. They crossed out the account against them of all logs cut, drawn and forfeited, on his bare back, much to his great comfort and delight. They made him wish he had never heard of pine trees fit for masting for the royal navy. Whiting said: "They almost killed me."

Quigley, his deputy, showed fight; they had to take up the floor over his head and beat him with long poles thrust down from the garret to capture him, and then they tickled him in the same way.

Their horses, with ears cropped, manes and tails sheared, were led to the door, saddled and bridled, and they, the king's men, told to mount; they refused, force was applied; they got on and rode off down the road, with jeers, jokes, and shouts ringing in their ears.

Eight of the offenders were later caught and brought to trial. Each was fined twenty shillings and the cost of the prosecution. This light penalty indicated clearly the court's sympathy with the offenders, a reaction that was characteristic of Colonial courts generally and that made enforcement of the law doubly difficult. When to the physical difficulty of ferreting out and apprehending offenders was added the hostility of their friends and neighbors and of the courts, the agent's task of protecting the mast timber became impossible.

As early as 1700 it was necessary to go twenty miles into the woods on the Piscataqua for a good mast. In another half century the Portsmouth supply had been noticeably affected. The solution lay in going farther eastward. It was the quest for lumber that colonized Maine. The first sawmill in New England was built in that state in 1623, and a considerable part of the lumber and masts shipped from Portsmouth came from the western part of the province.

Despite Indian scares, lumbering prospered in Maine, and Falmouth gradually gained on Portsmouth in the volume of lumber shipped, though Wentworth influence kept the larger part of the naval-contract business at the older port, which shipped five cargoes of masts to the Navy for every one sent from Falmouth. Not until 1772 did Falmouth forge into the lead.

The size of the great masts required a special type of cargo ship, and soon production began, principally in New England, of ships expressly made to carry masts. Usually they were of four hundred to six hundred tons burden, and one is known to have reached a thousand tons, a fabulous size for merchant craft in those days. They were built with oversize ports in the stern for taking in the unwieldy cargo, and had a capacity of from forty to a hundred of the largest sticks, together with lesser pieces such as bowsprits, spars, yards, and the like. They were handled by a crew of twenty-five men, and in time of war were attended by armed convoys. A frigate, often several, protected them from pirates, French privateers, or Dutch cruisers. They also carried passengers, and at times were used as troop transports.

The masting business was what colonized Maine, but while it was a great thing for the economy of the province, it was also harmful in certain ways. For the industry was so profitable, even to the lowliest worker, that many of the new settlers spent time masting to the detriment of their farms. They slacked off on their fishing, not bothering to dry cod or pollack for their own winter use. When winter came they found themselves in the odd position of men with hard money in their pockets and no food, nor any place to buy it. But being Yankees, they just tightened up their belts another hole and kept right on masting and building up their hoards of gold and silver, while their families existed on the fine edge of starvation.

The Government paid ship-owners a bounty of one pound a ton, the ton consisting of fifty cubic feet of rough or forty of hewn timber ("ton" timber). The price paid for the largest masts in 1770 was £110.

These were masts thirty-six inches at the butt and thirty-six yards long. The masts were always as long in yards as they were inches wide at the butt.

While we are speaking of "mast ships" and their peculiar construction, we must not neglect to say a word about "ton timber," which accounted for innumerable thousands of New England trees and awakened the spirit of resourcefulness in American lumber-jacks and shipbuilders.

It has always been strongly believed that hewn timber is stronger than sawn lumber. Both before our Revolution and after—when the peeved Britishers refused entry to the American colonists' boards, shingles, and such, but did allow squared timbers to come in—enormous raft-like boats composed of axe-hewn logs treenailed together in the form of a ship's hull, and fully as tall, were rigged with sails and sent forth to traverse the Atlantic under their own power. The members of the crew were snugly ensconced in a neat area hollowed out in the middle of the solid craft just to contain them.

Many of these curious contraptions made the voyage successfully, the record run of twenty-six days being held by a crew captained by a mariner from Newburyport, but many also foundered just as they approached the English or French coast, including one over three hundred feet long that sailed from Quebec in 1825.

The largest and most famous of these vessels came to grief off the Grand Banks. A Kennebecker named James Tupper, of Dresden, conceived it. In C. E. Allen's *History of Dresden, Maine* (1931) Dr. Tupper is described as a man "of strong and vigorous intellect, a deep thinker." He showed his powers on this occasion. At Bath he put together a monstrous craft of over a thousand tons burden, and correctly named it *The Experiment*. A one-tone timber was a log forty feet long, squared to 12 by 12 inches. Early in 1792 the doctor engaged a captain and a crew and even hoisted a lifeboat on top of his ship, as a concession to the crew, who at the last moment got cold feet and refused to sail.

For months *The Experiment* rode at anchor in Bath harbor, but at last Tupper rounded up another crew, of hardy New England whoresons who were afraid of nothing, and away they sailed, north by east. Somewhere off the coast of Labrador they ran into a heavy storm, and as *The Experiment* began to break into its component parts, the crew took to the lifeboat and rowed back to dry land.

The timbers themselves may have eventually washed back toward shore, to litter the ocean like the thousands and thousands of logs that each spring as time went on escaped from the booms of the St. John, the Penobscot, and the Kennebec to fill the coastal waters so thickly that ships could not pass through them, and often lay becalmed for a week at a time. As late as 1901 a freshet on the Penobscot loosed seven million feet of logs worth $100,000 at Bangor and carried them all out to sea.

As the Revolution was about to start, the British Government tried to seize all the masts available along the coast, but three hundred patriots turned out at Portsmouth and towed them hastily up the river, where a cargo ship could not go. The same thing was done at Falmouth, where the saucy rebels even fired upon a King's ship trying to load a few masts supplied by a Tory. That made the British very angry, so they sent a frigate that shelled Falmouth into the ground. Up the coast at Bath a hundred workmen were toiling at the masts when a band of local dissenters stepped out of the bushes and bade them cease and desist. The foreman, a sturdy King's man, was inclined to argue the point, but he was persuaded.

Ever rebellious against authority, the New Hampshire backwoodsmen, knowing that fire would spoil white-pine trees for masts, but would still leave them a good deal of salvageable lumber, started a forest fire in New Hampshire in 1761 that swept across the Maine border and raged for two months over a district fifty miles square, destroying a tremendous number of the finest pine trees in the world. Everyone knew the fire had been set deliberately, and everyone knew who set it, but proof was a difficult matter, especially after a farmer who had announced he would give evidence for the King suddenly disappeared. In 1762 an even worse fire swept through the Scarborough–North Yarmouth district in Maine, destroying woods, farms, sawmills, and animals.

It was limitless lumber that made shipbuilding the principal industry in New England. The first wooden ship built in America came from the mouth of the Kennebec. It was a "pretty pinnace" of thirty tons burden named the *Virginia*, of Sagadahoc, built in 1607, and it plied between England and America for twenty years. Wooden ships were still being built in South Portland as late as World War I.

The first warship to be built in America, the frigate *Falkland*, 637 tons, was launched at Badger's Island Yard, at the mouth of the Piscataqua, in 1690. Gundalows, topsail schooners, and brigs, all kinds of vessels for coastal and deep-water trade, were manufactured all along the New England coasts and up the rivers. More ships have been built in one three-mile-long area at Bath, Maine, than at any other place of equal area in the world.

The Revolution made all the shipyards hum, building warships, and every farmer along the coast who owned a stand of timber and had a spark of ambition built his own privateer and sailed out to make his everlasting fortune by capturing a British merchantman.

All this shipbuilding greatly encouraged the development of lumbering. Pine and spruce were needed for masts and spars, and oak was needed for hulls, as well as for the thousands of casks, barrels, hogsheads, firkins, and pipes required to carry everything from rum to gunpowder.

By 1800 the American lumberjack was already a distinct species, recognized and described by travelers, both domestic and foreign. In *Travels through the Northern Parts of the United States in the Years 1801 and 1808* E. A. Kendall, a visiting Englishman, wrote of him in 1809:

But, his habits in the forests, and his voyages (the river drive) for the sale of his lumber, all break up the system of persevering industry, and substitute one of alternate toil and indolence, hardship and debauch; and, in the alternation, indolence and debauch will inevitably be indulged in the greatest possible proportion. Nor is this all; the lumberer is nurtured . . . in the habits of an outlaw and desperado. The lumberer is usually too poor to possess land, it soon must leave him to pay for rum. . . . But, along with vice, where there is misery, we divide ourselves between anger and compassion. If his toil is unsteady, it is also unprofitable; and he suffers at least as much from the scantiness of his wages as from any deficiency in his work. The strength and execution of his arm almost exceed belief; and he fells the forest with at least as much activity as others plough the soil. Meanwhile, it is often amid cold and wet that all his labour is performed. It is often in marshes that he employes his axe whole days together. . . . To ward off damps and chills he drinks spirituous liquors; the liquors weaken his system. . . . Intermittents attack him.

The "intermittents" were called the "horrors" by New England woodsmen. They manifested themselves in visions of pink wildcats, red snakes, and the mystical Maine guyanousa, and they resulted from drinking too much rum. Rum, as all spirituous liquors were called, always did remain important in the life of the woodsman and the riverman.

In 1821–22 appeared in four volumes *Travels in New England and New York* by Timothy Dwight, who had died in 1817. Timothy was a poet, a preacher, a theologian, a president of Yale College, and a confirmed pessimist. Also, he enjoyed poor health, which caused him to spend his vacations traveling in the fresh air of the rural and backwoods districts, where he observed the doings of the quaint inhabitants with a sardonic and disapproving eye. He wrote of the loggers: "They are almost necessarily poor. Their course of life seduces them to prodigality, irreligion, immoderate drinking, and other ruinous habits."

These rather unsympathetic studies of the lumberjack were supplanted by a different viewpoint as the years crawled on. A writer in the *American Review* in 1845 described him as "reckless, generous and social," and Thoreau in his classic book on the Maine woods found him an admirable fellow. T. Winthrop in 1863 praised him highly in *Life in the Open Air*, and C. Lanman wrote in *Adventures in the Wilds of the United States and British American Provinces* (1866):

They are a young and powerfully built race of men, mostly New Englanders, generally unmarried, and, though rude in their manner, and intemperate, are quite intelligent. They seem to have a passion for their wild and toilsome life, and, judging from their dresses, I should think possess a fine eye for the comic and fantastic. The entire apparel of an individual consists of a pair of gray pantaloons and *two red* flannel shirts, a pair of long boots, and a woolen covering for the head, and *all* these things are worn at one and the same time. . . . Their wages vary from twenty to thirty dollars per month, and they are chiefly employed by the lumber merchants of Bangor, who furnish them with the necessary supplies.

So here at last we see the lumberjack (at first he was called a lumberer, later, a logger, and lastly, say from 1880 to 1940, a woodsman; in New England the term "lumberjack" was hardly ever used until Holman Day, who took it from the Michigan lumber-woods novels of Stewart Edward White, made it popular) in his habit and in his demesne: a man whose badge was the axe, a man who did not care for any other kind of work, preferring "indolence" to laboring out of his chosen place and season, who had a "passion" for the "wild and toilsome life," who was "reckless, generous and social." A man generally recognized as a separate species, as is shown by a newspaper account of a steamboat accident in 1912, which reported that "three men and a logger were drowned."

In short, a man well worthy of our attention.

4

Who Were the Lumberjacks?

THE earliest loggers in New England were, of course, Yankees, and they came from the "poverty" farms that bore most of the population. There was no labor-saving machinery, everything was done by "main strength and ignorance," and a dozen stout sons were a great help in clearing the land, picking stone, and tilling the soil.

But winter was always a slack season, and the farmer himself, along with his sons when they were big enough, would leave the womenfolks to milk the cows and do the necessary chores, and take to the woods to earn a few welcome dollars at the rate of fifty cents a day and "found."

For the most part they were steady, reliable men who already knew how to handle an axe or team, who took to the work naturally. They did not care to range far afield and one would see the same faces year after year in camps on the Nulhegan, the Saco, and other rivers.

But the professional loggers, especially the unmarried ones, were very often drifters. Urged on by an incurable wanderlust, by a taste for novelty, they enjoyed going from river to river, from camp to camp —partly, no doubt, to show off their prowess and match themselves against other redoubtable members of the craft.

But as Maine took the lead in the logging business there was not enough local talent to supply the growing demand, and skilled woodsmen from the equally poor farms of the Maritime Provinces crossed the line to help let daylight into the swamp. Those from Nova Scotia were called Herring-Chokers; those from New Brunswick were known as Blue Noses; but the term "P.I.'s" (Prince Edward Island) was often applied to all of them.

There were no better woodsmen than the P.I.'s, but as Bill Smart, walking-boss of the Connecticut Valley Lumber Company (C.V.L.), once said, "they were as ignorant as God is almighty."

Hugh Grogan was clerking at Nash Stream Bog in the spring of 1909 when he elicited a remark from a P.I. that became a North Country classic. Hugh was taking down the names and address of the men who were going to start the spring drive. Up stepped a strapping riverman. "Name?" said Hugh.

"Sure," replied the man in a brogue you couldn't have cut with a spade, "an' it's MacDonald!"

"Where do you come from?"

"Sure an' I come from the Island!"

"What island?" asked the clerk impatiently.

"Prince Edward Island, of course, ye goddamned fool! What other island is they?"

The men really from the Island were noted for the fact that they were always clad in pure-white wool—underwear, mittens, caps—spun and knitted by their mothers.

The P.I.'s were among the "Maine" men who followed the receding pines westward, taking their peculiar tools, methods, and know-how with them. Call the roll and you will find that it was New England men who, pausing briefly in New York and Pennsylvania, went on to the Lake States and then on to the Coast, showing the shanty boys there how to let in the daylight. An interesting study could be made, and partial ones have been made, of the role played in those regions not only by ordinary loggers and rivermen, but by those who achieved wealth and eminence. Their educational backgrounds and the moral qualities that put them on top of the heap are especially worth noting.

The sojourn of the New Englanders in Pennsylvania is attested to by a lumberjack ballad entitled "The Maine-ite in Pennsylvania," of which one memorable stanza goes:

> *There's the tomtit and the moose-bird and the roving cariboo;*
> *The Lucifer and pa'tridge that through the forest flew;*
> *And the wild ferocious rabbit from the colder regions came;*
> *And several other animals too numerous to name.*

Famous among many others who hailed from New England, we can name Michigan lumberman Horace Butters, from Maine, who invented the "Horace Butters Patent Steam Skidder," a steam-driven rig for hauling logs from the stump.

Wisconsin had a goodly number of old Maine loggers, prominent among them being Isaac Stephenson, who lived to be almost a hundred years old, and who, although born in New Brunswick, picked up all his lumbering know-how in Maine, whence he transferred it to Menominee, where it earned him several million dollars and a seat in the United States Senate.

But nothing he ever accomplished, he used to say, gave him so much pure pleasure as the memories of how, in the 1840's, he used to break in three yoke of green oxen and haul pine logs with them on the Aroostook, bigger loads than any of the other teamsters in camp.

Minnesota, too, had a big handful of lusty pine barons who came from New England, including Wesley Day, who had once been champion wrestler of Maine. Wesley, who was not exactly a spendthrift, used to challenge people to whom he owed money to a wrestling match—"double or quits." History says he never lost.

Along with the canny barons were hundreds of plain woodsmen and rivermen whom they had recruited back east, and of course there were many exchanges between the New England states themselves. George Van Dyke, most celebrated of the New Hampshire moguls, got his start over in Beattie's Gore in Maine. N. G. Norcross, after being a successful operator on the Penobscot, migrated to the Pemigewasset, as the upper Merrimack is called, in the 1840's and for years ran drives down to his big mill at Lowell, Massachusetts, a feat that J. E. Henry, a millionaire operator in the same country, could not successfully perform half a century later. Perhaps Norcross's success was due to the fact that, as contemporary newspapers stated, he sent back home "for some of the genuine double twisted Penobscot boys" to help him. In 1853 he employed 130 men who "were as tough and hearty as pirates," and as early as 1846 he was known as the "Timber King."

The New York *Tribune* in May of that year printed the following news item about him, sent in by the *Tribune* correspondent in Franconia, New Hampshire:

There's been a dragoon of a Down-Easter here, these two winters, with a company of red-shirted fellows from the banks of the Penobscot, making terrible havoc among the woods. His name is Norcross. They call him the Timber King. He's a perfect Bonaparte among the pines—he's fell a hundred thousand of 'em, I should guess by the noise, these two winters past, and has got 'em all into the water this spring, driving them down to a town in the old Bay State, by the name of Lowell, where they've put up a factory, they tell me. Norcross has built a steam sawmill down there, a purpose to saw up these pines. He's got 'em down out of the mountains on the top of last spring's freshets, and they lay in the Pemigewasset at the head of log navigation, all last summer. He kept them in a basin. This spring he has tapped his basin and let the logs all loose down stream. The Pemigewasset is alive with them now, for miles and miles, and Norcross and his red shirters are after 'em down the river like so many hounds. It is a sight to see 'em ride these mill logs down the rapids.—They'll jump right in among the white water, and they'll stay on a jamb where the water runs like a mill-tail, till the very instant it starts, and then they're off with their long, iron-shod hand spikes. This Norcross is everywhere among them, and he has got an eye like a kingfisher.

The native Yankee stock, the P.I.'s (the very last of the old-time woodsmen of the Androscoggin, Big Dan Murray, ninety-five years old in 1966 came from Nova Scotia), and a constantly increasing number of French-Canadians, constituted the bulk of New England lumberjacks and river-drivers right up to 1900 or a little later.

After 1840 there were also quite a few first- or second-generation Irishmen. The Irish tried to outdo the others in profanity, drinking, hard work and deeds of derring-do, and thus quite often naturally rose to the top, though by no means as often as myth would have it. Fred Gilbert, who came up from axeman to chief of the Spruce Wood Division of the Great Northern Paper Company, was a Frenchman. Frederick Noad, who advanced from cant-dog man to Deputy Minister of Lands and Forests for Ontario, was born in England. John Ross, the most famous riverman who ever lived, was a Yankee.

But as the years rolled on, and more and more trees had to be cut, local men could not meet the demand, and about the turn of the century North Country lumbering firms began to go to employment agencies in Boston and Portland and even New York, to find men. The agencies did indeed supply a few woodsmen, who had begun to get the habit of making those cities the scene of their pleasures, but when the supply of the genuine article was exhausted they would fill the rest of the order with anything that could stand up.

The agencies' main concern was to collect their "head fee," and they would send up "teamsters" wearing derby hats and pointed shoes who literally did not know which end of a horse-collar was up. "Axemen" would arrive who didn't know how to sharpen an axe, much less how to swing one; and men certified as sky-hookers who miraculously avoided killing themselves or someone else until the boss put them out in the road the day after their arrival, with a profane admonition never to return.

The old-timers resented them, for their ineptness gave the real woodsmen more work to do, but at least they were often good for a laugh. One man, shipped up to First Connecticut Lake from New York City, attacked a white birch as soon as his axe was ready. When shown that spruce was his proper subject, he exclaimed, "Oh! It's only Christmas trees you want, eh?"

A famous story that has to do with another of these "hard-hat" men was related by Tom Graham, a well-known woods boss on the upper Connecticut sixty years ago.

The man claimed he could use an axe, so Tom put him to swamping. During the day the boss came onto him as he was attacking a yellow birch about six inches in diameter. He was nibbling all the way around the tree, like a beaver. Tom was so thunderstruck he couldn't even swear. Finally he heaved a big sigh and said in a polite voice to the hard-hat man, "Which way do you think it'll fall?"

"How in hell do I know which way it'll fall?" retorted the axeman. "I came up here to work in the woods, not to be a goddamned prophet!"

Woodsmen who had shot their roll in places like Portland or Boston would go to an employment agency that the logging companies had begun to recognize, and the agency would take care of them—keep them overnight, feed them a few meals, and advance them train fare. The cost was charged up to them and they arrived at camp in debt. This procedure turned into quite a racket. The agencies padded the charges to the men, and quite often the men would desert the camp to which they had been assigned and go to another one, a practice which became a real source of trouble to the camp boss. It was commonly said, in the last days of long-logging, that every camp had three crews—one going, one coming, and one working.

In earlier days, when the increasing activity in the lumbering industry required more men than the native New England stock could supply, the French-Canadians were the answer, but even they sometimes presented a problem.

A noted C.V.L. boss was a Canuck named Joe Roby, who had once operated on the Nulhegan, but who had not been in that district for years. The French-Canadians, who were very clannish, would get off the Grand Trunk train at North Stratford, New Hampshire, and ask for Joe Roby's camp. When they learned that Joe had been transferred, they promptly took the next train home. After some head-scratching, the company simply named three of the Nulhegan camps "Joe Roby No. 1," "Joe Roby No. 2," and "Joe Roby No. 3." It worked fine and the men were satisfied.

Mushrat Hayes, who was walking-boss for the Odell Manufacturing Company on Nash Stream, solved the same problem by having one camp with a French boss, cook, and cookees, to which his depot-camp clerk, Hugh Grogan, who spoke and wrote French very well, sent all the Canucks who came in.

Many men shipped to the woods when they were drunk. I was at a camp on Perry Stream in 1919 when a Boston man with a respectable and profitable business arrived with the tote-team. He had slept most of the time. Now he woke up and learned he was in the north woods, twenty miles from a railroad—and he had two hundred dollars in bills in his pocket! In that same camp there were a New York City tailor, a Florida barber, an English remittance man, and two alleged murderers.

Speaking of murderers, an odd case was that of Bing Anderson, a young Norwegian woodsman from Berlin, New Hampshire. Bing was New England ski-jumping champion back in 1927. He jumped very well, and he was handy with an axe, but when you'd said that you'd said about all you could in his favor. In 1931 he found himself, broke in Moncton, New Brunswick. He scraped up an acquaintanceship with a man in a local flea-bag, then tunked him on the head, killing him quite dead, and took all his money—two dollars.

He left the rooming-house and walked out of town. After following a railroad track for ten miles he came to a logging camp, and hired out as an axeman. At that time radios were beginning to be popular, but they were always breaking down. The radio in camp was out of order, and Bing, who had worked in a radio store in Berlin, offered to fix it. After some tinkering he got the thing to working. And the first thing that came in was a report of the murder in Moncton, with a description of the murderer.

The camp boss took a long look at his new employee and summoned a sheriff. They arrested Bing and sent him to jail in Sydney, Nova Scotia. His numerous sporting friends did all they could to get him off, but it is much harder for a murderer to escape the penalty in Canada than it is in the United States. Poor Bing was hanged by the neck, and another woodsman transmigrated into a moose-bird.

For it is one of the pet superstitions of the woodsmen that moose-birds, also known as Canada jays and "gorbies," are the reincarnated souls of dead lumberjacks. These large, gray, silent birds appear from nowhere as you are eating your lunch out in the woods, in both summer and winter, and come so close, to get crumbs, that sometimes you can catch them in your hand. Tom Cozzie, of the C.V.L., did it once. "He squawk lak' hell!" said Tom. You must never harm one of them, even if he snitches a flitch of bacon, or dire evil will befall you. Any old woodsman or woods guide will tell you many stories to prove it.

As the old guard diminished, the French-Canadians, who often have more than a score of children in a family—and as a result sometimes run out of names and use numbers instead (I recall a Vingt-Six Gagnon from St. Augustin)—swarmed into the woods until frequently a camp would not have a single English-speaking lumberjack in it.

Finally came the Finns and the Slavs, strong in the back, weak in the head, as the saying went, but the Finns were equal to the Canucks, and the Slavs made up in brute strength for what they may have lacked in skill. Scandinavians, so plentiful in the Lake States, were always scarce in the North Country, but sometimes the city agencies would send up Italians. Perhaps as a result of this, the old Brown Company was bought out in 1964 by an Italian firm in Milano, and I have been told that spaghetti is replacing pea soup on the upper Androscoggin.

By and large, the Canucks were small, quick, trim men, fond of gay sashes and toques, and unsurpassed with an axe. It was their natural weapon and they handled it and practiced with it until they acquired unbelievable dexterity. They could throw an axe at a running rat and split it in two, or they could hurl it at a mark fifteen yards away and hit it three times out of three.

They were not good teamsters, they were not kind to animals, they were superstitious and easy to scare, and they never took a bath all winter. But they were gay, good-hearted fellows, and quickly learned to swear good, sound English oaths with a French accent that was amusing to listen to. When something went wrong they would fervently mingle the two languages.

The American woodsmen regarded them with tolerant superiority but often carried their French oaths home with them to use when needed—somehow a swear-word doesn't sound so profane when uttered in a foreign language. *Sacrémogee! You sunnybeech!* a farmer's wife would hear her husband yell when he hit his thumb with a hammer.

A curious phenomenon of nature was the "jumping Frenchman." Every camp had one, sometimes several. The affliction was obviously a functional disorder of some kind. Old woodsmen ascribed it to inbreeding. It is true that a Canuck seldom married outside his native village, where everyone was related to everyone else, as in all rural communities, but nobody seems to have made a scientific study of the "jumper."

If a jumper was shaving, or whittling, or just sitting on a riverbank, and someone came up behind him suddenly and cried, "Jump into the river!" (or "into the fire," if there was a fire), in he'd jump. If someone stepped up behind him and tickled him lightly, he'd jump through the roof. But one had to be careful if the man was holding a lethal weapon, for he would swing it around like old Brian Boru himself. Strangely, the victims of such mean practical jokes never got mad about them.

If a cookee was a jumper, the men would wait until he was about to place a dish of soup or some other spilly food on the table and then say, "Drop it!" and down it would come, right down the neck of the nearest man.

Many of the jumpers could not help imitating any quick physical motion that was made near them. A line of men would be sitting on the deacon seat and a playful lumberjack would swing his arm as if he were going to hit the man next to him. Every jumper in the line, if he saw the motion, would turn and strike at his neighbor. Or a man would take his pipe from his mouth and pretend to throw it on the floor. Then the jumpers could not help dashing down their own pipes.

The Finns were a silent, glum lot, compared with the volatile Frenchmen, but they were fine woodsmen, and they were very clean. The Finns in a camp would build a sauna, a little log cabin, handy to water, where they took sweat baths. The men would go there on Sunday, and when they were thoroughly steamed they would beat themselves with birch twigs and run out and roll in the snow, even at sub-zero temperatures.

While the Finns were unmatched as cutters and pilers of four-foot pulpwood, they were not as good with long logs, and they were often a special source of trouble to a camp boss, for in addition to the antagonism they showed toward the other Baltic nationals, there was—and still is—a clearly marked political, social, and cultural division into two groups of Finns, giving rise to friction if both were assigned to the same camp.

The Poles and the Russians seldom achieved the proficiency of the old-timers with axe and peavey, but they could cut down a lot of trees and cut them up, and as long as they stayed sober they would obey orders and mind their own business. Some of them, by sheer merit, became the equal of any woodsman Yankee, Canuck, or Indian. One of these was Tom Cozzie, a Russian who rose from swamper to woods manager of the St. Regis in West Stewartstown, New Hampshire.

In Maine, all the lumberjacks from eastern Europe, whether Russians, Poles, Balts, or Slovaks, are called, rather disparagingly, Polacks or Polanders. In northern New Hampshire they are all called Russians. They began to be numerous only after 1914, and when the Yankee camp clerks could not pronounce their names they put them down on the books as John Smith or John Doe. Harry Holme, who clerked at Hellgate, used to say of the Russians, "Most of them have no name. It's only a noise!" I knew one camp where 40 per cent of the Russians were called John Smith. One was on the books as Pat Duffy, and another man, a French-Canadian, as Hardstick Canuck.

But all these men, including murderers, underworld characters, hard-hat men of every description, once they arrived in the remote camps, far from their particular temptation, became industrious and companionable workers. And if they stayed, and came back, they developed into real lumberjacks. A couple of incidents about "Polacks" are worth telling:

On November 18, 1920, a motor launch carrying thirty-six woodsmen, most of them Polacks, burned on Chesuncook Lake. Half of the men were lost in the icy water. A camp clerk named Nelson Smith was so distraught that he shed every bit of his clothing, folded it carefully and put it on the wheel-house roof, and leaped overboard as the burning boat hit the dry-kye. One of the Polacks alone had the forethought to put his matches into his hair and protect them with his cap before he jumped overboard. Those matches lit a fire that prevented all the survivors from freezing to death. Fred Noad and George Cassidy, who were alone at the Moose Pond storehouse some distance down the shore, happened to look out the window and saw the burning boat. They threw blankets into a bateau and rowed furiously up the lake. The men shivering around the fire, especially Nelson Smith, were very glad to see them. That night was so cold that skim ice formed along the shore.

In the winter of 1919 a young Irishman from Boston was sent up by a Boston employment agency to work for the C.V.L. at a camp on Big Brook, near Second Connecticut Lake. The camp boss put him on as a sawyer with a big Pole, and the next morning, before daylight, the men started for the cuttings. It was cold, bitter cold, and the youngster was neither used to nor dressed for that weather. Presently, he stumbled and fell down. The other men told him to go on back to camp, but he was determined to stick it out. After a while he fell again, and this time he couldn't get up. The Pole, who could barely talk English, put him on his shoulder and ran a mile and a half to camp, tucked him into his bunk, and told the cook to give him something hot to drink.

There were always a few Indians in a crew. The red men were noted especially for their skill in handling canoes and bateaux in white water. To this day old men in the North Country tell stories their fathers told them of how in the spring of 1876 the Bangor Tigers (a group of virtuoso rivermen including Indians, Canucks, and Yankees) brought over to take the drive down the Connecticut ran the Pittsburg falls in canoes, and Bellows Falls in bateaux—feats never performed before, or since.

When the Depression struck in 1930, wages went down. The Government supplied a dole, or unemployment compensation, as it is called in these days of euphemisms, and while it wasn't very big, the lumber companies soon learned that a man could subsist on it.

In 1935 the Brown Company sent George Anderson down to Boston to hire men at the agencies. There were men enough lacking work, but George returned without any, quite disgusted.

"I told them what the wages were, how much would be deducted for board, and so on, and they just laughed. They said, 'Look, Jack, the Government gives me ten dollars a week just to sit on my arse and do nothing. Why should I go and work for you six days a week and clear twelve dollars?' "

The question, of course, was unanswerable, except to old rugged individualists who would sooner starve to death than to live on another man's money, even if it was distributed by a "government."

It was before the Depression that another Brown Company boss, Jack Lary, used to go to Boston to visit the employment agencies. En route he would pick up a section of telegraph pole, which he would place on the office floor. To men who asserted they knew how to handle a peavey or an axe, Jack handed the tool, and bade them prove it. No prove, no hire.

"Great Constipated Christ!" Jack used to say to the evident amateurs, "if you ever began to cut down a tree you'd have to stand in a washtub, or you'd cut off your own feet!"

Today's lumberjack is a suitcase-carrying, pomade-using, Coca-Cola-drinking gent who knows his rights. He toils from eight to five, and when the camp boss suggests a little extra effort, he consults his "shop steward." More often than not he takes his Chrysler and drives home on a good gravel road, on Friday night, returning only on Monday morning, leaving the camp deserted save for a lonesome cookee and a few old-timers who haven't got used to the new ways.

The great glaring difference is that the old personal touch has vanished, along with the old-fashioned, two-fisted, red-shirted woodsman, who wasted little time in thinking how he was being exploited—as he all too often was—but who would work himself to a frazzle and cheerfully risk life and limb for a boss who gave him a fair shake. Today's lumberjack is a grease-monkey who works for an Organization. How can he feel about a chain-saw and an Organization as the old woodsman did about his axe and his boss?

5

The Timber-Cruiser
and Woods Surveyor

WHEN lumbering first started in New England, "cruising," i.e., locating and estimating a stand of timber, was not necessary. Timber was everywhere, tall and thick, and all you had to do was to set up your mill beside a watercourse that made the overshot wheel clank lazily, while a pair of steers would drag in enough logs from right close by to keep you going.

But as the endless demand ate into the endless supply, it no longer sufficed to bring the mill to the trees. The trees had to be brought to the mill. So a man had to put up his mill where he could expect to find timber available to keep it going. There was, of course, speculation in timberlands by wealthy businessmen who did no crusing and who expected to make their profit by re-selling the lands to settlers. The most famous deal of this kind was the Bingham Purchase in 1793, along the Kennebec and east of the Penobscot, where a Pennsylvania politician named William Bingham bought a million acres and later a second million, at about ten cents an acre.

The whole history of the granting of state lands in New Hampshire and Maine to various educational institutions and private railroads, and of the final disposition of those lands, is a fascinating one which has never been treated completely. In 1870 the Maine legislature gave away its last 800,000 acres of forest land to the European and North American Railway, and even generously remitted $280,00 in taxes.

Cruising timber is done in one of three ways. First, your old-time woodsman, with long experience and a flair for estimating standing timber, can walk over a tract of from ten acres to forty thousand and make a report that is surprisingly accurate. He can tell how much black spruce and how much white spruce it will cut to the acre, how much of it is infested with bud-worm, how much basswood and ash and yellow birch is growing on it, and how much of it is worthless.

He can also supply a great deal of other useful information that a college-trained forester, just out of school, will refuse to accept until he has made a careful scientific survey himself and learned, to his astonishment, that his figures and the old-timer's just about coincide. Of course, on large tracts the cruiser does not carry all this information in his head; he uses a plan or book in which he makes a map or chart of each day's work, tracing his course from the beginning.

Just how the old cruiser has achieved his degree of excellence may not be immediately evident, but it was expressively explained in a celebrated case at law over a disputed estimate made on a certain pine tract in Canada some seventy-five years ago. The Honorable E. Blake, Member of Parliament, asked Bill Irwin, who was at that time Canada's most expert bushranger, as the cruiser was then called, if estimating pine was not like guessing the number of beans in a bottle.

Irwin replied that to him it was not, but that it probably would be to Mr. Blake. Mr. Blake then requested Mr. Irwin to explain how he did it, or how he got the necessary knowledge and information to be able to tell the quantity of pine on a large territory. Irwin, who was an Irishman not lacking in wit, asked Blake to tell him how he got his great knowledge of law.

And that answer, after all, gives the reader the best idea of the subject.

The second method of cruising timber is by airplane. There are men who claim they can fly over a stand of spruce and make a very close estimate of how many board feet or how many cords are in it. Many people, however, don't believe them. It is true that aerial photographs are particularly useful to show the types of trees, and they even give good impressions of the quantity and quality of the timber, especially since with stereoscopic views the trees can be seen as if standing straight up, but for accurate estimates, supplementary ground work is useful.

Third, today, if a good cruiser is requested to make an estimate of a stand of timber, he will ask about the topography of the region, the nature of the soil, the purpose of the cruise, the degree of accuracy required, the time allowed for the job, and the amount of money available for doing it. Also, he will want to know during which season the work is to be done, and the extent and condition of the survey lines and other lines which the cruise will be tied into.

The cruiser asks other questions, too, concerning maps, plans, and records of the region indicating areas cut previous to the cruise, and the date of cutting. He inquires about areas killed by fire, flowage, insect damage, and the like. If, as in the case of large properties, the cruise is to be made with the object in view of future cutting over a period of years, some attention must be given to growth studies, the age of stands, and the like.

Then your cruiser sallies forth into the trackless wilderness, blasphemously fighting black flies, frost-bite, or rotten ice, as the season may require, and presently he brings the report contracted for.

The cruiser's first problem, when he starts a new project, is to locate the test areas. He often has a good knowledge of surveying, and it helps him to find the old township markings which in these uninhabited woods supply the only points of departure for identifying particular tracts.

In the northern New England spruce area, where the land was originally divided into townships six miles square, the cruiser casts about until he finds a corner-post, usually a marked tree. Finding a corner-post is not always easy. When William Draper was logging the Pogy Mountain region in Maine fifty years ago, his best cruiser found one corner but couldn't find the next one. Like every good man he had long since mastered the art of making an adjustment in the number of his paces to accommodate variations in the surface of the ground—five hundred paces for him meant eighty rods, one thousand, half a mile, and so on. But all he came up against was a big red spruce tree, with no marks on it at all.

But it *ought* to have been the corner tree, and just as Bill Irwin *knew* the number of pine trees, this cruiser *knew* that it was the corner tree! After tramping all around the tree quite in vain, he stood back and looked farther up the trunk. A dozen feet above the ground he saw, or thought he saw, a slight depression in the bark. Philosophically, he spat tobacco-juice at the big tree and looked around for a smaller one, which he cut down and used as a ladder. When he had climbed up to the depression, hacked at it with his light woodsman's axe. A grin of satisfaction came over his weather-beaten face as his perspiring efforts were rewarded and he carefully uncovered the big blaze and inscription, buried deep under new growth, which had been made by a surveyor nearly a century before. There it was, clearly to be read:

I. D. BRECK
1829.

Breck, or whoever he had spotting line for him, must have been a very tall man, and he had probably run his survey in the wintertime, on snowshoes, when the snow may have been six feet deep. The man that made the blaze had reached up as high as he could place it—and there it still was. The cruiser's boss, Mr. Draper, was a city man, and he was so impressed that he went out with a good camera and took a picture of the thing.

Starting from a corner, a cruiser selects test areas, taken at intervals of five chains (twenty rods, or 330 feet). Each of these areas is in the form of a circle, with a radius of fifty-nine feet. The cruiser paces this distance from the center of the plot and only rarely is he off more than one or two paces. Of course, there are areas where particular conditions, such as an extra-heavy stand of timber, require special treatment.

On his test plots the cruiser records the trees by species, diameter, and height. An experienced man can guess height quite well, but sometimes he will use a curious instrument called a hypsometer. Then, knowing the diameter and the height, he consults a prepared volume table which specifies the board feet or cords yielded by trees of various dimensions. But as volume tables are based on sound trees, the cruiser must use his expertise in deducting for defects—decay, crooks, and the like.

Often, too, depending on his instructions, the cruiser must take notes on the "logging chance"——whether the land is rough or rocky, swampy or perpendicular. A good man will return with a map showing contours and possible logging roads.

In New England, cruising is quite generally done by two men, for the good reason that if some accident befalls a lone man he is a dead duck.

The timber-cruiser is often a surveyor, and vice versa. Such a man was John Locke, who later became general manager of the C.V.L. Such was Fred Noad. Such was Jack Carter, who worked for the Brown Company, and who once set a record of walking ninety miles on snowshoes in twenty-four hours (from Kicking-dash to Weymontachague, on the St. Maurice).

Jack had the habit of always singing hymns as he was dressing himself in the morning. About once in two weeks, the camp clerk would tie Jack's shoestrings into hard knots, after Jack had gone to sleep, and the boys were always overjoyed the next morning when, upon finding his shoestrings tied, he changed from his matutinal hymns to loud profanity without a pause. . . .

The winter life of a woods surveyor—and of a cruiser—is exemplified by the story of Fred Noad's 1921 survey near Umbazookskus Lake, Maine. A glance at a map will make the situation clear to the reader.

The Great Northern had just acquired timber holdings around Chamberlain Lake, on the East Branch of the Penobscot, and their paper mill was at Millinocket, on the West Branch of the Penobscot, above where the East Branch comes in. Not only would they have to get the wood back up the West Branch to the mill, if they drove it down the East Branch, but there was also a conflict with another company owning tracts on that river. So, if possible, the company wanted to find a way to bring the wood over the very low height-of-land into the upper waters of the West Branch.

This was by no means impossible, and indeed something like it had been done eighty years before, when a smart engineer named Coe had built at Churchill and Eagle and Chamberlain lakes a series of dams and lock dams that made the water run uphill and then overflow from Telos Lake, taking into East Branch waters logs that would otherwise have gone down the Allagash into the St. John.

This diversion of needed driving water from the Allagash made operators farther down that stream very vexed, and being forthright men, generous and social to be sure, but also reckless, they promptly dynamited Mr. Coe's lower dams.

A shrewd operator named Rufus Dwinel acquired control of the ditch that had been dug from Telos Lake into East Branch waters, and he proposed to charge Mr. Coe and other lumbermen a healthy toll for sluicing their logs through his ditch. This led to the famous Telos Cut War, one of the many famous serio-comic episodes in New England lumbering. Coe and the others said they would drive their logs through regardless. Dwinel, no puny man, armed seventy-five Bangor Tigers with large butcher-knives and stationed them at the Cut, with orders to use them if necessary. The state legislature promptly swung into action and upheld Dwinel's rights, but established his toll rate at a much lower figure than he had set. The old Telos Cut Company functioned until 1921, when it sold out to the East Branch Improvement Company.

The Great Northern's chief engineer was William Hilton (later he was the company's general manager, and he died only in November, 1964). In view of later decisions and developments, it is interesting to see just how the company envisaged the problem back in 1921. At the time it was decided to transport the timber to the West Branch, Noad was in the woods, working as inspector of a number of camps. Hilton pursued Noad from Bangor to Greenville Junction, to Lily Bay, to the Grant Farm, and finally to the Cuxabexis storehouse, telephoning from each stop, but in vain. Tired of the chase, and having to return to the Bangor office, Hilton penciled a note to Noad and left it with a scaler named Frank Mc-Kendrick at the Grant Farm: "We want to make a survey so we can determine if it is feasible to build a carrier, sluice, long hauler road, railroad, or what?" And then he went into details.

The winter cutting season was already over, but the ice had not yet gone out of the lakes. If the break-up, which would cover the flat country with water, came while Noad and his crew were frogging around there, their lot would not be a happy one. But Fred was not one to complain. At Suncook he picked up the surveying instruments, an 8 by 8 tent, a canoe, and the usual camp supplies and equipment, which Hilton had had the foresight to send up from Bangor, and being an authorized purchasing and contracting agent of the company, he proceeded to hire three Suncook natives and to buy all the groceries in the village store—real ham, steak, fresh pork, canned goods, and *butter*. No old woodsman can imagine real butter on such an expedition.

The company's regular purchasing agent, Charlie Curtis, who later became mayor of the city of Brewer, had once complained to Fred Gilbert, his boss, about Noad's predilection for good grub, but Gilbert, after hearing Noad's defense—that time and money were saved by his method of purchasing and packing for transportation—backed up the woodsman.

Noad and McKendrick built a sledge-like cradle for the canoe, loaded it to the gills, and away they went to the romantic shores of Mud Pond, beyond Umbazookskus. There they established a base camp in the deep snow, and Noad ran a rough traverse for a railroad, and figured out a holding ground in Chamberlain and a carrier scheme from Chamberlain to Mud Pond. Also, having discovered a beaver pond to give him the necessary water, he figured out a way to build a sluice from Mud Pond to Umbazookskus Lake.

Of course the water, like that of Chamberlain Lake, was originally St. John River water, but diverting it one more step from the Penobscot East Branch to the West Branch seemed all right to him—provided the East Branch people did not object. The East Branch had already stolen this water through Webster Brook and Telos. He found he could bring that water where he wanted it by using a short flume.

To make their final check of all the main points involved they had to cross Mud Pond each day, and as the season progressed the ice, which never had been very solid, began to get quite soft. Fred always went ahead and tested it with his axe, while McKendrick stayed behind with a great long pole, so that when anyone went through he could stay back from the hole and pull him out. Almost every day someone did fall in. As the dunking was more discomforting than dangerous, they at least got some laughs out of it.

Many little adventures have been omitted in this account, but when one realizes the conditions under which that survey was made in 1921—the fact that the men were cut off from all communication in the event of an emergency, with no shelter other than that which they could contrive for themselves, the uncertainty of weather conditions, and the urgency of their task—it is evident that the outing differed considerably from a Sunday School picnic.

In 1841, when Coe was building his lock dams, he vetoed a perfectly sound plan to dig a canal two miles long from Mud Pond to Umbazookskus Lake, in favor of the Telos Cut waterway, down the East Branch. Noad, in 1921, was in favor of the Mud Pond waterway, but the Great Northern turned it down, probably because of sensitivity to "public relations" and the objections of the East Branch people. However, in 1927 his alternate plan, for a railroad, bore fruit. Great Northern wood from Eagle and Chamberlain lakes was hauled on a railroad built the year before to Umbazookskus. From there it was driven by water to Chesuncook Lake, on the West Branch, and so on to the mill at Millinocket.

Winter is the best time to cruise timber, although life is no bed of roses even then. But one can cover a good deal of ground on snowshoes, especially on a crust, and the leaves are then off the hardwoods, making visibility better. Also, one can cross lakes, instead of having to push one's way through the mud and brush as one would in the summer. This last blessing, however, has its bad side, for one can never trust the ice, and many a woodsman had drowned when he broke through, while others have had well-nigh miraculous escapes.

In the summer, which is frequently dry, one can run short of drinking water, but this is no problem in winter, for one can always melt snow. Cold weather is not so pleasant as one might think. While working, one doesn't mind it, and a sheet-iron stove with a pipe passing through a hole in the roof (where it is well secured with tin) makes an ordinary tent quite comfortable. Probably the worst feature of timber-cruising in winter is having to use the hand compass with one's bare hands, for this work cannot be done with mittens or gloves on.

This last problem was sometimes solved by having one's wife, or girlfriend, knit a pair of mittens with the tops and thumbs open, the wrists extra tight so that they would hold in place, and the lower ends of hand and thumb fairly loose so that when one was not using them one could hunch his fingers and thumbs up into the mittens. Some men wore woolen gloves with the thumb and finger ends left open, but they were not so comfortable as the mittens.

Cruisers are only human, and they can err. Some eighty years ago Dartmouth College offered to sell the stumpage on the Dartmouth College Grant—27,000 acres of wild land on Dead Diamond Stream, in northeastern New Hampshire—to the Brown Company (then known as the Berlin Mills) for a reasonable sum. In fact, the Brown Company had a twenty-thousand-dollar option on it. They sent their head walking-boss, a huge man named Horace Frost, with another trusty woodsman named Tom Tracy and an office man named Jim Parker, to cruise the territory, which is very mountainous.

But Horace suffered from corns, Tom had rheumatism, and Jim got sick after a lizard showed up in the oatmeal and Tom, to plague him, told him it was poisonous. So the three heroes returned and reported adversely. George Van Dyke snapped up the option, and when the Brown Company bought it from him a few years later, they had to pay much more money.

All in all, the college received a million and a half dollars from the Brown Company over a period of fifty years, and the cutting on those 27,000 acres shows, in microcosm, how logging changed in northern New England during that period, between 1887 and 1937. The first cut was for long logs, fifty-six feet in length. The next was for spruce, fir, and pine with a minimum stump diameter of fourteen inches, breast-high. Then it was cut for four-foot pulpwood of spruce, fir, and poplar, at a nine-inch stump diameter. The next cutting was for old-growth maple and yellow and white birch for furniture making, at a stump diameter of over twelve inches. Finally all species of hardwood and softwood with a stump diameter of eight inches or over were cut for four-foot pulpwood.

To sum up, a cruiser must be skillful enough to know always where he is, and on whose land. He must be a good judge of timber, able to tell a sound tree from a defective one, and able to estimate closely the quality of lumber, reckoned in board feet (or in cords, if he is cruising for pulpwood), that each tree will be likely to produce when sawed at the mill.

He must examine the contour of the country where the timber is, determine how it is to be transported—by water, rail, or truck—and estimate how much money per thousand board feet or per cord it will cost to bring the logs to market.

In carrying out these functions he must be honest, industrious, and courageous. He must gain the other side of rivers that have no bridges over them, and he must cross lakes where there are no boats. He must find shelter when he has no tent, and make moccasins when his shoes are worn out. And he must be indefatigable, for he will often be tempted to leave some work half finished because of the physical obstacles that lie between him and the completion of his task.

He fords streams, or falls trees across them; he builds rafts to get over lakes; he climbs through windfalls—places where hurricanes have passed and left the trees twisted and broken, their trunks and branches pointing in all directions, generally with the trees tipped partly or entirely to the ground and their roots turned up. Getting through, over, under, and beyond these places, which vary from a few rods to miles across—especially in winter, when the snow hides the pitfalls and screens the rotten trunks and limbs from view—severely tests the courage, patience, and endurance of the woodsman. And all the time he must use his compass, keep his direction, and measure his distance, for otherwise he will not know where he is.

The cruiser has to cross miles of swamps where the bog bottom scarcely bears his weight, and where, when night comes, he must build a bed of poles to keep his weary body from the wet; he must travel all day in open and burned country, his bed and board upon his back, the sun's hot rays pressing like a heavy weight upon his head, while myriads of black flies swarm about him and attack every inch of his skin, even penetrating through the hair on his head. Bears and deer have been known to be blinded by black flies and go mad—and human beings, too.

Far from roads, telephones, or other living persons, he takes his chances with floods and forest fires. One old cruiser, in the late 1870's, records a forest fire he encountered:

. . . the sun was either completely obscured, or it hung like a red ball above the earth, now penetrating the clouds of smoke, now again being hidden by them. The smoke came at times in great rolls at the surface of the earth, then was caught up by the breeze and lifted to higher altitudes, and at all times was bewildering to those whom it surrounded. At times one became choked with the thick smoke. For many hours during one of those days I moved with my face close to the ground where I could breathe. When finally I came to open country where the currents of wind could lift the smoke, I was very thankful. . . .

It is true that in 1966 the cruiser's life is not quite so hard. His canoe has an outboard motor, and instead of cutting firewood—it took a cord or more to keep a campfire going at night, in the wintertime—he takes along bottled gas as cooking fuel. And in the winter he now gets around on a snowmobile and goes home, or to a camp, at night.

But the reader must wonder what in the world could ever impel a man to go out and endure the hardships we have just enumerated. The answer is not too difficult: he has health and appetite, which give him a buoyant spirit, and when he does come to a good piece of country with good timber, which inevitably occurs, the prospect makes him forget his trials.

Perhaps nothing contributes more to the joy of living than being in the solitude of the great unbroken forest, surrounded by magnificent, tall, straight, beautiful trees, on a day when the sun casts shadows through their waving tops and one can listen to the whisperings, formed almost into words, of the leafy boughs, to the warblings of the songbirds and the chattering of the red squirrels. On such days the woodsman who is alone in the forest approaches nearer to his Creator than at almost any other time in his life's experiences. And that, along with the feeling, conscious or otherwise, that he is pitting his individual strength and skill against the wilderness and is winning, that he is not a machine, an organization man, makes it worth while.

6

The Camp Boss

BY 1900, more or less, the "wild lands" of northern New England had nearly all come into the hands of great corporations—lumber and paper companies. It was about that time that the Great Northern Paper Company and the International Paper Company were formed. The J. E. Henry concern had bought out the various owners of their mountainous kingdom below Franconia Notch, New Hampshire, the Brown Company was the acknowledged ruler of the Androscoggin, Hollingsworth and Whitney had the upper Kennebec, and George Van Dyke, who built and directed various railroads, banks, and paper and lumber firms, was the undisputed master of the upper Connecticut. Of course, there were other big owners—Pingree and Coe, for example—and a host of individuals who owned a "lot" here and there.

The actual methods of logging did not change with this new type of ownership. October to March continued to be the cutting and hauling months, after which came the annual spring drive. Some duties formerly performed by one individual were shared among several in later days, but the nature of the work to be done remained basically the same.

In the earlier days, a canny businessman who had bought up the title to a quarter-section or two "on spec" but who had probably never seen it, would inveigle a capable lumberman of his acquaintance to log it for him. He would treat him to some good New England rum, tell him what a wonderful chance it was—it would cut fifty thousand feet to the acre, was handy to good driving streams, had no burn on it, was all down-hill haul, and so on and on—and he would offer a contract carefully drawn up in his own favor, with penalty clauses in fine print, in case the work was not completed according to specifications.

If the lumberman was interested, he would get himself a map, probably drawn from someone's memory, take a pocket compass, a frying pan and a tea-pot, no more supplies than he could carry on his back, and head up-river, in the month of August.

Using considerable woodcraft, an exact sense of direction, and possibly also his compass, he would search until he found the great old birch or pine, scarred with the cryptic marks of a long-dead surveyor, that constitute the corner-post of his township. Satisfied that he was in the right place, he would pace off his boundaries, hanging spots here and there. With a practiced eye to good water, good drainage, and nearness to the timber he intended to cut, he would choose a campsite; then he would climb up and down the hills, making tentative plans for the location of future roads, landings, dams, and other necessary facilities.

Next he would mark out his tote-road, generally choosing the short-est route to the source of supplies, and trying to avoid too-steep hills and streams requiring too many bridges. If he could, he would follow a stream, but in the rough and tangled hills of northern New England this was not always possible. Sometimes an ox tote-team would be on the road six days bringing supplies from Bangor. When Ed Lacroix, the millionaire jobber from the St. John, took on the job of cutting some two hundred thousand cords of pulpwood on Indian Stream, in northern New Hamp-shire, back in 1924, his best source of supply was the lonesome railroad station of Malvina, in St. Malo, Quebec. From Malvina his main tote-road ran eleven miles, first up over a steep height-of-land and down onto Halls Stream, then up another steep height-of-land and down onto Fisher Brook, then up another steep height-of-land and down onto Indian Stream. The ruts in that road were two feet deep, and the Canayen ("*Canadien*") teamsters couldn't haul loads of more than six hundred pounds over it, on drays.

An experienced man could calculate how much it would cost per mile to build a good tote-road, as well as how much more it would cost to build a better one. The amount of money he could allow himself de-pended on how much timber was going to be cut at that camp. A road to be used for several seasons could economically be much better than a road for one year's use only. It was estimated that two hundred tons of sup-plies were required for cutting and hauling a million feet of logs, and tote-road expenditures were based on those figures.

At the time of his first visit to the scene of his future operations, the lumberman would also spot his main two-sled road, with its one or more divergent branches, as well as chances for cutting crews, and would de-cide where to build a driving dam or two.

His next chore was to return to civilization and collect a crew. Strangely enough, the harder a boss was, the more he was respected, and the more eager men were to work for him. So (in those good old days) he would go to North Stratford or Berlin or Bangor and patiently make the rounds of the saloons, small hotels, and boarding houses where lumber-jacks were accustomed to congregate after a drive was in the booms. He would chaff with them, buy them drinks, tell them what wages would be paid to good men, and try to flatter each one into believing he would earn top wages. Word would soon get around that Frank Porter, say, was hiring a crew, and the men would come looking for a job.

But his worries would not yet be over. He would set a day and an hour for the start. He might have engaged sixty men, but when he counted noses he would think he was pretty lucky if he had thirty on hand. Where were the rest? Still in the saloons, boarding houses, and hotels, for not until their last cent was spent and their credit exhausted would many of these improvident, happy-go-lucky woodsmen leave their favorite haunts to go back and toil in the woods.

So the boss would shrug resignedly, load the more valetudinarian gents of his crew onto his supply wagon, and head north, the rest of the men tramping in the dust behind, singing, swearing, fighting, drinking, bringing a brighter gleam into the eyes of the farmers' wives as they passed, shouting humorous greetings, and a vague feeling of envy and nostalgia to the farmer himself. For no matter how nobly he denies it, no matter how truly he can compute that he is economically better off, your humdrum stay-at-homer does not feel entirely at ease in the presence of men who can sing, and mean, such fine old sentiments as:

> *I don't give a damn*
> *For any damn man*
> *Who don't give a damn for me!* . . .

And these men meant it. They would work their heads off for a good boss, but they remained independent. Jack Lary, a Brown Company boss, was driving up through the Thirteen-Mile Woods one winter day. He had been to Berlin on business and now he was heading back to camp, but he had made other stops besides the one at the company office and he was feeling no pain, as the boys used to say. Down the river road, his pair of black Arabians at full trot, came Mr. W. R. Brown, Jack's immediate superior. Brown wanted to talk to his boss, but he couldn't seem to make him understand. Finally he exploded:

"Lary, the trouble with you is you're drunk, and I know it!"

"Mr. Brown," Jack retorted, "the trouble with you is you're a damn fool, and you'll never know it!"

Eventually the wagon and the boss would arrive at the end of the road. The boss would put his crew into tents and start them building the tote-road. When they reached the campsite the first job was to build the camp. Many men did not care to go into the camp until it was built and in complete operation. Most camp foremen preferred to limit the building crew to old hands who understood the job. These experts did not have to be told how to notch the logs at the ends, how to cut them for windows and doors, how to make them shorter and shorter at each end as they approached the ridge-pole. The boss did not have to stand around and tell them how to raise the roof and how to lay the floor.

But he might decide where certain structures were to be built, or tell them that he wanted his own shack, where he lived with his clerk and scaler, to be made of peeled logs, with a little porch in front of it, and an extra bunk inside for visitors.

In fine weather it would take a week or ten days to set up a livable camp. There would still be a great deal to do: chinking the cracks with moss or mud, installing windows, doors, tables, and so on. The cook-shack was, of course, the first to be given consideration. Much would depend on the conditions at the site, the accessibility to suitable logs, and the number of men available who were accustomed to camp-building. Sometimes as soon as the men could be housed and fed in a rough-and-ready manner, the boss would be anxious to get to logging, and work on the camp would be continued more slowly for some time. The hovel, the office, the filer's shack, and the like might not even be started until the actual logging was well under way.

So, having put part of his crew to work building the camp, the lumberman would take another batch and set them to work clearing the stream of sunken trees, boulders, and driftwood so it would be ready for the drive in the spring. This task, about the meanest one in the woods, at least served to weed out the boys from the men. It had to be started in the summer, when the water was low, but it often continued until snow came and ice formed.

The accumulations of centuries in the form of driftwood and fallen trees frequently covered the stream-bed for miles, and all had to be cleared away. If the ground was swampy, horses could not work in it, and everything had to be done by hand. Tree by tree, stick by stick, the obstructions had to be lifted out and put far enough away so high water would not float them back in again. Islands and shoals had to be dug away; stumps, bedded deep in the mud, had to be grubbed out; embankments had to be made at sharp bends. The sunken tree in the bottom of the stream had to be cut and worked loose in its bed; then a chair could be fastened around it and the unwilling horses forced into the freezing water to haul it ashore.

All day long the crew would work, and as the days ran into weeks, and the short northern summer changed into cold autumn, the men would continue to grapple, lift, and carry the debris from the stream, wading in the icy water up to their waists, often bending down in it to their chins—week after week. Such work would kill a novice in a day, but these men it simply made harder.

There were men who tried the life of a logger, found it too rigorous, and walked out after a week or two. Of those who remained, the less nimble were often killed by falling trees, or crushed flat on a log landing. The spring drive, most dangerous of all woods work, accounted for a few more, and once the drive was in, a few died while celebrating. But the survivors were *tough*. As the saying went, you couldn't kill them with an axe.

While his crews engaged in the tasks just described, the lumberman set another gang to building the two-sled road. In the days of long logs, all transportation to the mill, save for a few logging railroads, was by water. New England was admirably constructed by nature for such an operation. The numerous rivers and streams offered free and easy transportation—especially during the short period in the spring when melting snows gave power and volume to the system.

Logs were hauled down and "landed," either directly on top of the ice that covered the rivers and lakes, or along the stream banks. Logs that were cut quite handy to a main watercourse could be hauled right from the stump to the landing or rollway, on a yarding-sled, or even by simple "twitching," but most of the logs arrived on "two-sleds," and for these a special road, appropriately called a two-sled road, had to be built.

The boss had already spotted this road out, in August, with a meticulous eye to securing a gradual descent, avoiding, if possible, grades of more than 5 per cent, and level stretches and cuts. On grades of over 5 per cent the load would acquire a great momentum, and had to be checked with hay or gravel. Occasionally, where a steep down-hill could not be avoided, a "hay-shed" was built, a solid roof to keep the ground bare of snow at all times, so that the ground itself could act as a brake. Some mountains were so long and steep that on the way down loads had to be snubbed three different times, and at times a steep up-hill could not be avoided. Various ingenious tricks were invented to take care of that problem. Most satisfactory was to get a donkey engine and set it at the top of the hill. The driver, having reached the bottom, unhitched his horses and hooked the endless chain onto his sled, and away it went up the hill, where he rejoined it at the summit.

The boss would do anything to keep his precious 5 per cent down-hill grade. Deep hollows were bridged with immense birch and maple logs piled trestle-fashion. Even today "Trestle Brook" is a common name on maps, and the trestles themselves are still there, some a century old. Today the birch logs in them, valueless then, are worth more than the spruce hauled across them in 1900.

If a heavy grade could not be avoided, it could often be lowered by a cut. Before the day of bulldozers, the lumberjacks tied into it with shovels and whittled it down to size. Streams had to be solidly bridged, marshy ground had to be corduroyed, curves coming down a hill were shored up on the outside by laving skids onto side-logs laid parallel to the road and covered deep with dirt. All stones were rolled out of the way, roots and stumps grubbed out, and by the time it was ready for the sprinkler to turn it into a twenty-foot-wide sheet of glare ice, the two-sled road was as smooth as a railroad right of way.

It generally followed a watercourse, and there were often low, marshy stretches and deep hollows that had to be filled or corduroyed. This cost time and money, and many years ago shrewd operators figured that it would be an easy trick to turn the stream into such spots, so that with the advent of cold weather the water would freeze and supply a long stretch of iced road at no expense. But they found that if a few warm days came along, which frequently happened, the road melted, and the teams floundered and swam, while the loaded sled rested on bare ground. So while this scheme is still commonly practiced in upper Canada, it is no longer used in New England.

The lumberman also had to figure out how many loads a teamster could haul in a day. If the landing was farther from camp than the men could be walked, or if the two-sled road was a turn-and-a-half or a two-turn-and-a-half road, a landing camp was built for the landing crew and the two-sled teams. In his mind's eye he had to foresee how many men and horses he would need to cut the millions of feet he had contracted for. He knew the proper time to begin work, he figured out how much timber he had on ground suitable for fall hauling—for by doing this in the fall he eliminated the need for a large yarding crew for a short time later on—and he made certain that the crew could finish yarding before the snow got deep.

The terrain dictated what kind of roads had to be made, and the kind of roads dictated the number of trips a teamster made each day from skidway or from stump to landing. One operation might require four daily trips by a yarding-sled, transporting from seven hundred to a thousand feet per load. Another, in hilly country, might not do better than two trips a day, using every minute of daylight available. An average load for a four-horse, two-sled rig was from seven to ten thousand feet, and weighed from twenty-five to thirty tons.

A famous slave-driver named Milt Shaw used to operate over on Dead River and Moosehead Lake, Maine. One day he met a Canuck teamster tranquilly returning to camp at 3 P.M. If the man had gone back for another load he would have been out long after dark. Milt gave him to understand that in the future he would make another trip. The very next day he saw him coming into camp. It was about 4:30, and the sled was empty. The lumberman lit into him. The teamster was unmoved.

"Trips you want, Mr. Shaw, trips you get!" he said. "You didn't say anything about loads. . . ."

Along in January, when the hauling season began, the camp boss gave his two-sled road a last smoothing, and dug his sprinkler out of the weeds and snow where it had been languishing for nearly a year and put it to work. Or perhaps a little earlier, before the hauling season began in earnest, he would have the old contraption out building up a road of solid ice, getting it all ready to haul those precious logs on.

The sprinkler was a humble and despised piece of wooden furniture, ugly, disagreeable, covered with icicles, but extremely useful. It was like a woman or a drink of whiskey: when a man needed it, he needed it awful bad. It was simply a wooden tank made of iron-bound planks, with a capacity of some five hundred gallons, mounted on a sled—or on two-sleds. Above an opening in the center of its top was erected a solid frame from which hung a pulley, through which passed a rope.

Sometimes the sprinkler was used by day, but usually it was at night, when the roads were clear and the rest of the crew were settling down for a good night's rest, that the sprinkler crew would hunch their mackinaws up around their ears and creak away in the frosty darkness to the water hole in the stream or lake.

There, in the sparkling moonlight, with only the howl of a melancholy wolf or owl to cheer them, one man would unhitch a horse and attach him to the free end of the rope on the far side of the tank from the waterhole. The other end of the rope was tied to a barrel. Another man would set up a slide, consisting of a couple of poles fastened together like a ladder, at the side of the sprinkler, below the framework just mentioned. The barrel slid down the slide, plop! into the waterhole, whose ice another man had just broken. With a long pole the barrel was forced down into the water. When it was full, a yell to the driver made him start his shivering steed, and the sloshing, dripping barrel mounted the slide to the opening on top of the tank. One of the men upended it with the aid of a long pole, and the water ran down into the tank. Then the man with the horse returned, the rope went slack, and the barrel slid back into the waterhole. It took about half an hour to fill the sprinkler.

Then the horse was put back on the team, the crew climbed on top of the tank, and away they went to the two-sled road. Arriving with the loaded sprinkler, a man got off and with an axe knocked out two wooden plugs that stopped up holes in the rear of the tank-body, just over the sled-runner tracks in the road. Out of the holes came streams of water that spread as they left the little metal trough at each hole. The horses ambled along and the sprays of water froze almost as soon as they hit the ruts, for the sprinkler was aboard only on very cold nights. When the tank was empty, back they went to the waterhole.

In New England the two-sled rigs were eight or ten feet wide. Out in the Lake States they went up to twenty feet, but the terrain is different out there. Ruts of the correct width were made in the road, and once the sled got started it stayed in those ruts. Since the road was down-hill, and surfaced with glare ice, enormous loads could be hauled on a two-sled road, but it had to be kept in careful repair. The constantly watered road built up to a thick layer of ice that stayed bravely erect on the road-bed long after the surrounding snow had melted to show the bare earth in the spring.

The camp boss knew that swampy ground could be hauled across until it was frozen, and that rough ground required more snow than smooth. He knew that the two-sledding season was limited to about ten weeks, which necessitated the hauling daily of about 1.7 per cent of the total amount of lumber. He estimated the amount that could be yarded and two-sledded per day per team, and that was how he determined how big a crew he would need.

The boss also had to determine the location of "turn-outs" for his tote-roads and two-sled roads, and "go-back" roads. For after the yarding teamster or the two-sled teamster had brought down his load to the landing and rolled it off, he was not allowed to go back for another load on the same high-speed road he came down on. Oh no! Those snub-hills he came careening down in twenty minutes he clambered painfully back up again in an hour and a half, or more, his sled empty, to be sure, but with no more nice smoothed road to go on. The go-back road was a crude affair that an empty sled could painfully but adequately negotiate, and bad as it was, cheaper than building a parallel road of two-sled quality.

While attending to all the tasks just described, the camp boss could not neglect the building of some driving dams, in order to be sure of a sufficient head of water to drive his logs come spring. More than one boss did neglect to do this, to his sorrow. Clarence Roby put in three million feet on East Inlet, at Second Connecticut Lake, in the winter of 1894, and there they lie to this day, rotting on the skids, proving that even the best of men can err. The dead water of the Inlet wouldn't float them out.

An even more unusual case, grotesque if it weren't pathetic, occurred in Minnesota many years ago. A logger named George Day went out late in the fall with a small outfit and built his camp on the shore of a small lake near Little Pokegama. That winter he cut 300,000 feet of pine that he put onto the ice. When he got ready to drive his logs out in the spring, he found the lake had no outlet. It is still called Day Lake.

In the high White Mountains around Franconia Notch, the terrain called for novel methods, but there were always ingenious woods bosses who would come up with something to cope with the situation. Ave Henry logged the East Branch of the Pemigewasset. He built a logging railroad up the valley, but he had to use horses to bring the logs down to the road. The wonderful pattern of logging roads, one above the other, that he slabbed across those almost perpendicular mountainsides is as discernible today as when they were built, fifty-five years ago, some of them, although in the interim the slopes between the roads have filled in again with spruce and mixed growth.

One of Ave's Canuck teamsters, Pete Morin, recalls with pleasure the visit made to Lincoln, many years ago, by a Hollywood movie firm eager to film a colossal "epic of the timber."

The handsome, beardless hero took the reins and stood bravely on the front end of the load of logs along some of the less steep stretches, while the cameraman ground madly, but when they came to a steep pitch he gingerly dismounted and let Pete take his place.

"Hell!" Pete told him, "you're doing all right. Don't you want to take it all the way down?"

"My God!" said the handsome hero, blanching as he looked down, far down, into the valley below, "I wouldn't go down that mountain for a thousand dollars!"

Pete shrugged pityingly. "I do it all day long for two dollars and a half," he told him.

Down in that country they used "hot" gravel on the roads in winter. Many of the roads were steep, with grades in excess of 5 per cent, and when they iced over, the heavy loads came down at break-neck speed. Therefore, dry gravel was spread over the ice to serve as a brake. Supplies of gravel were stationed along the road at needed spots, to be spread in the tracks by the road monkeys (the men or boys who tended the roads, sweeping off the horse manure and scattering hay or gravel on the steep pitches).

But sometimes the snow or sleet would come on suddenly and the foreman would neglect to put on enough men to scrape the existing gravel off and renew it with fresh, dry gravel as the loads approached. Another problem occurred when, in slightly snowy weather or in icy rains, the gravel was heated to keep it dry: if it was too hot, the gravel could make the road even more slippery by thawing the ice or snow, as it hit the runner track, just enough to form a coating of ice on the track—causing a load to be sluiced. Sometimes the road monkeys would get the gravel too hot in the hope that doing so would save them the labor of cleaning up the ruts. Or perhaps they would not have time for cleaning, and tried the easy way. After all, they liked to have a warm fire. They were often old birds, just one step from becoming a gorby, says Pete.

Some years ago I met a barber in Meredith, New Hampshire, who had been shipped up as a hard-hat man by a Boston employment agency to drive team for the Henrys back in 1905. He did know how to harness a pair of horses, and as all he had to do was to follow another rig up the mountain, he got along all right—for a while. He drove up under a roll-way, the men obligingly loaded his sled and fastened his chains for him, and then he clambered onto the load, tipped his derby hat back a little, and naively asked them where he should go.

"Oh, just go straight ahead, the horses know the way," they assured him.

In about a minute he had turned a sharp corner, and caught a brief, terrifying glimpse of all of New Hampshire spread out right under him, three thousand feet below; then his horses were galloping like mad, his hard hat came down over his eyes, and he knew his end had come. But he was too scared to let go of the reins, and when, a long, long time afterward, the horses slowed down and with a trembling hand he had pushed back his hat, he found himself down in the valley. He had survived, and in time he became quite a fair teamster.

Another peculiar feature of logging at an elevation of three thousand feet or so was the wind. Down in the swamps the trees mercifully protected the woodsman from the wind—it was an old logger saying that the forest was the poor man's overcoat—but when he got up toward treeline, especially when the mercury was hovering around zero, the wind could blow hard enough to knock him down. Came a mile-a-minute gale and choppers clear-cutting spruce on a rollway or sled-tenders shoveling out logs on a brush road at that elevation couldn't even see, let alone keep from freezing.

It was always the rule, before the days of power-hauling, never to haul logs up-hill. It couldn't be done and it shouldn't be done, and that notable fact preserved quite a few stands of fine timber for many years. Jim Keenan, who worked for many years for the Brown Company, won fame in 1902 when he invented a half-mile sled-and-cable line—unique at that time—which pulled timber from a tributary of the Androscoggin valley near Pond-of-Safety over the height-of-land into the Upper Ammonoosuc valley. He used a donkey engine and two drums, each of which could hold only half of the ⅞-inch crucible-steel cable, and a halfway landing where the log sleds were held while being hitched to the second drum. At the height-of-land, horses and sleds took over.

George L. Johnson, reputed to be so crooked he could hide behind a corkscrew (some men say he was so crooked "he couldn't piss a straight hole in the snow"), and a smart lumberman about whom more will be said in a later chapter, came from Monroe, New Hampshire, and landed down in Woodstock, beside the Henrys, and at about the same time. A town and post office were named after him there; he skinned the timber off the eastern slopes of Mount Moosilaukee, and then he moved into Kinsman Notch, to the famous Bunga (pronounced "Bungy") Jar, at the height-of-land between the Wild Ammonoosuc and Lost River.

In this forbidding country all the readily accessible spruce had already been skinned off, but there was a large patch left above and behind a rugged eminence known as South Niggerhead. The former owners had not logged it because they didn't know how. But Johnson had a woods boss named Jakey McGraw.

Jakey looked at the lowering black crag and the black timber above it and did not quail. Starting above the lower ledges he built a logging road, first edging westward around the crag, and then climbing steeply southwestward into the precipitous Stark Falls valley, itself high in the crag and still covered with virgin spruce. All that remained was to devise some means for lowering the long logs from the base of the crag-side road to the meadow below. McGraw soon had a drum secured to the upper terminus, and with logs snubbed back with an endless wire rope the teams could slide safely on their haunches down the slope. "They sure looked handsome," he told J. Willcox Brown, who recorded it in *Appalachia,* "like they were ready for a fancy drive, with the long sticks rearin' up behind them."

In later eras, the work just described was done by various members of the company hierarchy—the manager of the Timberlands Division, the walking-boss, a cruiser, a scaler, a dam-builder, and so on. But in both periods the camp boss at this point came onto the scene, as he does even today, ready to spit on his hands and sail in now that the preliminaries were out of the way.

It was the camp boss, or foreman, who assigned cutting crews to various chances. In consultation with the head chopper of each crew, he would lay out a road into the strip he planned to cut, and that "road" would wriggle around so as to make it possible to reach the most logs in the easiest way.

When the crew reached the strip on which they were to cut, they swamped out their own road as they began cutting. Where the strips were roughly parallel there was often friction at the place where the cutting of two crews met. When there was good timber along this boundary, the crews raced to get there first; if it was bad timber, hard to get, they would slow down to let the other guys reach it. A good camp boss would usually hang a few spots to let each crew know exactly what was to be cut, and he would vary the line of division between crews so as to give each an equal chance.

To superintend all these multifarious jobs, the foreman had to be constantly present, ordering, advising, showing how. Against him were arrayed all the weapons of a perverse Nature, in the shape of too much snow, or too little snow, too high water (which would carry his logs into the brush and dry-kye), or too low water (which would leave his drive stranded on ledges and gravel bars). And he had to look out for wind, fire, and pestilence. The men would kick because the cook was no good; there would be half a dozen sick horses in the hovel; supplies ordered three weeks ago wouldn't arrive; the last box of axes would be cheap metal, not worth a damn. . . .

In short, it was more than any one man was meant to bear, and who could blame him for uttering Great Loude Othes? I'll tell you who could blame him—the state legislature of New Hampshire, which in 1964, when a bill was proposed which repealed a Colonial law making profanity punishable by a year in jail and a two-hundred-dollar fine, voted overwhelmingly against repeal. The occasion engendered some of the nicest oratory that has been heard in Concord since the Indian Stream War.

But a camp boss could—and did—use his knowledge of human nature to good advantage. If a teamster with a splendid pair of horses was hauling smaller loads than the others, he might solicitously ask him, in the presence of the others, if he would like to trade teams with someone. The resultant ribbing from the men in the ram-pasture put the teamster into action immediately. Or to a sawyer whose daily total was behind the others he would say, "Perley, can't you get as many logs as Sam, in the same timber? Why? I thought you were the best man of the two. There must be something wrong with your saw."

In wages, the camp boss received three or four times as much as he had as a common woodsman. And he earned his pay. After the preliminary work had been done, and logging had begun in earnest, he went out every day to make the rounds of six or more cutting crews, which more often than not were operating on the sides of steep hills, entirely separated from each other. At each one he made sure that the drag roads were properly laid out, that the first and second choppers, while falling and limbing, were respecting the edict that they save the small trees under a certain diameter for future growth; that all choppers were falling and salvaging the diseased and lodged trees; that all merchantable trees above a certain diameter were being taken; and that the sled-tenders and the teamsters kept up with the head chopper, who had cleverly felled the long logs in parallel rows at the side of the drag roads.

Visiting firemen who went out with a camp boss on a slippery winter day to see if he was earning his pay were never heard to say they thought he wasn't.

He had to see to it that the crews didn't run yarding roads too close together, that they didn't cut off and leave big tops, that they cut small hardwoods for skids instead of small spruce trees. He had to act as a banker, a peace-maker, and a doctor.

For use in this last capacity he included in his stores, doled out by the clerk, or himself, or even the cook, in whose charge they were often left because he, at least, would be in camp if a sick man showed up, Epsom salts, Johnson's Anodyne Liniment, and Jamaica ginger. After those staples, the list of medicaments varied according to the fancy of the individual boss.

French-Canadian woodsmen preferred something that had, as they said, "a little taste to it." Beneficial for any internal complaint was a "French hot-crop," a dose composed of the following: black pepper, Johnson's Liniment, one tablespoonful each, in a pint of boiling water, well sweetened with molasses, taken as hot as it could be drunk.

For a cut or bruise, a fresh chaw of tobacco or a slice of salt pork was applied directly over the wound; while for a sprain, beef brine was of great value. Often they would take four tablespoonfuls of kerosene, which they believed "toned up" the system. Frost cracks were sewn together with needle and thread, while rotten pine wood was used in lieu of talcum powder to soothe chafed skin.

On drive, if a man's toes became scaly from too-long immersion, white lead was painted on, and a tub of lard was always kept handy to the sleeping tent, for in the morning many rivermen would put lard inside their socks before drawing them onto their feet. Young rivermen learned the hard way that it did not pay to leave their spiked boots too near a fire at night, to dry out. Leather shrivels fast, and in the morning, when they started to draw on the boot, it would fly into pieces.

In 1880 an epidemic of smallpox swept through the New England logging camps. Thirty-six men died of it in one camp in Conway, New Hampshire. At another, near Crawford Notch, there remains to this day a melancholy monument: far out in the woods—the camp has long since vanished—stands a solitary gravestone, and five mounds nearby mark the graves of five others who died of the dread disease. Of the six only one had any friends or relatives interested or caring enough to come and put up a marker.

Smallpox struck again in the winter of 1903-4. That season any man who applied to the Brown Company for employment had to be vaccinated and fumigated before being allowed to enter any of the company camps.

But on the whole the loggers were a healthy and hardy race, and while cuts and bruises were frequent among them, only a tiny minority ever suffered from the ills that other men are heir to. Without doubt the principal reason for their sound health was their long hours of vigorous toil in the pure air.

A camp foreman seldom put his own brawny shoulder to a task, although he was not too proud to do so when the occasion demanded. Indeed, he sometimes pitched in just to show the young men what an expert could do, and sometimes he did it just to encourage them in a difficult spot, as did Tom Graham one sleety morning when the drive was going down the Nulhegan.

Logs were piling up on a gravel bar in the middle of the stream. There was no bateau handy and half a dozen shivering rivermen stood on the bank, reluctant to plunge into the black water that was dotted with swirling chunks of rotten ice.

"Come on!" cried the boss. "It isn't hot! It won't scald ye!" He seized a peavey from the nearest man and waded out into the waist-deep water to the bar. The men followed him. He worked with them until lunch call, and if they got a kick out of seeing their boss get wet, the work also seemed to go more easily that morning, the peavies clicked a little faster, and the logs slid off into the current with more zest.

So the camp boss rose up every morning with steadfastness and courage, but no matter how great his experience, there was always some new problem arising to test his ingenuity and the toughness of his fiber.

How, for example, would *you* have tackled the problem that faced Mr. Charlie Henderson, a lanky, rather sour gent, but a first-class mountain logger, who had charge of a camp far up on the Swift River in Conway, New Hampshire, one freezing Sunday in December, 1909?

On this occasion there had just been two days of blizzard, with a mountain wind bellowing down through the Notch, and snow swirling so thick that a man could hardly make it to the five-holer. Work had been suspended. Then came a holiday, followed by a Sunday. Woodsmen usually loaf on Sunday, but Charlie, fuming at the work just lost, ordered the men to shoulder their axes and betake themselves to the tall timber.

"The company's been paying out a lot of money just to feed you fellers while you've been loafing," he informed them, "and now you've got to get out and work, even if it is Sunday!"

A few of the men did pick up their tools and depart, but most of them—great, surly giants—spat dispassionate tobacco-juice at the glowing ramdown stove and regarded their boss with a look that meant as plainly as words, "Just try to make us!"

"I'll give you just five minutes," he told them grimly.

Not one of them had stirred by the end of the fourth minute. Henderson wasted no time in argument. He had delivered his ultimatum; now he had to make it stick. He went to the storehouse and got a stick of dynamite and a length of fuse. Then he shoved the dynamite under a corner of the camp, lit the fuse, and opened the door.

"I just put a stick of powder under this camp," he told them, "and I just lit the fuse. I guess it'll go off in less than one minute. I told you once to get out and work. I'm not going to repeat myself!"

The men seized their axes and fled to the woods. The boss calmly stamped out the lighted fuse and took the dynamite back to the storehouse.

Dynamite really has a very moving effect on people. Some years ago the management of the Pejepscot Paper Company, operating up around the Rangeleys, had listened to the then-new gospel of conservation, and had fired an old-fashioned camp boss and replaced him by a college-trained forester. The camp crew, mostly "Russians," took a dim view of the change, and they refused to go to work when they should. When the new foreman ordered them out, they just said, "No hurry, boss man."

At last he had to give up, and the company sent in a Canuck boss of the old school named Frank Pepper. The crew, enjoying its new status, told him the same thing they had told the forester, but Frank had never been to college. He lit half a stick of dynamite on a short fuse and threw it into the bunkhouse. It rolled under the stove. The stove went right up through the roof, but just a few precious seconds before, the door and windows were full of Russians diving head first out to work.

There is a saying in northern New Hampshire that the law never crossed Errol Hill—even the road went around it. Here, winding along the Maine–New Hampshire boundary, flows the Magalloway River to join the Androscoggin, and the inhabitants of the Magalloway River area were very rusty characters. One of the rustiest was Percy Ripley, lumberman, guide and dam-builder, who had sailed the seven seas, and was quite a figure of a man. That he hunted and trapped out of season was well known, but nobody seemed to care. Not until a fellow named Jorgenson was appointed game warden and announced that he was going to bring Ripley in.

One day, when Jorgenson was not in his cabin, Percy put a short stick of dynamite into the ashes of his stove. When he came home and started to cook, he was quite surprised to see his frying pan go up through the roof. Jorgenson hadn't been to college, either, but he could add two and two correctly. He departed to the hither side of Errol Hill and never came back.

Your woodsman was not more careless with powder than the next man, and its use was not carelessly entrusted to employees unacquainted with its vagaries. But the best of men can make mistakes. Sometimes too heavy a charge was tied around a pole and jabbed into a log jam, with funereal results. *Usually*, but *not always*, one can thaw out dynamite, which freezes easily, by putting it close to a fire, or inside a stove oven, and it won't go off. But sometimes it does go off, in spite of what anyone may say to the contrary. Kim Day's big three-story house on Indian Stream was blown up by a mess of dynamite that Kim had obligingly permitted the rivermen, who were driving the Stream nearby, to thaw out in his oven.

Ice jams had to be dynamited, and so did the boulders in stream-beds that hindered driving, but the majority of dynamite accidents in the logging industry occurred in road-building. Rocks, stumps, and other heavy obstructions had to be blown up to make the two-sled roads smooth, and dynamite is like a woman—no matter how much experience you may have had with it, it can make a monkey out of you. The Woodsville (New Hampshire) *News* of March 10, 1905, records a typical accident. "One of the most frightful accidents since the annals of the lumbering business of J. E. Henry & Sons, occurred in Lincoln on Thursday, last. Richard Sweeney of Colorado, who was one of the firm's oldest road makers, had been blasting out a piece of road at the camp. A charge not having gone off after an hour, he went to see what was the reason and tried to dig out a charge, when there was a terrific explosion. His left foot was crushed to a pulp, his right hand blown entirely off, while his face was one mass of cuts and bruises. The jawbone was broken to pieces."

How would *you* have solved the brand-new problem that faced an old camp boss named Barty Gilman on New Year's Day, 1909, at his camp on Tim Pond, above Kennebago Lake?

Into his camp office that night, doubled up and white-faced with pain, came a young axeman, a Herring-Choker.

"It's my—my penis, Mr. Gilman," explained the axeman between raspy gasps. "It's killing me!"

"We don't have any women in camp," said the puzzled boss. "How come you've got trouble with your—what did you call it—penis?"

"I've never touched a woman in my life!" groaned the sufferer with virtuous indignation. "It's just swollen up, that's all. I can hardly walk, and I can't stand it! Ow!"

"Let's see it," said the boss. "Hold the lamp over here, Ralph," he ordered his clerk, Ralph Sawyer.

The poor youth's organ was swollen to an imposing size, and getting more majestic by the minute.

"Looks like a woodpecker had been at it," said the boss. "Trouble is, young feller, you've never had to do with a woman, and your foreskin has suddenly got too tight. And we're thirty miles from a road and more than that from a doctor. But never mind, we'll fix it.

"Tell the cook to come in here and hold his legs," he bade the clerk, "while I strop my old razor.

"Take down your pants," he told the woodsman, "and lay down on that bench. Sit on his chest and hold his arms, Ralph. You, cook, wind your arms around his legs under the bench, for this may hurt!"

Then Mr. Gilman spat a generous mouthful of Spearhead tobacco-juice onto his razor-blade, to sterilize it, and attacked his problem. With one careful, quick stroke he severed the cord. Immediately the patient felt better. His swollen organ went down like a pricked balloon, the beads of sweat stopped beading on his brow, the pallor of his cheeks gave way to a natural hue, a great feeling of relief flooded through his being. The next morning he took his axe and went to work with the rest of the crew.

"What would you have done, if he'd died under your knife?" asked the clerk.

"Just like the other doctors!" answered the boss. "I'd have buried him!"

It happened that two days earlier the Brown Company had distributed to their camp foremen a new order of the day concerning illnesses and accidents suffered by the men. From now on, a great long form was to be filled out for each case, telling just how and why and where the "accident" had occurred, how much time had been lost, what measures had been taken to remedy the situation, and so forth. And on the last page was a large blank space on which the foreman was requested to make a drawing or diagram showing just what had happened. In short, just the sort of thing office help dream up to bedevil busy men out in the woods. Old Barty, who had never heard such fol-de-rol, had listened sardonically while his clerk read it off to him.

But now had occurred the first accident of the season. "You're a handy man with a pen, Ralph," said the boss. "You write up this here accident on one of those new-fangled accident report sheets, and send it to Mr. Brown himself. I feel that he will allow this is one of the goddamnedest accidents on record!"

Ralph went to work, and the report, picture and all, duly dated and signed by all concerned, went in to the head office in Berlin. More than forty years later, Ralph happened to be in the office of Mr. W. R. Brown, in charge of company woodlands. After their business talk was over, Mr. Brown said, "Oh, Ralph, I want to show you something," and he took from a desk drawer the report and picture the young clerk had drawn four decades before.

"I've had more fun," confessed Mr. Brown, "showing this to visitors. . . ."

7

The Logging Camp and the Diversions of Its Denizens

THE old-fashioned logging camp consisted of a combined cook-shack and dining-room; a men's bunk-room, known in the New England woods as the bar-room or ram-pasture, an office; a filer's shack for the man who sharpened the saws; a blacksmith shop; sometimes a separate shack for the teamsters; and downstream from the drinking water, a five-hole backhouse (in the days before Sears, Roebuck this was furnished with the *Farmer's Almanack*) and a hovel, as the horse-stable was always called. Since the backhouse had an open front, it was well ventilated and washed by wind and rain.

The curious word "hovel" was also used as a verb. A man might say, "I hovelled with Pete Boyle on Squeeze-hole Brook last winter." Or, "I wouldn't hovel with that son of a bitch if I never had a job!"

The tote-road at a new site was generally done by summer or early fall; then the crew moved in, and, along with other duties, started to put up the camp. A couple of horses would twitch in the logs, tree-length—forty feet, sixty feet, eighty feet, as required—on each side, and men at each end would quickly notch them and roll them up, one on top of the other, to form the sides and ends of a building. In earlier days the roofs were made of poles and covered with bark, and the floors (when there were floors at all) were made of faced poles; these were later replaced by cheap boards, toted in from outside. The roofs were covered with tarpaper, held on by poles and nails, and mud or moss was stuffed into the chinks between the unbarked logs of the walls.

The very earliest bar-rooms, and they persisted here and there even into the 1880's, were low structures with a large square opening in the middle of the roof, over which was built a log cupola plastered with mud inside to prevent it from catching fire. There was indeed a door, but usually there were no windows and no bunks. It was commonly said that the woodsmen lived considerably worse than their oxen, who at least had fresh straw to lie on.

Under the cupola of this primitive hovel was built the camboose (cambus, caboose), or fire-place: four large logs were laid in a rectangle, and the interior was filled with sand, on top of which the fire was built. A rude swinging crane was erected at one side, on which hung kettles for boiling water and for cooking. In one corner was dug the beanhole. The beans were almost inevitably exposed to the admixture of sand and wood-ashes, but the cooks asserted that these were as good as pepper, and aided the digestion.

The smoke from the fire, it was hoped, would go out through the hole in the roof, but as a matter of fact much of it stayed inside, where it penetrated every thread of clothing, so that one could smell a logger half a mile away. What was worse, the omnipresent smoke caused sore eyes. When it got too bad, someone would open up the door to thin it out, but the sub-zero weather did not permit the open-door policy for very long. On the other hand, when the fire burned low, the cold air came through the open cupola and the men half froze.

There were no bunks and no chairs. The men ate standing, out of a common kettle. For a bed, fir and hemlock boughs were sometimes strewn on the bare ground and on these was laid a twenty-foot-wide spread stuffed six inches thick with cotton batting. When one of those things got wet, twenty men could hardly lift it. Such spreads were still being used on drive as late as 1930. On top of the first one was spread a second, and about a dozen men crawled in between, lying spoon-fashion. Those great covers were especially hard on small men sleeping in the center. If a man wanted to turn over, he cried "Flop!" and everyone, without waking up, flopped. Old woodsmen aver that the worst thing about them was when some man would crepitate underneath them. And of course, the inevitable lice found them a favorite roosting-place.

By 1860, however, these windowless, stoveless bunkhouses had largely been improved by the addition of a couple of windows, a floor of poles faced on their upper sides, and an immense cast-iron box-stove, five feet long, placed in the middle of the chamber. Also, two-men bunks were introduced. In most New England camps these were built in two tiers and were of the "muzzle-loading" variety; that is, one crawled in from the open end. Upright logs or hand-hewn timbers, 8 by 8 inches, separated and supported the bunks. Sometimes into these timbers auger-holes were bored, into which sturdy wooden pins, a foot long and two inches through, were driven to serve as ladders. The rows of bunks continued the whole length of the room, and often around one end, while in front of the rows extended the famous deacon-seat. This was the split half of a log, its flat side up, supported on legs stuck into auger-holes.

The deacon-seat usually was about the only article of furniture. There might be a chair made from a flour-barrel, or a crude stool, but that was all. There was no mirror hanging on the wall to tell who was the loveliest of all. The lumberjack was not coquettish. On the contrary, it was widely believed that whiskers kept one's face from freezing.

If he wished, the logger could cut some hemlock boughs, or some marsh hay, to put on his hard bunk, but he frequently did not choose to. Typical was Joe Powers, a robust gent who could carry a barrel of flour under each arm. Joe worked for the Brown Company, and later for International Paper, on the Kennebec. He once had to go down to Rumford Falls, supposedly for three weeks, but he cut his visit short. The beds there were too soft for him.

"I never had a night's sleep in the whole time!" he declared, as he rolled gratefully into the blankets on his bare board bed, closed his eyes, and in an instant was snoring like a baby.

Of the tiers of bunks, where the men slept two together, the upper was the more fetid. My own uncle, ninety-two years old in 1966, once told me that starting in October of 1892 he stayed for 125 days at a camp on Indian Stream, New Hampshire. "It snowed every day," he said. "I never saw another winter like it. And I never saw the camp by daylight, except on Sunday. The first night I arrived I slept in an upper bunk, but the air was so bad that the next day I took the only lower one left, in a corner. It had an icicle thick as my leg and three feet long lying between two logs, right beside my nose. I slept beside that icicle for four months and I never had a trace of a cold. I never was sick and I never weighed so much again in my whole life as I did that winter, living on baked beans and salt pork and working from before daylight until after dark six days a week!"

There you have one of the many sound reasons why the lumberjacks liked their hard life with its hard work. Instances are many of farmers who stayed home all winter, suffering from colds and asthma, but who hired out in the spring to go on drive. Working in ice-water up to their belly-buttons fourteen hours a day, sleeping in wet blankets, eating coarse food, constantly risking their lives, they found their illnesses dropping from them as if washed away. They never could explain the why of it, but you couldn't fool them as to the fact.

Connected to the bar-room by a passage called a dingle was the cook-shack, with its stove at one end. Beside the stove, curtained off, was the cook's bunk, and over it, on the rafters, was the berth of his assistant, the cookee. The rest of the building was the dining-room, where the long plank tables, covered with oilcloth, were set three times a day for the hungry crew.

Each camp differed in some details from the others, but in general, in the old logging camps the cook's dingle, which served as a storeroom for the cook's supplies, was an extra room at the far end of the cook-shack, while at the other end, between the cook-shack and the bar-room, was another dingle—the wash-room—containing a sink, a water-barrel, a grindstone, and firewood. It was preferable to put the grindstone there so that water from it wouldn't slop all over the floor of the ram-pasture, though sometimes the grindstone was put in the latter chamber, right at the end of the stove.

In the days when horses were used, a set of log buildings with cheap board roofs and flooring, for seventy-five men and thirty horses, cost about $1,500 to build. Of course, some camps were much better than the average, and some were much worse. The Eastport (Maine) *Sentinel* of March 19, 1873, has this to say of certain camps on the East Branch of the Penobscot:

Some of these camps belonging to Bangor parties are fitted up in magnificent style. A party of us visited Mr. R. Parks' camp one evening last week, and to one only accustomed to seeing those low, smoky dog-holes which are designed as camps on Schoodic River, it is a matter of some surprise. The camp is fitted up to accommodate thirty-five men; it is high and airy, neatly floored with boards; the sleeping berths are built about two feet above the floor on one side, a table the entire length of the camp on the other; two stoves, one for the cook and another for the men occupying either end. The camp is furnished with the best provisions the market affords, and a cook who has no superior in the profession. Mr. Parks plays the violin, and keeps two *fancy dancers* at his camp, who do nothing but perform before his crew two or three times a week. His camps are models of neatness and good order. . . .

To a city dweller the life of a logger may appear hard and bleak, but the logger loved it. A stanza of a popular lumberjack ballad goes:

> *Oh I've left those pretty maidens fair*
> *And I've gone to Black River Stream*
> *Where the wolves and the owls*
> *With their melancholy howls*
> *Do disturb my nightly dreams.*

But as a matter of fact, neither wolves nor owls held any terrors for the hardy man with the axe, though in the old days, when the camp was made of pine logs, the pine borer did often keep the men awake as it bored and chewed into the sides of the camp.

A borer worm is about an inch in length, and has a "machine" on each end like an augur gimlet. He makes a quarter-inch hole out of which the sawdust drops just as it does out of a hole bored by a gimlet. The creatures always keep an upward course, so that the sawdust they make will drop out of the hole of its own accord, and when they attack a standing pine you will often find a pile of sawdust several inches deep at the foot of the tree. Hundreds of borers work in the same tree at once. They seldom go in a straight line, but pursue a zig-zag course, and they fairly honeycomb the timber, rendering it useless for boards. They never leave a tree until it loses its sap substance, and is virtually dead; on the other hand, they attack only trees that will die, such as pine through which a fire has run.

Another insect pest eternally associated with logging camps is the louse. But along with plenty of exercise he also afforded the lumberjack good clean fun: a louse fight would be held on a Sunday. A newspaper was creased down the middle and two lice, from different jacks, were placed on opposite sides of the crack. When the lice met they would fight until one was killed. The interested spectators placed bets on the outcome and proffered loud and excited advice to their favorite.

Woodsmen of the Connecticut Valley Lumber Company used to claim that some of those great old cooties had "C.V.L." stamped right on their backs, but this is probably an exaggeration.

The diversions of the logger in camp were as rugged and elemental as his habitat. In the ram-pasture, at the ends of bunks and on poles and wires strung overhead, as near the stove as possible, were always hanging steaming socks and boots and other articles of clothing, redolent with indescribable fragrance. And in the evening, until nine o'clock, a hanging kerosene lamp shed its dim rays over the whole rugged scene.

After supper, the men sprawled in their bunks or along the deacon-seat, and fearsomely they spat and swore, and fearsomely they lied. Buchanan and Lyall (B.L.), "black" or "light," was the favorite chewing-tobacco, and it was also used for smoking. A lumberjack could drink raw alcohol without ever taking his chaw of tobacco out of his mouth, and he could send his spittle fourteen feet to the side of the red-hot stove, where it hissed like an angry rattlesnake.

Cigarettes were not tolerated in the camps until after 1900. To the old-timers they were the mark of a man of doubtful character and even of doubtful sex, and more than one smoker of coffin-nails, as they were prophetically called long before the surgeon general made his famous report, was "put out in the road" without further ado the moment the camp boss saw the heinous spectacle.

The French-Canadians came down with the frightful "Canada shag," made from home-grown tobacco, and it is curious to note that the Yankee woodsman, whose boiler-plate constitution, inside and out, could take incredible abuse, balked at Canada shag. As soon as the men left for the woods the camp boss would slip into their bunk-room and resolutely replace with a more humane brand all the shag he found in their turkeys and kennebeckers. (The Penobscot riverman carried his worldly belongings in a meal-sack tied together at two corners, and called a turkey, and he considered the Kennebec logger a "gentleman" for using a flowery carpet-bag, which came to be known as a "kennebecker," the term still used in the Maine woods for a woodman's knapsack.)

The men occupied themselves in various ways. Some darned their socks—many a woodsman could darn as neatly as a woman. Big Ed Hilliard, whose fingers were as big as bananas, could even knit. He had learned how from a nurse when he was laid up in a hospital with a broken leg. Some oilstoned their axe-blades, others whittled out wooden toys, played pitch or old sledge or euchre, or read an ancient newspaper. Or they told stories.

For the greenhorns the old-timers invented gruesome tales of the hodag, the side-hill elk, the high-behind, the Dungarven-whooper, the Maine guyanousa, and the lethal tree-squeak. Stories of this last horrible monster were brought out especially on stormy nights, when the mysterious noises made by the bare branches of the hardwoods wrestling protestingly with one another rendered his reality audible.

As for Paul Bunyan, the old-timers had never heard of him. As nearly as can be ascertained, Paul is the comparatively late (about 1910) invention of some Minnesota newspaper reporter. Certainly he was unknown to the New England loggers.

The younger woodsmen had various games and diversions that, if not peculiar to logging camps, were at least very popular there, in the evenings and on Sundays. One was called Shove-Shove (other names for it were Shove the Brogan, Shuffle the Brogan, and Hot Ass): the men formed a circle, and "it" bent over and hid his face in his cap. Each player was armed with a long woodsman's boot, and somebody would give him a mighty thwack across the posterior with the boot; to escape further punishment, the victim had to guess correctly who had hit him. Thereupon, that individual would replace him in the middle of the ring. A powerful lumberjack, meaning no harm, might whang a comrade so hard he would be driven head first through the circle.

Or again, they would persuade a greenhorn to balance an apple, or an empty tin cup, on his chin, his head thrown back. A tin funnel was stuck down the front of his britches, and ostensibly the trick was to make the apple or cup fall into the funnel. But actually the trick was to maneuver the unsuspecting victim backward into the vicinity of the water-barrel, where a scout who had slipped around behind him would quickly pour a dipper of cold water into the funnel.

Or (this was an outdoor trick, played on greenhorns who were boasters) they would inveigle the victim into climbing high into a big yellow birch by telling him it couldn't be done, and when he was crowing disdainfully near the top they would set it on fire. If he had displayed his boasted-of agility in going up, it didn't hold a candle to the rapidity with which he came down!

Sometimes the men would box a little, but contests of skill and agility were more common than those of mere strength. For example, they would set up a couple of empty flour-barrels side by side and a man would stand in one and leap into the other without using his hands.

"I saw a man lose the family jewels once, trying that trick," Vern Davison told me.

Or they would bet on who could chop through a log the quickest; or one would hold a broomstick in both hands and jump over it with both feet. If you think that's easy, try doing it backward.

Then there was, especially in camps with French-Canadian lumberjacks, music and dancing. The source of the music was most often a mouth-organ or a violin, or even an accordion. If he broke a string of his fiddle, Ba'tiste could easily replace it with a piece of haywire, and neither he nor his audience minded the substitution.

Haywire constituted the omnipresent and omnipotent repair kit of the lumberjack. "To go haywire," "as easy as falling off a log," and "log-rolling" itself, are three authentic American locutions that come directly from the woods and the drive, and the greatest of these is "haywire."

A "haywire" camp was one where things were slipshod and always going wrong. The haywire itself—it came into the camp wrapped around bales of hay and straw, on tote-teams—was used for repairing everything: a broken chain or piece of harness, a cracked peavey-handle or whiffletree (always pronounced "whippletree"), a violin, a stove-leg—or even a human leg. There is a story about an old logger who ran a hay farm on the Dead River and who, while pursuing a family of bears one day, somehow lost his false teeth. He shot the bears and got them home. Then he extracted the teeth of the bear cub and with a piece of haywire rigged himself up a usable set of dentures and proceeded to eat the bear with its own teeth.

The camp boss was usually boss because he was better than his men at all kinds of work. It was always a pleasure to watch a Canuck boss when the jigging began. He would let the young fellows show off first, but finally the music would be too much for him and he would descend from his bunk—separated from the others by a curtain—and gravely advance to the middle of the floor.

G. Dupin, in a little book entitled *Les Anciens Chantiers du St. Maurice*, printed some thirty years ago by a provincial press, has a fine description of such a spectacle:

His body straight, his head thrown back, his arms level with his chest, his elbows sticking out, he appeared motionless, so little did he seem affected by the movements of his legs and feet, which would tremble and shake without once losing the beat.

The same movements were ofttimes repeated, performed now by one foot, now by the other, then done again, with a variant, like the music, that rippled along with a simple but lively rhythm. From time to time the dancer's foot would strike the floor more forcibly, as if to scan the changes of movement.

By now all eyes were fixed on the boss's feet. The connoisseurs squatted on their heels to watch the leg movements more closely and in order to lose nothing of the intricate steps performed with a grace and agility that evoked shouts of admiration.

The boss kept the interest of his audience awake by increasing the difficulties. Now he would cut a pigeon wing, three inches above the floor, striking his feet together while in the air; then would come the most complicated and unexpected cross-capers. With a sudden light bound he rose from the ground, and before touching it again would have time to cross his legs twice; and all these elegant acrobatics were performed within the space of a square foot.

It looked like a contest between the musician and the dancer; at each variation of the beat, the boss invented a new step. In the heat of the action a lock of his hair fell down and kept time on his forehead, while the long fringe of his sash would fling about in a mad saraband.

The music grew wilder and wilder. It might last ten minutes when suddenly the musician slackened the tempo, struck two or three chords that marked the finale, and the accordion would fall silent just as the dancer stopped.

Both men were dripping with sweat. While the boss wiped his face on a large red handkerchief, the men, filled with excited wonder and admiration, would give him a big hand. To which he would answer nonchalantly. "When I was a young fellow, I could do better than that, but what can you expect—when one grows old? . . ."

The young Yankee woodsmen, not wishing to be outdone, quickly learned how to do jigs and reels from their Canuck colleagues, and sometimes even surpassed them. Vern Davison came off the Connecticut River drive in 1915 with several hundred dollars burning in his pocket, and he went to Boston to celebrate. One night, as he related it, "I was full of cockalarity and was showing off to the assembled multitude how a real woodsman can jig, and I was throwing in some whirls and twirls of my own and a feller happened to be there who was connected with the Orpheum Circuit. Damned if he didn't offer me fifty dollars a week to go into vaudeville, doing tap dancing and such on the stage!"

"Why didn't you take him up?" I asked.

"I know my failings," he answered. "I wasn't cut out for a stage actor."

A word should be said about other Sunday occupations. It is true that the majority of old-time woodsmen believed that taking a bath in the winter season would bring on galloping consumption, and so forbore, and it is true that some loggers kept putting on one pair of socks over another and one suit of long red underwear over another (they were always red, except for the white wools of the P.I.'s, because the common belief was that red was especially warming), and were quite surprised, come spring, when they had their first wash, to find several layers of socks and long-johns that they had forgotten about. But there were always some members of the crew who on a Sunday would fill up a kettle with water, get it to boiling on the stove, and immerse their clothes in it. This killed the lice, and enabled the wearer to sleep comparatively louselessly for several days.

On Sunday some men would go out and pick a little spruce gum, or visit a trap-line they had laid out, or do a little deer or moose slaughtering in a nearby "yard." The "moufflon," or prehensile upper lip of the moose, was the choicest tid-bit, just as the best part of a beaver is his flat tail.

In later years, especially in Maine, where French-Canadian woodsmen abounded, an itinerant priest occasionally appeared to celebrate religious services. One Saturday night in the winter of 1914, Fred Noad and Charlie King arrived at a camp on the West Branch of the Penobscot run by Johnny Bryce and inhabited by a crew of Canucks. They drew a pair of clean blankets and turned in. The next morning there was a priest present to perform the divine service. Charlie claimed he was a Roman Catholic, but it is more likely he was just putting on a show. Anyway, he and Fred were in a bottom bunk, and Charlie crawled up to the deacon-seat, where he rested his head on his hands and went through the motions of participating. In the midst of it, a young Frenchman who had not crawled out to join in the service reached over and kept tickling Charlie's bare feet. Noad lay in the blankets and enjoyed the situation immensely.

But finally Charlie could stand it no longer, so he pulled his head back into the bunk and in a loud voice roared out, "Cut it out, you French son of a bitch or I'll kick the shit out of you!"

It caused quite an uproar. The crew were all French and there were a couple of women and some children there. Some of the men wanted to throw Charlie out, but others thought it was a swell joke. The priest got into the act and finally got everyone calmed down. Noad hid his head under the blankets and laughed without restraint.

The older woodsmen in a crew might not participate in the jigging and other feats of strength and skill, but they had plenty of dry wit to dispense. They had lived long and seen much, and if a man listened to their frank and pungent remarks about men, women, and things in general, he would be considerably edified.

One, watching two young lumberjacks jigging to the music of a violin, spat philosophically at the stove and remarked, "With young people, energy begets action; with old people, action begets energy."

One warm March day, forty-five years ago, at a camp on Soper Brook on the Penobscot, the men were coming out of the cook-shack after dinner (their mid-day meal) and a full score of them were standing around, smoking, singly or in groups, and blissfully enjoying the warm weather. Their lice were enjoying it, too, and every man jack had one hand inside his shirt, scratching busily.

"Look at those bastards!" said Al MacNeill, their boss, affectionately. "Every damn one of them thinks he's Napoleon!"

One day Bill Smart, the C.V.L. walking-boss, and his employer, George Van Dyke, were watching a crew of rivermen breaking out landings (high piles of logs on the bank) on the Nulhegan. The face of a landing hauled—that is, got loose and rolled down onto the men working below—and a half dozen men dropped their peavies and rushed wildly out into the water among the floating logs.

Said Bill to George, "Just look at that for good drivers! They don't even use cant-dogs. They just breast them out into the stream!"

On another occasion, before daylight one raw and bitter morning, the men had finished breakfast and gone down to the river. In front of them a jam had formed on a gravel bar out in the middle, but no man knew how deep the water was, and it was full of chunks of rotten ice besides. As they stood there, leaning on their peavies, smoking their pipes and wondering why they had been born handsome instead of rich, Smart came along and encouraged them to wade in.

Said big Jack Fraser, "Only one man ever walked on water, Bill, and you know they crucified Him!"

Vern Davison was a big man and a tall man. I once heard a logger say, admiringly, as he watched him towering over a crew of smaller men, "Old Vern looms up there like a poplar god in an alder swamp."

Harry Holme, who was an English remittance man, clerked for years at Hellgate Depot Camp. He once summed up a lazy cookee there by saying, "He's afflicted with hyperplumbum glutei."

Wade Thurston, a well-known woodsman on the Magalloway, was telling one night about how he had broken a dangerous jam: "God, Christ, and I got out on those logs, and believe me, we made them go!"

Said Jack Haley, who for years was in charge of the drive in that country, "With that crew, you shouldn't have had much trouble!"

It seems proper to say something about hay farms. When a firm intended to log in a remote district for some years, it would often clear a "hay farm" in the forest, since it was cheaper to grow hay—and sometimes vegetables as well—than to tote it in. In the early days of oxen it might take six days for a tote-team to go from Bangor to a camp on the upper Penobscot.

One such was the Chamberlain Farm, on Chamberlain Lake in Maine, where six hundred acres of hay and potatoes were harvested annually. Another was the Pittston Farm, situated where the North Branch and the

South Branch of the Penobscot join to form Seboomook Lake; there five thousand bushels of potatoes were raised in 1924. The importance of Pittston Farm as a depot for operations in that region cannot be overestimated. In 1916 sixty tote-teams a day passed over the tote-road coming up from Rockwood.

The Brown Company had a three-hundred-acre hay farm on the Swift Diamond, in New Hampshire, that for years was run by Owen Crimmins, about whom a book has been written and many stories are still told. Even earlier, prior to 1850, lumbermen were accustomed to cut marsh hay on old beaver meadows and stack it for the winter.

The solitude-loving woodsmen who chose to do that kind of work claimed solemnly that they were witnesses of strange sights: a bull-moose mating with a mare—the offspring had the hind-quarters of a horse and the fore-quarters of a moose and made good saddle-stock, for they would lope through the woods all day at an average speed of eight or nine miles per hour; a bear being pursued by a panther; wolves chasing deer; or a fisher-cat fighting to the death with a porcupine.

The mild, slow-moving, self-confident, tail-rattling, camp-eating porcupine is a peaceful critter, but like his peaceful cousin, the skunk, he gives no trail. It is interesting to speculate on what would happen if those two animals should meet on a narrow bridge.

Vermont, New Hampshire, and Maine have wavered for years in their view of the porcupine. It is evident to anyone who has traveled in the woods that he does gnaw and kill quantities of trees, and that he eats up a good many summer cabins as well as old logging camps. On the other hand, there have been periods when state legislators regarded him as the woodsman's best friend, the only animal so slow-moving that an unarmed man lost in the woods could catch and eat one and so avoid starvation. In such years, state laws protecting them were passed.

But of late, as timber becomes scarcer and more costly, and as most woodsmen would rather starve to death anyway than eat a porcupine, it has become the style to declare the porcupine a pest, and to pay a state bounty on him, even if this results, as it has in some years in Vermont, in the payment of nineteen thousand dollars in one year for noses brought in to town clerks.

Now there is one animal that does not fear the fretful porcupine, and that is the lissome, hip-swinging fisher-cat. This rare fur-bearing animal, which may weigh up to fifteen pounds, while a porcupine may reach twenty, had become practically extinct in Vermont when the state forestry department re-introduced it about 1960, hoping it would eradicate its hereditary enemy, for just as a mongoose will attack a cobra, and win, the fisher will cheerfully assault a porcupine. It is true he doesn't always win, and Ervin Palmer, a woodsman, trapper, and violin-maker who lived at Four-Mile Brook on the Swift Diamond once witnessed a draw, where each animal killed the other, but in most cases the fisher emerges red-mouthed, red-eyed, and victorious.

But Vermont has found, as did New Hampshire, where the same experiment was tried, that the remedy is worse than the disease. The trouble with him is that he also kills animals other than porcupines. Nor is he afraid of men. The *Maine Outdoorsman* in November, 1956, reported one running up the inside of a woodsman's pants-leg, much to the woodsman's surprise.

But if there aren't any more porcupines to eat, neither are there any lumberjacks to eat them. I saw an advertisement in a North Country newspaper in May, 1966, crying for "woods technicians"! Today the tar-paper flaps forlornly on the roofs of the old log camps. The modern camp is often portable, is made of pre-fabricated materials, has individual iron beds; the floors are tiled and clean; shower-baths with hot and cold running water are available for everyone; there are electric lights, radios, and television sets; the deacon-seat has been replaced by nifty easy chairs; and instead of singing, the men of the crews listen to Elvis Presley and the Beatle boys. Yes, times have changed. . . .

8

Choppers, Sawyers, Cant-Dog Men, and Filers

UNTIL the late 1890's, a chopping, or cutting, crew consisted of three men, a head chopper, a second chopper, and a sled-tender. Old-timers differ as to exactly what year the cross-cut saw became a weapon of the cutting crew. Omar Sawyer, who for many years was manager of timberlands for Hollingsworth and Whitney, operating on the upper Kennebec, puts the change-over definitely in 1897. Harl Pike, who worked on the upper Connecticut in 1892, laughed heartily when I asked him about "sawyers" in a cutting crew. "We had nothing but axes," he assured me. Dan Murray remembers when saws were not used, but cannot name the date when the change took place. At any rate, by 1900 the saws were in universal use.

But in both eras the head chopper was the boss of the crew. He had more experience, he knew more tricks, the responsibility was his. He and the camp boss worked together in deciding what to do in any particular strip. The head chopper was not infallible—no man is—but it was marvelous how he could size up a tree, especially a crooked or leaning tree, in one short glance, and then calmly step up to it, spit copious tobacco-juice onto the fresh snow, and notch it smoothly without another glance, while his second chopper whaled confidently away on the other side—and the tree fell exactly where they wanted it to.

Accidents could happen. A tree might split, and fly sideways or backward with the speed of sound. Or a widow-maker—a loose, dead branch suspended in the top of the tree—might fall viciously and silently down on the axeman. That night there would be silence in the ram-pasture while someone passed a stained and battered hat into which each man, as a matter of course, quietly put a week's hard-earned pay, which would go to the dead man's widow "outside."

Sometimes the tree, aided by a contrary wind, would turn on the stump and land in the high crotch of another tree, where, one would think, the devil himself could not loosen it. The usual thing was to fall the crotched tree, which was a dangerous piece of business, but it was often possible for a skillful axeman to fall a third tree against the first one and dislodge it. Such tasks were for experts, not for hard-hat men.

Sometimes when the wind blew in the wrong direction, a tree would remain upright even if falling-wedges were used. This was a dangerous situation, for even an expert could not be sure which way the tree would finally fall.

Before the cross-cut saw was used for falling, it took four good men to fall by axe and to saw into logs twenty thousand feet of timber in a day. But two men could equal that daily cut when they used the saw for falling.

The second chopper kept his end up, and learned how to become a head chopper by dint of watching his boss. He learned how to fall the trees in long parallel rows beside the skid-road, where they could be easily loaded onto the yarding-sled, he learned how to use a killig pole to make a crooked tree fall straight, and if, as occasionally happened, a green teamster showed up, he would show him how to load his sled and bind on his chains to the best advantage. He learned how to knot—many a careless chopper who had not mastered this art and who did not realize that an axe will slip on frozen timber, especially on knots, was laid up for months with a foot nearly cut off. And he learned to believe his head chopper's reason for sometimes leaving uncut a fine stand of big spruce on their strip: "It's so blamed cold, those trees are frozen solid. If we cut 'em now they'll split, sure as hell. We'll just leave 'em till spring."

After 1900, when cross-cut saws became common, the cutting crew consisted of the head chopper, two sawyers, a sled-tender, and one or two swampers. Their duties were pretty well defined, but in practice in a harmonious crew everyone pitched in and helped everybody else when his own particular chore was finished. The head chopper would face-notch even the biggest trees with the axe, and the two sawyers would saw the back of the tree while the chopper watched that they sawed evenly across, parallel to his cut, or if it was necessary to "throw" a leaning tree one way or another, he would have one side of the saw held back so that there would be a "bone" that would serve as a pivot.

In later days, the swamper prepared the bed for the log, made the road, such as it was, for the yarding-sled, and helped the sawyers limb out—that is, cut the limbs off the fallen tree.

In earlier times, the sled-tender had those jobs, along with the particular chore that earned him his name. Old woodsmen say that tending sled caused more friction, sometimes including fist-fights, than any other job in the woods. The teamster would come struggling up the "road" into the cutting strip with his yarding-sled. The road was narrow, and no attempt was made to widen it. The snow could be deep. The well-trained horses obediently turned in their tracks, but the heavy sled had to be lifted by the sled-tender. He would get the bar of the sled up onto his shoulders, close to the back of his neck, and swing it around close to the ground so that he could rest while the team was being swung around. A tongue and neck-yoke added to the total weight; the bunk and chain were usually removed before the sled-tender took hold of the sled. Very strong sled-tenders would not bother to remove them, but few had that much strength. A good sled-tender was usually a medium-height, heavily built guy with a strong back and a weak mind. Since the heavy sled rested on the man's back, mostly on the back of his neck, he was subjected to great pressure if the team, often up to their bellies in brush and debris, eased ahead too much. Most *good* sled-tenders wouldn't work for a teamster unless they knew him—real well.

An old C.V.L. woodsman told me that when he was quite a young fellow he tended sled for one of the Kennedy boys, from Bloomfield, Vermont. "One of the greatest head choppers the C.V.L. ever had," said my informant reverently. "His own tender was in camp sick for a few days and he asked me to carry on for him. I had one hell of a time for the first few trips because I was not heavy enough for the job, but suddenly Kennedy came over to the teamster and told him, 'The next time you do that, I'll kick your arse till your nose bleeds!' The job was new to me and I was giving all my attention to swinging the sled, so I didn't see anything the teamster was doing, but that night one of the sawyers told me that when the horses and I were in a tight place, the S.O.B. would ease the horses up when there was no need to and at the same time put on a crafty smile. A long time afterward Kennedy told me he would have punched the face off him if he had done it again."

The humble swamper was either a green man who could do nothing else, or a veteran woodsman whom old age had brought down to that lowly level. On the other hand, more than one good man with executive ability and a sense of observation began as a swamper and worked his way up to ownership of the lumber company. The professional woodsman loved the woods, just as the riverman loved the river. The work was dangerous, the work was hard, but as long as he could lift a hand to earn his living, he stuck to it. Old broken-down woodsmen reduced to swamping were usually old head choppers, cant-dog men, rivermen, and the like, and were wonderful company. Get a few of them together at night in the bar-room, or at lunch-time out on the job, and with the stories they could tell of ancient days, of mighty deeds, of incredible courage and daring, of teams sluiced and men killed, of wild orgies in Bangor and Boston and Holyoke, or epic fights and practical jokes—they had no need to talk of Paul Bunyan!

Among the real-life lumbermen who daily performed deeds of bravery and skill, the cant-dog man, who loaded and unloaded logs, was certainly to be numbered. Logs were usually yarded from the stump to skidways in the woods built beside a two-sled road, whence they were transported by four-horse teams to the stream. The mere making of one of these skidways called for some skill and knowledge. When they were piled high with logs they became dangerous to work on, for the logs could roll forward and down and crush a man quicker than two winks.

And quicker than one wink they could fly, slide, or jump blindly back when being rolled up onto a sled, and kill a man. Even when being piled up, tier on tier, the top ones being brought up by means of a "cross-haul" (a block-and-tackle arrangement pulled by one or two horses), they could slide backward, fly around, and otherwise disturb the men guiding them. Logs that were a little crooked, as many of them were, never seemed to want to lie where they ought to. "It's like screwing a whore on top of a pile of apples!" I once heard an exasperated cant-dog man say as he nimbly leaped out of harm's way for the third time in ten seconds.

A two-sled rig was a simple affair, consisting of two sets of runners with a heavy piece of squared timber, called a bunk, extending crosswise on each one. In New England woods operations, this bunk was usually eight feet wide, although bunks of ten feet were not unknown. In 1909 the Brown Company had twenty-two two-sled rigs hauling from four camps around Little Kennebago, all of them with ten-foot bunks.

This sled, heading down-hill, halted on the lower side of the skidway, and the first log was rolled into the middle, to balance the bunks. Then a log was chained to each side, after which logs were packed in between, and the loading continued. When the sled was fully loaded, chains were wrapped tightly around the front and rear ends, to keep the logs from spreading, and away it went to the landing on the stream, loaded as heavily and as high as the condition of the road and the drawing-power of the horses would stand.

At the landing, the sled was driven out onto the lake, where two men unloaded it. Usually, when they knocked out the fid hook in the binding-chain the logs simply cascaded off the load, but sometimes it took hazardous work with the cant-dogs to start them.

Any teamster worth his salt welcomed the chance to pile on and haul a record load. Sometimes this was done purely and simply for exhibition purposes, but even so the most expert work was required to build the load up and draw it. As a matter of general interest, the world's champion two-horse load of logs was loaded and hauled out of the woods on the Ontonagon River, in Michigan, one Sunday in February, 1893, and was on exhibiton at the Exposition in Chicago that year. The load was more than thirty-three feet high and scaled 36,055 board feet, and the logs were each eighteen feet long. Back around 1910, when school children still studied geography, a photograph of this load appeared in many school geographies.

And, load to top all others—on Thief River, Minnesota, the playful jacks piled up 56,000 feet and a teamster hauled it fifteen miles, with six horses! (It is true that this consisted of two two-sled loads hitched one behind the other, but it was an incredible feat of loading and hauling just the same).

Just as a matter of everyday hauling, I like the 16,000 feet of twenty-foot spruce logs brought out of the woods by four horses in the spring of 1902 on Paul Stream, Vermont.

The cant-dog, or cant-hook, was used for lifting and prying logs both in loading sleds and on drive. It originally consisted of a straight, heavy handle, set into an iron socket that might or might not be pointed, and fitted with a swivel hook that had nothing to hold it in position and was as likely to miss catching a log when a logger made a pass at it, as it was to grab hold. In 1858 Joseph Peavey, a blacksmith at Stillwater, Maine, was watching, through the cracks of a wooden bridge, the rivermen working beneath him and swearing at their refractory hooks. Right then and there Joseph had an idea that revolutionized the logging industry. Returning to his blacksmith shop he made a rigid clasp to encircle the cant-dog handle, with lips on one side. These lips were drilled to take a bolt that would hold the hook, or dog, in place, allowing it to move up or down but not sideways. It was a marvelous invention and it rolled billions of feet of logs into American rivers, but Joe got drunk on his way to get the thing patented and a friend stole the patent from him. It is good to know, however, that regardless of patent ownership, he manufactured his brain-child and did right well with it. The Peavey gravestone in the Bangor cemetery bears a large letter *P* crossed by two beautifully carved peavies.

For many years a peavey factory in Brewer sported a ten-foot sign above the door. It bore only two letters, one at each end: P   V

When a man was top-loading, especially the upper layers, he had to have a quick eye and nimble feet as the logs came up at him on a par-buckle (a kind of rope sling). If they came up in a normal manner and landed in the position intended when the dogs of the parbuckle were set by the ground-loaders, everything went fine. But if one end of the log gained on the other so as to carry it to one or the other end of the load, the situation wasn't so good. If the log gunned and came up endwise, it was worse: a big log would sometimes stir up some of the logs already on the sled; in that case there always seemed to be a lot of spaces between logs to keep his feet out of. Many a man was maimed or killed by the "peak" log of a load.

But there was a skill about cant-hook work that fascinated. Working

on the ground, a man gripped suddenly with the hook of his strong instrument, stopping one end of a log that the other might slide; he thrust
the short, strong stock between the log and the skid, allowing it to be
overrun; he stopped the roll with a sudden, sure grasp applied at just the
right moment to be effective. Sometimes he allowed himself to be carried
up bodily, clinging to the cant-hook like an acrobat to a bar, until the log
had rolled once; when, his weapon loosened, he dropped lightly, easily, to
the ground. And it was exciting to pile the logs on the sled: first a layer of
five, say; then a layer of six smaller logs; of but three; of two; until, at the
very apex, the last log was dragged slowly up the skids, poised, and, just
as it was about to plunge down the other side, was gripped and held in-
exorably by the little men in red shirts.

Chains bound the load, and if they broke or loosened and the load
quashed out—woe to the teamster. A saw-log was heavy, and fell through
anything that happened to be in its way. Twenty or thirty of them falling
fifteen or twenty feet could crush a man into strange shapes and frag-
ments. For this reason the loaders were picked and careful men.

Like good cooks or good rivermen they got a reputation. Al Sprague
was a cant-dog man from Rangeley, and a good one, but he was hard to
work with. One winter he was working with Charles Adams, who was
boss on the Spotted Mountain operation. Adams got so angry with him
that he was going to fire him, but he made the mistake of telling him,
"One of us must go. We can't both get along on this job!"

Al saw which way the wind was blowing, and replied promptly, "I'll
go. I can get another job, but you probably couldn't."

The saw filer was a man apart. Every woodsman could file a saw, but
the professional filer could do it better. At some camps the filer would
wander around to the various cutting crews and set up shop on the spot.
All he had to do was to cut off the tops of two saplings a couple of inches
in diameter and standing some four feet apart. Then he cut a deep slit into
the top of each sapling, laid the saw upside down into the two slits, and
began his ear-rending work.

But in most camps the filer had a shack to himself, which he kept
neat and comfortable and in which the louse-bearing lumberjacks were
not welcome. There is a legend that saw filers had professional "secrets"
and always worked behind closed doors, but this legend seems to have
originated in the fact that they kept their shack door locked to keep out
lousy visitors. As a matter of fact, the filer was usually nothing but a
woodsman a little more mechanically inclined than the rest.

Bunking alone, the filer, if he was on good terms with the cook, seldom got up to breakfast with the crew. Outside his shack, under the roof
projection, were numbered pegs. A member of each crew brought in his
dull saw and hung it up at night and the filer would take it in and replace

it with a sharp one. Notches corresponding to the numbers on the pegs were filed into the ends of the saws, so there was never any question as to who had whose saw. Extra saw-handles were in a box nailed to the shack and the men could make replacements themselves when necessary.

A good filer was aware of the nature of the timber in which his crew was operating—whether it was frozen hard or full of sap, for instance. The amount of "set" and the difference in angle between the cutting teeth and the rakers (which cleaned the sawdust out of the kerf) had to be just right for the condition of the timber being cut. The angle of the edge of the cutting teeth also had to be considered. Some old filers, proud of their craft, would study their crews, and for crews that were careful with the saw would give the teeth a little sharper bevel. For rougher, careless crews, the bevel would be slighter. The difference probably didn't really matter much, but the filer would tell them what he was doing, and kid them into being more careful with their saws.

Some fifty years ago the Chemical Lumber Company suddenly decided, very late in the season, that they wanted an extra million feet of logs by spring. It was almost Christmas, and experienced camp bosses refused their offers. They finally approached a Blue Nose named Millbury, who, anxious to make a reputation, told them he could put in a camp and cut them the million feet before the snow went off. He got a crew together and started. For a filer he hired an old but capable man from Rangeley named Peg-Leg McPherson but he was so hell-bent on keeping costs down that he objected to Peg-Leg having heat in his shack to file by.

"You sauerkraut-eating son of a bitch, get yourself a new filer. You ought to have polar bears working for you!" said the disgusted McPherson, and straightway took his turkey and limped back to Rangeley.

9

The Scaler

"SCALING" logs (that is, measuring them according to a scale) was necessary in order to arrive at a suitable figure between buyer and seller. In the early years, when trees were so plentiful that a millman would sell a load of boards for a dollar, or a whole pile of them for ten, and loggers took only the best log out of a tree, leaving the rest to rot, scaling was not so necessary as it became later. Teamsters were paid by the day, and the camp boss saw to it that they made their prescribed number of "turns" per day, according to the terrain and length of haul, between stump or skidway and landing. A scaler appeared about once a week, laid his measuring stick lightly over about three logs in each pile, estimated the rest with a rapid glance, and entered the figures in his book.

But as lumber became scarcer and more expensive, the process naturally tightened up. A scaler was stationed at the landing, measuring each log as it was unloaded, and another man, an expert axeman with incredible dexterity, cut the company's or the owner's "stamp" into each end of the log, and into the middle as well, for identification. The mark in the middle became necessary because certain interested parties often sawed the stamped end off a log, making it a maverick to be picked up by the first comer. These log marks were of countless fancy kinds. When George Van Dyke ran the C.V.L., the company stamp was four cross-marks cut into the end of the log like this: ×✕×

So many individuals and firms operated on the Penobscot, all anxious to get their logs down to the mills while the river was high from the spring run-off, that they got in each other's way and a great deal of enmity and fist-fighting resulted. After a while they realized how stupid this was, and the Penobscot Log Driving Corporation was formed, which drove everybody's logs at once, and sorted them at the sorting booms and "gaps" above Bangor so that each log was delivered to its proper owner.

A list of the log marks ran into the hundreds and the symbols and strange combinations of letters are fascinating. Old river-drivers could read them as easily as we read goverment-agency abbreviations in our newspapers—probably even more easily. They included a diamond, a double-dart, a cat's head, a crow's foot, a rabbit's track, an anchor, a reel, a hat, a notch, a girdle, a belt, a long-forty, a square-forty, and so on:

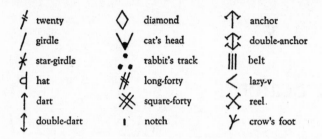

These characters, combined with monograms and initials, were registered with the Penobscot Log Driving Corporation. They were supposed to be filed also at the register of deeds in Bangor, but this was not always done. The marks changed from year to year so that a man could distinguish his logs of one year from those of another. Frequently, too, an extra mark was added to show from which tract or township the logs had come. Sometimes marks consisted of unusual combinations of letters, such as three connected *H*'s: The reader can judge from the marks shown here how skilled a man had to be with an axe to cut them:

M girdle *R* cross

J M belt star-girdle

notch *E* star-girdle *W*

hat *E* hat

E K N six notches

As axemanship deteriorated, the marks were made by an embossing head on a pole-axe, or a simple stam-hammer was used. Today the old brands have given way to blotches of paint, but the principle is the same. A small pistol-grip paint gun is pressed against the end of the log or stick of wood, and pushed. A piston arrangement creates air pressure, and a spray of color adorns the timber.

Today's standard log scale was unknown in the early days of lumbering. At first, measuring lumber was called surveying. Then the word "scaling" was substituted, to avoid confusion with the measurement of land. Various formulas and tables were in use as early as 1825, and the scale or board-foot, rule was invented as an aid to computation. This became popular because pine, the chief lumber scaled, was straight and therefore easy to measure. Just before the Civil War the so-called Holland, or Bangor, rule became popular, generally replacing the hitherto common Scribner rule.

The Bangor rule came to be used for scaling four-foot pulpwood, and is still employed. Tables were worked out by head scalers for the large companies, and presently the board feet shown on the "stick" or on the printed form were replaced by figures giving cord measure for the same logs.

A little anecdote about a Bangor rule, related by Vern Davison, comes to mind: "I was scaling pulpwood one winter on Island Brook [a tributary of the Androscoggin] and I'd seen where a beaver had a little trail down through the deep snow, angling off from the tote-road. I came along there one afternoon with my Bangor rule in my hand and I thought it would be cute to corner him in that deep snow.

"I followed in on his trail, and there he was, and of course he was cut off from the stream. Do you suppose he tried to dash off into that snow? Or that he cried for mercy? Not much he didn't! He whined and he grunted, and he came at me with his mouth wide open and his eyes shooting sparks! One bite of those long, steel-hard teeth and a six-dollar rule would have been in two pieces. Or one very valuable leg! I jumped right out into the snow and let him pass."

In Maine, early regulations about measuring lumber were bound up with the law of Massachusetts, not only because Maine was under the jurisdiction of Massachusetts, but also because Maine shippers to Boston were obliged to abide by Massachusetts procedure. This soon caused much grumbling and dissatisfaction, for the Boston "surveyors" would nonchalantly throw out as "refuse" a forty-foot board that had two feet of rot in it. Such "refuse" had to be sold at half the price of "merchantable" lumber. Angry Maine shippers retaliated by diverting their lumber to other ports, which made the Massachusetts governor see the light, and in 1830 he took proper steps to correct the abuses.

From New Hampshire came the Blodgett rule, which largely superseded the Bangor one in the measurement of long logs, even in most of Maine. This scale stick has a quaint mechanism worth mentioning—a rimless wheel with which the scaler measures the length of the log (fifty or sixty feet in the old days) by the number of revolutions. He then returns to the middle of the log and measures its diameter with the calipers on his scale stick. The volume of the log is computed by formulas, and the figures for different lengths are indicated on the main bar of the scale.

Long logs were scaled at various points, depending on the operation —in the yard, at the landing, at sorting gaps at the end of the drive, at the mill—but in northern New England, usually at the landing on the river.

One camp would have, say, half a dozen teams hauling logs, each one assigned to a cutting crew. Some smart scaler—nobody knows where or when, but his practice became universal—invented the "bucking board," which wasn't much more than a piece of paper or cardboard hung on the inside of the door of the men's bunk-room. Its purpose was to develop the spirit of competition among the teamsters, and its result was to get many more logs hauled for the camp boss. Also, it occasionally caused hard feelings, when the crews or the teamsters felt that the scaler had not given them a fair scale. The teamsters usually received nothing extra for their efforts, except to see their names at the top of the list that was posted each week. But that was all they wanted. It was a matter of pride with them, and to them, as to all men, pride was of very great importance.

Some camp bosses would give three pounds of tobacco to the top teamster, two pounds to the second, and one pound to the third. One winter, Al MacNeill's teamsters worked so hard to get top place on the bucking board that he voluntarily raised their pay.

In the winter of 1906 Ed Bateman, scaling at a C.V.L. camp on the Nulhegan, made up a particularly fancy bucking board to hang on the door. The teams were numbered, and the scale was marked against them every Sunday morning with paper stars. The star for first place, of course, was gold; for second, silver; for last, black; the intermediate teams received stars of plain brown paper. The date for each week's tally and the amount of the scale were recorded on the back of the bucking board so that the scale for each team could be added up, showing at any week-end the total scale for any team during the season. But as we have mentioned, some scalers objected to such a system because it often embroiled them in arguments about the correctness of the scale for certain loads. They also asserted that it promoted friction among the cutting crews.

There was always a big difference between woods scale and mill scale, and it was always to the advantage of the millman and to the disadvantage of the logger, as we explain in our chapter on the sawmill. The C.V.L. had its own mill, a big, modern plant at Mt. Tom, Massachusetts, and one might think they would not have had this trouble. However, shortly after Van Dyke's death in 1909, the company became perturbed by the astonishing difference between the quantity of sawn lumber at their mill and the volume of logs put into the river at the beginning of the spring drive. By 1911 they were convinced that not many logs had been lost or stolen on the way, and that the trouble lay at the mill.

So they sent down a trusty scaler named Cleve Dore to stay at the mill and find out what the difficulty was. Cleve found it all right. Some time previously, the Mt. Tom Sulphite Company had built a sulphite mill a furlong away from the C.V.L. sawmill. The Sulphite people cheerfully paid the mill help for their slabs, which in those days would otherwise have been burned up as waste. The boys had rigged up a narrow-gauge track, with rolling stock of one four-wheeled car, pulled by one horse, and this rig ambled back and forth hauling slabs and enriching the millmen's pocketbooks. The fatter the slab, the fatter the pocketbook. And the smaller the lumber scale! It didn't take Cleve long to spot the trouble, and another railroad went into receivership.*

When long logs gave way to pulp, the scaler's duties multiplied. A war of wits was carried on between the pulpwood cutter and the scaler. Pulpwood is measured by the cord: the tree-trunk is sawed into sections four feet long. These, in a pile four feet high and eight feet long, make a cord of wood—128 cubic feet.

The first year the Great Northern cut four-foot wood, scalers marked only one stick in a pile, one of the end sticks in the top tier, usually adding the date of scaling. After the scaler was out of sight it was a simple matter to throw the marked stick into the brush. The scaler on his next trip would amiably scale the pile again, recording it as a second cord. All piles looked alike to him.

The second year, all the sticks in the top tier were marked with the scaler's crayon. Did this deter the wily woodsman? Not noticeably. He sawed an inch off the marked end of every stick, and tore down the pile and re-piled it across the road. Or he built his pile fan-wise, the butts all one way, so that the front was much longer than the back. He often piled his wood over stumps or over a blow-down, using short ends to accomplish the deception, and the fact that he could have cut half a cord honestly in the time it took to cover up his tracks never seemed to occur to him.

As a matter of fact, he was not mainly motivated by a desire for gain; it was a contest of wits. This seems to be proved by the fact that not only were men cutting by the cord to blame, but also company cutters who worked by the day. To them an increase in scale could have no money value, but they were even more ingenious than the others in devising snares and delusions for the scaler off his guard.

Sooner or later, however, the scaler usually did notice the various tricks. He knew when much of the wood was poorly knotted. And he discounted another 5 per cent for rot.

Thus a pulpwood scaler had to have an observant eye and an alert mind if he was to protect his firm's interests. It was an old adage that if the crew complained about a scaler, he was a good scaler. Indeed, an honest and capable scaler was to a lumber company what an honest and capable teller is to a bank. Orton Newhall was such a scaler for the

---

* The railroad wasn't really liquidated, but corrective measures were taken. That Mt. Tom sulphite mill was the first one in the world *designed* to run on sawmill leavings.

C.V.L., George Anderson for the Brown Company, Charles Langley for International Paper, and Shed Scott for the Great Northern.

I have heard men say that old Shed was the world's greatest scaler. "He wouldn't *give* or *take* enough wood to make a perch for a chickadee," they assert. His motto was, I'll give you a scale upon which you can buy or sell, and he had it all set out in a kind of a creed:

1. Large wood piles closer than small wood.

2. The same wood put up in one pile with sizes mixed occupies a little less space than if the larger and smaller sizes are piled separately.

3. Smooth, round wood eight inches and up in diameter has eight-tenths of its contents in solid wood, or yields 102 cubic feet of solid wood to the cord.

4. Small pulpwood, from three to eight inches in diameter, contains about seven-tenths of its stacked volume in solid wood, or ninety cubic feet to the cord.

Shed carried out those propositions *in extenso,* but his rigid honesty was not always appreciated by some of those concerned. We have been talking here of four-foot pulpwood, but Shed was equally good on long logs. A scaler was supposed to deduct for crooked logs and for defective logs, and naturally the seller's scaler and the buyer's scaler both favored their own boss. The resulting differences in estimates often led to bitter arguments. After all, the scaler is a human being, not a machine, and individual judgments in estimating the amount of cull—wood unusable because too small, to rotten, and the like—are bound to vary, no matter how good the scaler is.

Shed Scott would insist upon measuring a very long log in two lengths, even when using the so-called New Hampshire rule. He claimed, and rightly so, that to scale long logs, especially where the form factor was pronounced, on a mid-length diameter would not hold out in stacked cords. Some of the jobbers and cutters cutting on a cord basis knew of this feature, and there were some great old battles over it between them. But no one ever got the best of Shed.

The woods scaler was high up in the hierarchy: he bunked with the boss, not with the lousy lumberjacks; he got up an hour later for breakfast, since his work could not be performed in the dark; and his salary was of course higher than that of a manual laborer.

He did not, however, have many friends. On one side were the teamsters and the cutting crews, and on the other his employer. No matter how conscientiously he did his work, both parties were inclined to believe he was rooking them. As a matter of fact, sometimes he was. A few years ago the Shevlin-Clark Company, operating in western Ontario, was stuck with a fine of over two million dollars, and a number of scalers drew prison sentences as the result of a Royal Commission inquiry into their odd practices.

Sometimes a scaler, to show his independence, built his own shack, where he lived in lordly solitude. A remarkable example is the hemlock-bark dwelling of bearded Josiah Woodbury, photographed in 1906 (see picture section) when Si was scaling in Victory, Vermont, for George L. Johnson's Moose River Lumber Company. Note the old patriarch's calipers, his measuring stick, and especially his unique parasol.

10

The Teamster and the Teams

BEFORE the horse, there was the ox. The ox has many advantages: he is stronger than a horse; he is less apt to be scared; he is less inclined to flounder in snow or mud; he is not so given to sickness; he is less expensive to buy and to keep; and if it becomes necessary; he is better to eat.

On the other hand, he is slower than the wrath of God, and he is not equipped by nature to hold back a load and thus check its speed. It is true that it was not unknown to put a collar and breeching onto oxen, but the strongest part of the beast is his neck, and usually the oxen hauled loads by means of a heavy wooden yoke fastened around their necks. So there are the two principal reasons why horses supplanted oxen in the logging woods.

In the North Country in the days before horses a team of three yoke of oxen, hitched tandem, was ordinarily used to haul logs to the river. It took a skillful teamster about two months to break in a green team. Senator Stephenson says that when he was a bull-whacker on the Aroostook in the 1840's he received sixty dollars a month. This must have included payment for the use of his three yoke of oxen.

The New England ox-teamster used not a whip, but a goad, a straight stick about four feet long, five-eights of an inch thick at the butt, one-half inch at the tip, with a sharp brad one-half inch long fixed in its tip. Many teamsters punished their cattle unmercifully, sticking the brad into their hides until the poor animals were covered with hard lumps.

Wesley Day, the Machias lumberman who later moved to Minnesota,* wore a goatee, and his favorite by-word was "Oh, b'God," uttered as one word, with emphasis on the first syllable. His methods were direct and efficient. A man once came into his office and applied for a job as an ox-teamster. Wes said, "Oh, b'God, how do I know you can handle oxen? If I pay your fare up-river and you can't drive, I'll be out. Here, I'll be the ox. You show me how to drive." He handed the man the goad-stick and bent over on the floor on his hands and knees.

* This story is related in a sprightly 43-page booklet by Joseph A. De Laittre; *A Story of Early Lumbering in Minnesota* (1959).

The man timidly waved the stick around and said, "Get up."

"Oh, b'God," Wes said, "you'll never do."

However, work was hard to get, and in a few days the man applied again. They went through the same performance, with Wes playing the ox again, but this time the man said, "Get up, damn you!" and rammed the goad into Wes's rear.

The lumberman promptly jumped to his feet and said, "Oh b'God, you'll do! I'll send you right up on the train tonight!"

In the early days, the days of independent lumbermen, oxen were often taken far into the woods on an operation and when spring came they were simply turned loose to forage. In the fall the boss would return, hunt them up, re-tame them, and start logging. He did not always find them, however. Sometimes an ox would wander into the camp root-cellar, probably to escape the flies; the door would blow shut, and the animal would starve to death there. Sometimes an ox was found in the fall with its hind-quarters half eaten by a bear or wolf. Of course, then it had to be killed.

Oxen didn't get sick much, but they frequently got lame and galled, and when the snow was crusty they were always cutting their legs below their dew-claws. So, by 1890, although there were still old-timers who swore by them and patiently removed the ice from their legs each night by rubbing them with their bare hands, the beasts had generally been replaced by horses in the New England lumbering woods.

Before big western horses became common, the lumbermen depended on the home-grown product. Not many farmers kept stallions, but every farmer had a mare or two, and when she was in heat he'd take her to the nearest neighbor who had a stud-horse and have her bred.

Also, in the late spring and early summer certain horse-breeders used to travel a stallion around a regular circuit in the farming districts for the service of mares. Some sixty years ago a man used to travel a fine big gray stallion out of Colebrook and make stops along the Mohawk and other farm areas. Many of this horse's get found their way into Van Dyke's hovels when they became mature. If you were traveling through the upper Connecticut valley you would see posters announcing the place of meeting, and the description of the horses would be tacked on trees at cross-roads, at blacksmith shops, and at the horse-sheds behind stores and churches. Usually they ended with the clincher: "Guaranteed to Get a Colt that Will Stand Up and Suck!"

And those horses were just as important to a logging operation as an axe or a cant-dog. Like people, horses can be docile or mean, quiet or nervous, co-operative or balky. They can be cribbers, be sweenied, be as temperamental as a female college professor, have heaves. People today, brought up in an automobile era, cannot imagine the tremendous amount of interest, of work, of chicanery, of double-dealing, of training, expended by *Homo saps* on horses. Some of the most amusing stories in the world have to do with horse-trading. There is a famous one about Lincoln, whom a sharp neighbor offered to swap horses with, "sight unseen." When the deal had been agreed to, he triumphantly brought to the rendezvous a spavined old swayback, blind in both eyes. But Abe arrived carrying a sawhorse under his arm.

Before tractors and trucks had largely replaced horses in the New England woods, every lumber company had a trusted and capable horse-buyer who would go out West, either to the stockyards in Chicago or straight on to the mid-western farms, and pick up a carload or more of horses when needed. Gene Andrews, a horse-dealer down in Maine, bought the C.V.L. horses, Doc Gibbons, a Berlin veterinary, outwitted many a western farmer for the Brown Company. And so on.

The tricks of a horse-seller were many and wonderful, and it was the business of the buyer to know them. "Heavey" horses were not uncommon, and of course nobody in his right mind ever bought one. There was a way of temporarily "curing" this defect, but even if a heavey horse had been thus "cured" and looked to be sound in wind and limb, his anus, unlike that of a healthy horse, always remained sunken in. Even a smart buyer seldom knew enough to lift a horse's tail and look at his anus.

Many a farmer and teamster who has handled horses all his life doesn't know what to do with a balky horse except to beat the living hell out of him with a trace-chain. Yet there are other ways. Will Andrews, now of Woodsville, was in Lisbon, New Hampshire, one summer day in 1906, talking with a friend in a drugstore, when a top-buggy driven by a local man came to a sudden halt in the middle of the dusty street, right outside the store. The driver hadn't wanted to stop, but his horse had. The driver plied his whip savagely. In vain. He cursed, he prayed, he wept, equally in vain. A curious crowd soon gathered and offered free advice, from biting the equine's ears to building a fire under him.

"I'll bet you could start him, Will," said his friend.

"I know I could," said Will indifferently, "but it isn't any of my business."

Presently the owner of the store grew restless. "Listen, mister," he said to Andrews, "if you can get that damned horse out of there, I'd be obliged to you. I'll give you two dollars if you can move him."

"All right," said Will. "Just give me a bottle, say a Moxie bottle, full of plain water."

Bottle in hand, he went out. The crowd made room. "This man will start your horse, Len," said the druggist to the dejected and red-faced driver. Will stepped to the horse's head and carefully poured half of his bottle of water into the animal's left ear. The horse, who had been standing like a statue, lowered his head a trifle. Will went around to the other ear and emptied the bottle into it. The head went lower and lower.

"When his nose touches the ground," the miracle-worker said as he stepped back, "you'd better be well braced, for you're going to be moving!"

The driver grasped his reins firmly and braced his feet against the dash-board. It was a good thing he did, for when, a moment later, the horse's nose touched the ground, the critter suddenly uttered a horrible roar and took off like a rocket. Every fifty yards or so, all the way down Lisbon's long main street, he would slide to a halt and shake his head violently to get that water out of his ears; then he would go into orbit again. But he didn't balk any more.

Another trick that will sometimes work with a balky horse is to point a finger into his ear and blow along it, making a sound like *b-z-z-z!* The horse will think it is a bee, and will start off quickly.

Sometimes sterner measures are necessary. One winter this same Will Andrews worked for the International Paper Company in Wildwood, where the terrain was very steep and ledgy—so steep, in fact, that the yarding-sled had to be chained to a stump while it was being loaded—and one afternoon he came flying down the mountain when his off mare over-reached, tripped herself, broke the whiffletree, turned a complete somersault, and broke her neck. The other horse was unhurt. The next morning the camp boss gave him another mare.

"That mare is balky, and you know it," objected Will. "I don't want her."

"Aw, she's the only replacement I've got on hand, and you're the best man with horses in camp," soft-soaped the boss. "You can make her pull."

Will went up the mountain and put on a good-sized load of logs. The mare refused to budge. The teamster swore softly. He didn't have any Moxie bottle of water, but he had something else. The load came down past the camp to the landing. The boss saw it and couldn't believe his eyes.

"How did you ever get that good-for-nothing so-and-so to pull that load?" he marveled, after the logs had been unloaded.

"Nothing to it," Will assured him. "You just say 'Gee-wug, Polly!' to her and she'll pull like blazes!"

The unbelieving boss took the reins and stepped onto the sled. "Gee-wug, Polly!" he cried. The other horse wasn't quite ready to go, but Polly started off with such a bound that he was dragged along unwillingly, and the boss fell backward off the bunk.

He wasn't camp boss for nothing. He looked the mare over carefully for signs of a beating. There were none. But he had to know, and he kept pestering the teamster until the latter took a .38/55 rifle shell from his pocket and showed him. It had been filled with cement, and out of the cement stuck a sharpened ten-penny nail.

"I jabbed her with that," Will explained, "right up under her fore-leg, where it's tender. And at the same time I hollered, 'Gee-wug, Polly!' A horse doesn't like to be jabbed in that spot. . . ."

There was a great difference between driving four coach-horses, with a plug-hat on your head and pigskin gloves on your dainty fingers, or even driving a pair of horses on an express-wagon in a big city, and driving the same horses in the logging woods. A teamster had to be able to guide his horses, by little steps, over, through, and around slippery and bristling difficulties. He had to acquire the knack of facing them squarely about in their tracks. He had to hold them under a control that would throw into their collars, at command, anywhere from five pounds to their full power of pull, lasting from five seconds to five minutes. And above all he had to be able to keep them out of the way of tremendous loads of logs on a road which constant sprinkling had rendered smooth and glassy, at the same time preventing the long tongue from sweeping them bodily against leg-breaking debris when a curve in the road was reached. It was easier to drive a horse-drawn fire engine than a logging sled.

In any heavy sledding in very cold weather the steel shoes on the sled runners froze fast in the snow if the load was allowed to stand still for a few minutes. It was then that a good team and a good teamster displayed their qualities. If the horses had been poorly trained and handled, they grew nervous after one or two failures to start the load, and began to see-saw on the evener, pulling alternately instead of both at once. In fact, the best of teams would often be unable to start a load once fairly "set" if they pulled straight ahead, relying on their own strength; an experienced teamster would pull the horses a few inches to one side, so that the tendency was to wrench the front runners loose, but not too far, or the pole would certainly be broken. At a quiet word the big fellows would move into the collar, gently at first, but increasing their effort as they felt the resistance. Harder and harder they would strain, the great muscles of their buttocks ridged and shining. For six seconds they would hang mo-tionless. Then another quiet word would recall them to parade rest. After a few moments the teamster would cause them to pull sideways in the other direction, and then again would send them forward.

Then would come a squeaking, grinding noise as the frost loosened its grip, and the front runners moved to the side, following the pole.

A good teamster cherished his horses, and they had entire confidence in him. Sometimes, perhaps too much. Ed Hilliard taught a team he was driving one winter to chew tobacco, for a horse likes a chaw as much as a man does. But the horses became so accustomed to their eleven-o'clock nicotine that they would refuse to work until Ed had provided it.

The teamster was up at four o'clock, taking care of his pets, though most camps had a "feeder" or "barn boss" who gave them hay and grain long before daylight. Then he woke up the teamsters, who frequently slept in a "teamsters' shack," separate from the ram-pasture. This shack was off limits to the other hired help. Its sanctity was guarded as jealously as that of a Southern California golf country club, though it was generally agreed that no one in his right mind would want to go into it anyway. It was especially fragrant on nights when the men came in with their clothes all wet with fresh snow. The barn boss would have the old box-stove heated to a cherry red, and fairly jumping. Wet clothes, wet, manure-soaked horse-blankets, the greenish smell of Royal Gall Cure, sweaty collar-pads, stained with liniment: only the toughest men could survive. But the teamsters were strong. Just to smell them would convince you. As a matter of historical fact, they claimed, and really believed, that the peculiar aroma of their living quarters was what kept them healthy.

If teamsters were paid more than other woodsmen, it was because they earned more. Their hours were longer. Frequently they came in from the landing long after dark, held up by some accident—a broken chain, somebody sluiced (upset), a busted snub-warp—and their first care was to blanket their horses, knock the balls of ice out of their hollow hooves with a mallet, and with the aid and advice of the barn boss, take care of any cuts, sprains, or other troubles that they were aware of. Many horses developed "scratches" back of their fetlocks in the winter, and if the snow was deep they would bang their knees against the neck-yoke. Bean-grease from the cook was a sovereign remedy against both maladies.

Every teamster, and the old barn bosses, who were usually "retired" broken-down teamsters themselves, believed in the efficacy of horse-liniment in relieving strains and sprains. The more evil it smelled, the better they knew it was. It never occurred to them, in spite of their vast specialized knowledge, that liniment, or any other liquid, does not work through the skin into the sore muscles. If the suffering horse obtained any relief at all it was from the concomitant rubbing, not from the liniment. Strange as it seems, many teamsters even drank the horrible stuff. It had a high alcoholic content, and the drinker became happier at once.

A disease common in hovels where there was a careless barn boss was "Monday leg," or "blackwater." This afflicted horses who were accustomed to work and exercise but were left tied up in the barn for a couple of days or so. Their legs swelled up, and they suffered other complications as well. If they didn't die, they eventually got better. The only real remedy was Gilfillan's Horse Powders, procurable from only one source —Gilfillan's drugstore in Orleans, Vermont. It was concocted by an In-

dian, who refused to sell the formula to Gilfillan, and when the red man
went on to the Happy Hunting Grounds, Gilfillan's Horse Powders went
with him.

Most of the old lumber barons, among them the Coburns, in Maine,
were fond of horses. Van Dyke had a stable of sixty blooded trotters in
Canaan, Vermont, along with a private race track, and until the automobile came along and he bought a Stanley Steamer, which killed him, he
dashed like mad up and down the Connecticut, behind a pair of matched
blacks or bays. He once bought a trotting mare named Esperanza, for ten
thousand dollars, and promptly bet ten thousand on her in her first race
—and she won.

W. R. Brown had a big stud of pure-bred Arabians in Berlin and
even wrote a book about them, *The Horse of the Desert.*

Ave Henry was another very rusty character who had a soft spot in
his heart for nags. Twenty-eight of the forty-seven "Rules" posted at his
camps concerned the care and handling of horses, and he saw to it person-
ally that those rules were obeyed. Here are some of them:

1. The proper length to tie a horse when in the stable, is two and a half
feet, and positively not over that.

5. Do not feed the horses on the ground, but have boxes for them.

7. If teamsters will let their reins drag on the ground, they must expect to
be charged all loss by so doing.

10. Teamsters are supposed to throw sticks out of the road instead of driving over them day after day, as they are liable to kill or injure the horses.

11. Teamsters are hired to drive their horses and not let them go loose; if
any horse is injured by a teamster neglecting this rule he will be held responsible for all damage done.

12. Do not tie a horse with either strap or rope around the neck.

14. Every teamster is expected to take good care of his team, see that they
are cleaned night and morning, watered at least three times a day when standing, and at least five times a day when at work.

16. Do not trot horses down grade when it can be prevented, that is, do
not get the habit of trotting down every hill on the road.

42. Any person found watering a horse immediately before going into
feed shed or stable, will be fined $1.00.

43. Any person found letting a horse or horses go loose to and from landings and stable, will be fined $1.00.

44. Any person found feeding hay at noon or hiding hay or grain to feed
horses, unknown to the hostler, will be fined $1.00.

47. Any person but teamsters, found leaving their work before 6 o'clock at
night, or until dark, will be charged with one fourth day lost.

When it was reported to Henry that one of his lumberjacks had met
a violent death in the woods, he said, "Worry about the horses, for they
make you money."

This remark ranks with Van Dyke's classic cry when a riverman fell into the water: "To hell with the man! Save the cant-dog!"

For years, Will Fuller had charge of Van Dyke's woods horses. A famous barn boss of the Great Northern was Bill Appleby, still working when he was eighty-four. Down in Thornton, New Hampshire, John Hines died in May, 1965, aged eighty-five. He had been a barn boss all his life, and knew more about horses than they knew about themselves. Such men remembered every one of the thousands of horses that had passed through their hands, and could tell you years afterward which horse made the best mate for each, what ills they suffered from, and what their temperamental peculiarities were. George Van Dyke himself remembered every horse that had ever worked in any of his camps. One summer he and 'Phonse Roby, one of his bosses, were together in New York. They saw a pair of horses hauling a dray. Old George stopped. "Look!" he bade 'Phonse. "Those horses worked at Charley Leighton's camp on Teapot Brook last winter. Go look!" Each C.V.L. horse was branded painlessly on the fore-hoof with a number and letter indicating its serial number. Since this would grow over in six months or so, a description of each horse was entered in the books. 'Phonse went over and looked. Sure enough, they both had the C.V.L. mark.

In the spring, the C.V.L. horses were brought out from the camps in the woods, the sick and lame ones were doctored up, and those the company wanted to keep were turned out to pasture. The others were put in the company barn, doctored up, and exercised every day until they could be sold. A few dozen transported the C.V.L. rivermen's wangan (the tents, stoves, blankets, and other impedimenta needed by the men) down on the drive and hauled stranded logs off the meadows and gravel bars. When the drive ended at Holyoke, sometimes these horses walked back to West Stewartstown, sometimes they were shipped back by freight on the railroad, and sometimes they were sold.

"Ginseng" Willard, who was quite a man with horses, was sent up to a camp on Indian Stream one winter by the C.V.L. to rehabilitate a pair of horses that had been sluiced. It took a lot of expert re-training to make the horses of such a team useful again. Often it was cheaper to take them out and shoot them, but this was a good pair and the boss wanted to save them. So Ginseng came in, and worked with them for some weeks, winning their trust and re-establishing their confidence in themselves. At that camp they were yarding directly from the stump to the stream. Ginseng chawed his tobacco and took good-naturedly the joshing of his fellow-teamsters concerning his small loads, but the day came when he told them to watch out, for the blacks were going to bring down a big load. And they did—three thousand feet of forty-foot logs on a yarding-sled. But just before coming down into the stream there was a snub-hill, some eight hundred feet long. Vern Davison, who was just behind him, waiting for the snub-warp, tells the story:

"We used three binding-chains for that kind of work, two bunk-chains, one on each side, on top of the sled bunk, and then a thirty-five-foot top-chain full of logs, on top of the first two. Ginseng had a hell of a big load, but then, he was a hell of a good teamster. When he came to the top of the hill he stopped and threw the warp, which was a two-inch manila rope, around the bunk and the load, tied a bowline knot in it, and started down. The snubber, the man who pays out the warp off a stump at the top of the hill, was a little French-Canadian.

"He had three coils of rope wound around the stump, and separated by big wooden pegs driven horizontally into auger-holes bored into the stump. I've seen snubs where they just threw one coil of warp around the stump, and paid it out by hand, but that can be mighty dangerous if it's slippery. On this one, the snubber had a wooden lever set in a mortise, and all he had to do to slow up the load was to bear down just a little on his lever, which tightened the warp.

"Ginseng had gone down about two hundred and fifty feet when the snubber got careless and bore down too hard on the lever. Consequently, with all that length of rope out, one of two things had to happen—either when the slack was taken up the load would be jerked back up the hill, or else the warp would break. Well, the warp didn't break—that time—but the load, horses and all, leaped backward up that icy hill a dozen feet, as if they'd been shot out of a cannon.

"Only Ginseng, standing on the front end of the logs, kept right on going down the hill. He shot out on the pole between the two horses, right over the neck-yoke, and landed on his face and hands in the middle of the road. It jarred the soup right out of him. I thought he was killed, and so did he. He slid more than three rods down that road on his face and stomach. But he wasn't killed. He had sense enough to realize what had happened, and knew that if that snubber eased off on the warp again, the horses and logs would come smashing right down on top of him. He rolled off into the snow beside the road as fast as he could.

"But the snubber had heard him yell when he went diving over the neck-yoke, and he saw what had happened. So he held the warp tight until Ginseng got back onto the load and started again. But that last yank on the rope had been too much for it. It was getting old and weak, and he was just easing down onto the next hog-back when it broke.

"He didn't look back, but he knew the instant it parted that he was sluiced. I tell you, young feller, I've been in some pretty tight places in my life, and I've never been scared, really scared, but just that once—watching another man riding to hell. God! Even today I can remember just how prickles of fear went all over me, from my scalp to my toes!

"There were ledges and trees on both sides, so it was impossible to turn the horses out of the road. Ginseng should have jumped right there, but he wouldn't leave his horses. And a second later it was too late, even if he'd wanted to.

"The road down that snub-hill wasn't straight, nor was it level. There was a curve near the foot, and there were hog-backs, or benches, maybe ten feet long, before each steep pitch all the way down. When the sled struck the first bench, I thought the binding-chains would break. They groaned like a wounded bear.

"Ginseng told me afterward that right then he felt something clutching at his foot. He tried to move it, but it wouldn't come. He looked down. The logs had begun to roll and they'd caught the rubber heel of his boot and held it like a vise. Lucky for him he was wearing felt boots like everybody did those days. He pulled his stockinged foot out of it in a hurry. The logs rolled right up that boot-leg half-way to the knee! Of course, they rolled back again after a while, but that wouldn't have done him any good.

"He went shooting down those pitches hog-wild. The horses couldn't hold back. They weren't even really running. They'd jump and strike, jump and strike, and every time they hit the edge of those little flats, the logs would come sliding down the pitch behind and jam them forward something desperate.

"Ginseng stood on top of the load as firm as the Rock of Gibraltar, helping 'em all he could, and a teamster who knows his business can do a lot with horses, even in a place like that, so he managed to keep them on their feet and in the road till they got to the last curve. It was just at the foot of the last pitch, and he couldn't swing the horses around!

"By God, he *couldn't* swing 'em around! That three thousand feet of green timber gave one last hellish lunge just as he tried to swing 'em, and it pushed 'em ahead so fast they shot straight across the road. There was a big spruce tree, three feet through, blown down, or uprooted, rather, right in front of them, leaning at an angle of maybe twenty-five degrees, its top lodged in the crotch of a big yellow birch.

"The heavy load fairly hurled the horses right up that tree-trunk, one on either side, and they hung there by the neck-yoke, kicking into space. The pole lay along the trunk, and when the bunk of the sled hit the tree, of course the whole thing stopped. It's a wonder it didn't break that big spruce right in two.

"Ginseng didn't feel like taking another header off that load, and just before the bunk hit, he jumped. He landed in a couple of little balsams and bounced off them into a snowdrift. He wasn't hurt. He picked himself up and ran back to his team. Their hind feet was on the ground, but they'd have choked to death pretty soon, lying on the neck-yoke that way. They were too tight to unhitch.

"He had an axe sticking in one of the logs on top of the load. He grabbed that and crawled out on the pole. Those horses knew he'd come to help 'em. They stood as quiet as kittens while he chopped the neck-yoke in two and let 'em down. So all the damage was a broken warp and a chopped neck-yoke. Oh yes, and one missing French-Canadian snubber.

"After Ginseng had got the horses free, he came back up the hill to talk to that snubber. He had the axe in his hand. I'd run down the hill to meet him, but he never noticed me at all. I don't know whether he intended to kill the snubber or not. But *he* thought so. When he saw Ginseng coming with blood in his eye, swearing at the top of his voice, and swinging that four-pound tomahawk, he turned and ran like a fox. He must have run clear to Canada. Anyway, they never saw him on Indian again."

A special kind of teamster was the tote-teamster. He preferred driving a tote-team to hauling ten thousand feet of slippery logs down slippery hills, but his own work was not devoid of incident nor of importance. His team might consist of from two to eight horses, and he drove them in good weather and bad, over rutted and muddy roads, over stumps and boulders that shook his false teeth loose, over wide frozen lakes where he might lose his life in a blizzard, or break through and get drowned, or nearly freeze to death when the north wind came screeching across the open expanse.

His job was to bring in the food, the mail, and all other necessary supplies for men and beasts. Sometimes his haul was short. Sometimes he was on the road for six days, stopping at makeshift camps or making his own and taking care of himself and his team. In the winter he shoveled his way through snowdrifts. In the fall and summer he toted on a dray or "jumper," a rig that dragged on two poles behind a pair of high wagon-wheels. Sometimes he got stuck in a mud-hole and had to unload everything before he could move. Sometimes he broke an axle or slid over the side of a steep side-hill. I have seen both happen, but the ingenious teamster always thought up a way to extricate himself.

A well-known tote-teamster for the Great Northern was Charlie King, who died in Rockwood, Maine, in the mid-1950's, at a great age. Fred Noad says he was the best tote-teamster he ever knew. In 1921–22 Fred was running a winter survey up north of Moosehead Lake, near Big Bog. The crew lived in tents, of course, and frequently changed their location. Charlie did a mighty fine and unusual job that winter: with no road, no hovel, no liniment, but a hell of a lot of good woodcraft and horse sense he guided his team through the deep snow of that silent forest and brought them out in the spring as fat as seals.

Sometimes a tote-teamster went beyond the line of duty. Vern

Davison told me that one fall before the men had come into the woods he was staying at a camp on Mooselookmeguntic Lake. There were three other men with him—Jack Haley, Johnny Arsenault, and Mike McCabe. This was during the Prohibition era. Said Vern:

"We were staying in the cook-shack, which had a separate bunk-room behind it, connected by a door. Bob Campbell came in driving a tote-team and bring the mail, and he had four mail-pouches full of pint bottles of whiskey. And he had two cute little whores with him—they came from Rangeley, so they said. So there we were, half a dozen men and two women and rum enough to float a bateau. Well, I stayed on the wagon. I didn't want to see the camp burn down. It damn near did. They got to fighting over the women, and three times that red-hot stove tipped over, and three times I got it righted before anything caught on fire.

"McCabe would have killed Johnny Arsenault that night. He had him by the throat with one hand and struck at him with an axe, but I had a little bull-bitch that Johnny had been kind to, and it saved his life, for when Mike swung up the axe the dog jumped on his back and grabbed him by the collar—he had on a roll-neck sweater—and he was drunk enough and off balance enough so that the dog sent him to the floor and then the stove went over again and one of those crazy fools—it was Jack —drew a revolver and began to shoot out the kerosene lamps.

"Bullets were flying wild and Johnny and Mike were tearing into each other like a pair of wild bulls, and the stove was on its side and the women were yelling in the bunk-room, and there was I, cold sober, the only one in the lot who wasn't happy."

"What did you do?"

"I finally yelled to Jack to open the door and I picked up the two warriors, one under each arm, and threw them outside. 'Fight there all you please,' I told 'em, 'but I'm tired of picking up that hot stove for you!' At long last everyone calmed down, but it was really quite a night."

A good teamster loved his horses, and he was proud of them. Thus old Rut Steere said, when relating the drawing power of his team, "I'd just had 'em new-shod, all around, and I was drawing a load of logs across the river and there was a covered bridge there. We slowed down and stopped right in the middle of it, but by God! neighbor, when I asked them horses to pull, they dug in their calks and left every one of their shoes sticking in the planks!"

A story is told of a boss who told one of his teamsters to drive his four horses and a load of logs out onto the river ice to unload. The teamster refused, saying the ice would not hold up the load. The boss said he would get someone else to drive the team. Then the teamster said he would drive out his horses with that last load of the season. The horses and load were lost in the water. The teamster was saved. For some days he stayed around the camp, saying little to anyone. Then he disappeared. No one knew where he had gone. A little later, when the ice had melted, the men in the camp decided they would go down to the river and salvage the sleds and harnesses of the drowned team. They found the teamster with his arms clasped around the neck of one of his lead horses. They took him up and buried him on the bank of the river. A big boulder was rolled over his grave and on it the camp blacksmith chiseled the teamster's name.

An old Green Mountain Lumber Company teamster named Dan Steward tells a similar story of a teamster named Corrigan. Corrigan was a little man who had been shipped up to Fayston, Vermont, by a Boston employment agency. He couldn't do anything right, not even cookee, but he was willing. The men rather liked him, and so did the camp boss, who was constantly threatening to fire him, but never got around to it. Corrigan didn't talk much, but the men thought he had once been a horse-jockey and had come up into the woods for his health. Finally, when a teamster broke a leg, the boss, at Corrigan's request, gave him the team. His name was soon high on the bucking board, and he cherished the two big bays, named Colonel and Major, as if they were his children.

In the spring, just before the ice began to break up, when most of the men had already "gone out," Steward and the camp boss went out to examine the ice on a lake over which passed their main tote-road. The boss told the clerk not to let any teams leave the camp until he came back, but the stupid pen-pusher, when the boss had not come back by the next morning, ordered Corrigan to load up with boom-chains and go out. Coming back to camp, Steward and the boss noticed a big hole in the ice, and the fresh sled-marks in the road. When they got to camp and learned Corrigan had left, the boss would have killed the clerk if Steward had not stopped him. They went back to the lake, and found that Corrigan had dived down and unharnessed both horses, all but one buckle. He had died there with his team. They buried him on the bank in the grave with the two big bays.

Scaler Josiah Woodbury's hemlock-bark camp at Damon's Crossing, Victory, Vermont, 1906. Note his calipers, his measuring stick, and his parasol.

A timber cruiser (below) and his wigwam at Long Pond, Maine.

An old-fashioned logging camp, Hellgate Depot Camp on Dead Diamond Stream, 1920.

The "ram-pasture" in a base camp.

The autocrat of the breakfast table (below left), *ye olde woods cook. At right: George "Ginseng" Willard, a woodsman, alongside a coffin he made and slept in for two years in order to get used to it.*

Left: *Albert Lewis (Jigger) Johnson, one of the most famous camp bosses in New England.*

Tom Cozzie (above right), *recently retired timberlands manager of the St. Regis Paper Co. (successor of the Connecticut Valley Lumber Co.), in 1926 when he was a cook, with his "mouse-trap," at Camp 8, East Branch of Dead Diamond.*

Ed Lacroix's Depot Camp on Indian Stream, Pittsburgh, New Hampshire, 1924. *Left to right: a scaler, a clerk, a stumpage inspector, C.V.L. walking-boss Phonse Roby, and two timber cruisers.*

Modern, portable camps at dusk, Tim Pond, northwestern Maine.

Pictured below: *the axeman, head chopper and second chopper, and a modern woods laborer cutting a hardwood with a chain saw.*

Bill McKelvie (left) and Ed Bateman, two old C.V.L. scalers, sawing firewood with a crosscut saw at Camp 8, East Branch of Dead Diamond, 1926.

The scaler.

Charles Langley, head scaler of the International Paper Co.

Shed Scott of the Great Northern Paper Co. was described by some experts as the world's greatest scaler.

Logging in the high White Mountains brought many new problems, one of which was how to lay out roads. This photo shows the north and east slopes of Mt. Hancock, near Lincoln, New Hampshire, with North Fork Junction in the right foreground, 1938.

Sluiced! A pair of horses running away, down-hill, with a load of four-foot pulpwood. No driver in sight.

Charlie King, said to be the greatest tote-teamster the G.N.P. ever had.

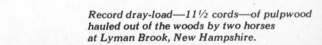

Record dray-load—11½ cords—of pulpwood hauled out of the woods by two horses at Lyman Brook, New Hampshire.

A woods yard showing two loaded yarding sleds coming in and one loaded two-sled rig going out, with cant-dog men on top. Below: the old road-sprinkler, festooned with ice. Note the pole that was used to tip the barrel. Note also the two-pole ladder-like "slide" lying beside the rear runners; it was placed upright against the side of the sprinkler and the full barrel of water was hauled up along it by means of a rope attached to a pulley on the frame on the top of the sled. A horse hitched on the other end of the rope, on the far side of the sled, pulled the barrel up to the edge where it tipped.

Today's method of loading logs—with crane and tongs.

An early Lombard steam log-hauler, guided by a horse, at a C.V.L. operation on Paul Stream in northeastern Vermont, 1906.

Left: *a typical "barn boss," John Hines, of Thornton, New Hampshire. Died in May, 1965, aged eighty-five. At right: in 1921, Al Edgerley (center) was walking-boss of G.N.P. His right-hand man was Jack Duchene (left). They are with Al MacNeill, another G.N.P. boss of great fame.*

A home-made locomotive on a track of peeled spruce logs, hauling loaded cars, at Damon's Crossing, Victory, Vermont, 1905.

Tintype of Harl E. Pike (right), old logger and railroader, with his engineer, Ted Nourse, taken in 1903. Above right: Fred A. Gilbert, 1866–1930, the first manager of the Spruce Wood Dept. of G.N.P.

Diesel tractor hauling train of pulpwood. A St. John operation.

VICTOR BEAUDOIN PHOTO, COURTESY BROWN CO.

Breaking out rollways in Thirteen Mile Woods on the Androscoggin.

Joseph Peavey in 1857 (at left) invented the tool that bears his name and that revolutionized the logging industry. He is shown here as a young man, jauntily leaning on the hookless "handspike" that preceded his epoch-making invention.

Three men on a log.

A touched-up photograph of a riverman (right) running a log.

River-hog, 1900.
Taken on the Connecticut River near Plainfield, New Hampshire.

"The Spring Drive" (at right),
a painting by Gordon McCough,
published in Outing Magazine in March, 1907.

*Sluicing pulpwood on the South Valley Branch of
Swift Diamond Stream, 1939. Below: Lower Dam on Misery Stream,
a Kennebec tributary, during driving season, 1914.*

Above: two rivermen "tending out" at a bad place on the South Valley Branch of the Swift Diamond Stream in 1939. Below: rivermen running a bateau through the Slewgundy Heater on the Mattawamkeag River, a tributary of the Penobscot. Many rivermen have been drowned here.

Above right: *whenever a Penobscot riverman was killed on drive, his comrades hung his spiked boots on a tree, to mark the spot. This pair, belonging to J. P. Brown, who was killed in 1907, remained on a tree beside Pollywog Stream for more than twenty years.*

Above left: *cookees equipped with yokes carrying lunch and tableware to a crew of rivermen on Diamond Stream. Below: rivermen eating lunch in early April. It was too cold to sit down.*

Picking a small jam on Dead Diamond Stream, northern New Hampshire.

It was hard work.

"Powder"; sticks of dynamite tied onto poles; they were thrust into jams to loosen them.

Dynamiting a jam at the Diamond Peaks, northern New Hampshire.

Connecticut River Drive, 1896, looking upstream from the mouth of White River (at left). Note the horse rafts and Mary Ann, the cook raft.

Looking down on the Connecticut River at Brattleboro, Vermont, 1902, after a log jam formed on an island (left) and backed up.

The Connecticut Valley Lumber Company's spring drive in 1897 took out two sections of the Boston & Maine railroad bridge over the Connecticut River at Windsor, Vermont. It took nine years of litigation before the C.V.L. finally paid for the damage.

Jack Haley, noted drive boss of the Androscoggin.

Rivermen eating lunch at the wangan on a nice June day during the spring drive on the Androscoggin.

Winfield Schoppe, one of the great names in logging on the Upper Connecticut in northern New Hampshire.

Dan Bosse, greatest riverman in the North Country (he died on August 10, 1951, aged seventy-four).

John Ross, the most famous riverman in the world.

DRAPER PHOTO, COURTESY MAINE STATE LIBRARY

A "headworks" raft in operation. The men are warping a boom of logs down a lake. Below: rivermen reinforcing a boom, Mooselookmeguntic Lake, Maine.

VICTOR BEAUDOIN PHOTO, COURTESY BROWN CO.

New Hampshire lumber king, J. E. ("Ave") Henry, in 1880, when he was fifty years old.

John H. Hinman, a New England logger. He got his start scrimmaging with George Van Dyke on the Nulhegan and later made International Paper the biggest paper company in the world.

Vern Davison, a well-known logger.

Head rig in Nicholas Sawmill at Bow, New Hampshire, still operating in 1936, as shown here. It was the last up-and-down saw to function in New England. Below: a modern carriage and headsaw.

Lumber King, George Van Dyke, 1846–1909.

Frederick A. Noad (above), former axeman and river driver for George Van Dyke, in 1921 when he was wood engineer for the G.N.P. At right: when he was Deputy Minister for Lands and Forests of Ontario in 1934; his good work in timber conservation was directly due to his earlier training. Today, at eighty-four, Fred is living on the Olympic Peninsula.

COURTESY U.S. FOREST SERVICE

Owl's Head, Lincoln, New Hampshire, fire of 1907, from Camp 12.

11

The Versatile Blacksmith

ISAAC STEPHENSON, who drove six-ox teams on the Aroostook in the 1840's, says in his memoirs that in those days, about every woodsman one met, although he held some special job, such as teamster, axeman, filer, blacksmith, and the like, was quite capable of doing any of the rest.

This versatility, so strikingly absent in today's workingman, lingered on in the woods until the 1920's, though getting scarcer all the time.

In a class by himself was the woods blacksmith, and old lumberjacks will argue heatedly about the superiority of smiths they have known. Fred Noad, who has had a very considerable experience in the woods, from the Penobscot to the Stillquamish, asserts that George Cassidy, a Great Northern veteran, was the greatest woods blacksmith New England ever saw. Sleds, dams, sprinklers, log-raft towboats, horse-shoes—wherever iron was called for, George had the answer. Fred recalls that once he had an accident with a transit and the spindle became sprung. He would have had to lay off a survey party if George hadn't been around. With no other tools than those he used in his ordinary work he trued it up so that it gave accurate readings, and there was not a mark of any of his tools on it.

George Anderson, who was a Brown Company boss for many decades, gives the palm to Elmer Page, who was blacksmith and wood-butcher at the company's Cupsuptic storehouse about 1910. Once, on a bet, Elmer went into the woods, cut the material and hauled it into the shop, and in one day hewed out runners, bar, bunks, and tongue, and left a yarding-sled, all ironed off ready to hitch a team on, that night. The biggest one-day job ever done for the company, says George.

Elmer and his brother Bill were both blacksmiths. In 1898 they built —at least they were the principal mechanics—the company's big tow-boat, the *A. E. Rowell*, on Lake Umbagog. When the boat was launched, the woodsmen brought in a big load of booze from Errol to celebrate.

W. R. Brown, woods manager of the company, had sent word that he would be coming with a party to take charge of the launching, and had told them to have everything ready. Everything was ready all right. So ready, in fact, that when Bobby, as the old-timers of the company called him, arrived with his party, they were met with as glorious a gang of drunken woodsmen as had ever been seen together at one time. They wouldn't let Bobby and his party aboard. One drunk actually fired a few rifle-shots over their heads before someone, probably less drunk, disarmed him and threw the rifle into the lake. Somewhat crestfallen, the party returned to Berlin, while the howls and oaths of the woodsmen continued to echo from the forested hills. The celebration lasted several days—until the hotel in Errol refused to sell them any more booze. It was probably one of the most successful launchings in maritime history.

A blacksmith was paid more than most woodsmen, and with good reason, for his hours were long and his work hard. Something was always broken and needing repair or replacement—sleds, chains, neck-yokes, whiffletrees, cant-dogs, and so on. Experienced top-loaders, who had the most dangerous job in the woods, except for river-drivers, would bring their peavies to the smith to have the dogs set and sharpened just so, and a good smith knew how to do this. For the hook on a cant-dog as it came from the factory was a glauming, crude-looking, drop-forged atrocity that would miss as often as it would catch on a log. In nearly every camp the blacksmith made a few extra shekels or plugs of tobacco by hand-forging and tempering hooks to order for *real* cant-dog men. Some of them were works of art. Each blacksmith had his own design, and it was surprising how they would take a great deal of trouble to put the weight of metal where it would do the most good.

The woods blacksmith really exhibited great skill in his work. One wonders how, without any academic knowledge of the theory of mechanics or the strength of materials, he gained the ability to proportion each part of the things he created.

On operations involving several camps, the smith might travel from camp to camp, working all night at shoeing the horses so they would be ready to go out at daylight. Sometimes he would leave a number of shoes at each camp, and the teamsters, or the camp boss (versatility again!), would nail them on when necessary. Today, how many woodsmen would even know how to pick up a horse's hind foot?

Still more complicated was the task of shoeing an ox. Because an ox's hooves are cloven, each one took two shoes, and in addition, when he was to be shod, the critter had to be lifted off the ground, for one cannot pick up an ox's foot as one does a horse's. So he was driven into a kind of narrow pen called an ox-sling that had a slide rail on each side. Then a wide leather sling was passed under his belly, and a winch, laboriously turned by hand, hoisted him off the floor. This leather sling had a hole in it for the ox to pee through (just like the hole in a medieval chastity belt). The leg to be shod was thrust into a kind of vise and then hauled out straight and pegged—a peg was slipped into one of a series of holes, to maintain the proper position.

An ox-sling was no place for a horse, but if he had to deal with a kicker, a smith who had no time to waste, or who was short-tempered or scared, would sometimes lead a horse into a sling and give him a hasty once-over.

During the winter of 1910–11, Ralph Sawyer had charge of the storehouse at Windigo on the St. Maurice, in Quebec. Old Charlie McArthur, the blacksmith, had somewhere got hold of a supply of one-inch pine boards, and when a couple of woodsmen were drowned in the fall and had to be shipped out, Charlie put together a couple of quite passable coffins to carry them off in.

One day in January, when it was 45 below zero, Ralph had a phone call from Eleven-Mile Camp. A woodsman had been killed by a falling tree and they were sending the body up to the storehouse, to be shipped home. So Ralph went to see the blacksmith and told him to build another coffin.

"What size?" Charlie wanted to know.

"Oh," said Ralph, "these Frenchmen are all small. A six-footer will be about right."

The coffin was in the office, sitting on a couple of cases of canned goods, when the body arrived. It was on a pole stretcher, covered with a blanket, and frozen stiff. Since the blacksmith built the coffins and lined in the sheet, Ralph always gave him the honor of laying in the body. Charlie flipped the blanket off the poor fellow, jumped back, and yelled, "My God, Sawyer, he's a giant!"

And in fact, the man was over 6 feet 8 inches tall.

Old Charlie said, "The only way to get him into that box is to break his legs and double them under."

"Go build a bigger box," said Ralph.

Meanwhile, the dead man lay by the hot box-stove. By and by, up came Charlie with a couple of men carrying the new eight-foot box. Charlie had them set it on the canned-goods cases, ready for the body. Just as they were lifting him into the coffin, his arms fell to his sides, because they had thawed. Said Charlie, "Damn you, don't you go to flopping and flaying around, you big bastard. You've caused me trouble enough. You're going into that box, like it or not!"

And in he went, and on went the lid.

"Now," said old Charlie, "ship him to hell out of here."

Yes, a blacksmith had to be versatile.

12

What's Cooking?

And there on a morning about all you could see
Was a dirty old cook and a lousy cookee.

— OLD WOODS SONG

IN THE earliest logging crews, no man was brought along exclusively to cook. All the inmates took turns, and as the food consisted principally of pickled beef and baled codfish, sourdough biscuits, and flapjacks (beans did not become common until after 1850), one cook was about as good as another.

But "new occasions teach new duties," as the old hymn says; and as the lumbering business flourished, cooks began to appear in the camps. Like many an innovation, the cook soon became a necessity—and then a tyrant. He could be fired by the camp boss, it is true, but on the other hand, if he felt aggrieved he took his turkey and walked out, leaving the boss in a hell of a fix, for woodsmen of course won't work unless they are fed. A boss usually stepped softly around his cook.

In the winter of 1917 Charlie Glaster was running a camp for the Great Northern on Chesuncook Lake. The spruce bud-worm had just ruined most of the fir in that region, and this particular camp had been built of small, upright fir logs from trees killed by the worms. There was plenty of baled codfish in the dingle, but for some reason the cook wouldn't use it. After a few weeks, Glaster angrily told him that there were a lot of Catholics in camp, and that he damned well wanted to see codfish on the table the next day, a Friday.

Silently the cook took off his apron and handed it to Charlie. Silently he reached for his turkey.

"To hell with you and your camp!" he said to the bemused boss.

Then he drew back his foot and disdainfully kicked a hole through the side of the wall, and went out through the hole.

"I wouldn't even walk out the door of your damn rotten camp!" he flung over his shoulder as he departed.

Some cooks became famous for the grub they put out, and some became infamous. There is a song that pays homage to John LaRoche, a Penobscot cook, and there is a story about another, Mickey Dunroe, showing how bad a reputation could get: A bateau crew came rowing down Ambajejus in the evening and saw a smoke ashore, which meant wangan and supper for the asking; they hailed, "Whose wangan?"

"Mickey Dunroe's," was the reply.

"Head boat!" ordered the bowman, and the crew rowed away.

The real test of a great cook is to make poor food, or even ordinary food, taste good, and some woods cooks could do it. Men still talk of Barney McHugh, a Penobscot cook, and of Tom Brackett, who cooked on many rivers, but principally for the C.V.L. His reputation in the North Country was such that when you went out to hire men for your camp, the best pitch you could make was to tell them Tom Brackett was cooking there. Fred Brooks, Dan Kelliher, Joe Buckshot, and Tom Cozzie were other excellent C.V.L. cooks. Tom's doughnuts would have taken a prize at any county fair. Equal to these men was Champlain Realty's Albert Cullen. It takes know-how to cook for a hundred men, four good meals a day. Albert did it, on drive, and Neil MacDonald, who recently retired from the Great Northern, on occasion cooked for three hundred men.

A cook could make mistakes, especially when he was feeling low and had been imbibing freely of lemon extract. Sometimes they weren't entirely his fault. The story is told of a cook who made up a lot of lemon pies, employing the usual pie-filling, which was shipped in wooden tubs. But the cookee, who had brought in a kettleful of the ingredient from the tub in the dingle, had taken it by mistake from a tub of petroleum grease, and the cook had not noticed the difference. The boss and the crew, who gagged on the lovely looking pies, were not amused.

The cook was generally known as a boiler or a sizzler, depending on whether he boiled most of his food, or fried it, but you didn't call him by either name to his face.

In the old days of the open fire-place surmounted by a smoke-hole, a favorite food in New England logging camps was flapjacks. These were made, very large, in a light, long-handled frying-pan. Into this, the thick batter was poured, and the pan was held over a bed of coals. When one side was well browned the pancake was thrown upward from the pan and caught again as it descended, the uncooked side down. An experienced camp cook could do it a hundred times and never miss.

At a camp on the Saco River the men got to teasing the cook one day about his dexterity, and he boasted that he could throw a pancake out at the smoke-hole in the roof and catch it outside the camp as it came down. A wager was instantly laid and the experiment tried. A great, spreading batch of batter was poured into the frying-pan, everybody was commanded to clear the track, and the crisis came. Turning his eyes toward the hole overhead, the cook estimated the distance, calculated the time

that would be required for his cake to descend, and bracing himself for
the supreme moment, sent the steaming flapjack on its way. He turned
and rushed for the door, but struck his head against the low lintel and fell
like a stunned ox. He was not seriously injured, but for the rest of the
season he had to endure bad jokes about his flapjack.*

One of his most persistent bedevilers was a teamster who for some
reason detested goose, and never wanted to hear *it* mentioned. The cook
got back at him a few days after the pancake episode. While making his
biscuits for supper the cook discovered that he had mistakenly used goose-
grease as shortening. Unwilling to waste good flour, he decided to take
the risk of being found out, baked his bread, and placed it upon the table
as if nothing had happened. The men's appetites appeared unusually
hearty that evening and they eagerly devoured the warm biscuits. Even
the teamster declared aloud that the cook had beat himself, that he had
never made any bread half as good before, and asked for the secret of his
success.

"Well, Sam," replied the cook, "they ought to be good, for I short-
ened 'em with goose-grease." The rest of the winter the crew, instead of
spending all their wit on the cook, spent half of it on the goosed teamster.

The cook was highly paid, but he worked hard for his wages. Up
about 3 A.M., he was still working at 8 P.M., but of course in the middle of
the day he could relax and read his favorite literature—the *Police
Gazette*, with its entrancing pictures of ladies with magnificent calves, and
the *Farmer's Almanack*. He kept one or more cookees busy splitting
wood, building fires, washing dishes, cleaning up, and in general learning
to cook. Often, too, one or more cutting crews would be so far away from
camp that they would lose too much time from work if they came in to
dinner (the mid-day meal) and then walked back again. So, instead, a
cookee was sent out with big buckets of food slung on a neck-yoke across
his shoulders. Arriving at the cuttings, he unhooked his burden, built a
little fire to thaw out the frozen food some, and yelled for the men to come
and get it. If the weather was fair, the men would drink their hot tea and
down their beans with relish, and then light their pipes and fool with the
moose-birds a little before picking up their axes and going back to work.
But if it was snowing, or below zero, the men ate the half-frozen food
while standing, and departed as soon as they had finished.

Big Dan Murray recalls that he had charge of a camp near Little
Kennebago Pond one winter and a sixteen-year-old cookee was sent out
to a cutting crew with thirteen dinner pails suspended on a pole over his
shoulder. The youth got lost. When their lunch didn't show up, the
axemen sounded the alarm. The whole camp went out hunting, but they

---

* This story used to be a favorite in logging camps. The earliest version I have
found is in G. T. Ridlon's *Saco Valley Settlements and Families* (1895).

did not find the cookee until late the next afternoon. He was still carrying the thirteen pails on his shoulder. Arriving at camp, he was hungry as a wolf, and ate and ate. It had never entered his head to eat the food he had been toting all that time.

Young cookees were not the only ones to get lost in the woods. It happened to old experienced woodsmen. The Brown Company had a big Irish camp boss named Henry Mullen who was running a camp on the Little Dead Diamond. One day in the fall, a telephone message came that a forest fire had been spotted behind a hill over east of the camp and that he was to take what men he could scrape up and hustle over there. So Henry gathered up the clerk and a few loafers and stormed out into the pathless forest. After about an hour and a half he broke out of the trees into a clearing, and in the clearing was a logging camp, and sitting on a block of wood in front of the cook-shack was a bald-headed cookee peeling potatoes.

Mullen knew there wasn't another camp within five miles of his, and he couldn't figure out where he was. He strode up to the cookee, bawling, "What camp is this?" The cookee looked up at him, his mouth agape.

"I asked you what camp this is!" Mullen roared.

The cookee sat back against the wall of the camp, his paring knife in one hand, his potato in the other. "If you're such a damn fool that you don't know your own camp, Mr. Mullen," he said, "I ain't a-going to tell you!"

Orrie Crawford, who became the owner of a prosperous little restaurant in Colebrook, New Hampshire, got his start cookeeing in the last century for Joe Boulay, usually called Joe Bully. Joe was not so good a cook as Tom Brackett, but he was even more widely known. Even though he passed nearly all his life cooking just for the C.V.L., Joe was spoken of in camps from the St. Croix to the Nulhegan as "the dirtiest cook in the woods."

"The dirty cuss put out food that was palatable, as long as you didn't see him," says one man who knew him well. "I have seen his cook-room floor so dirty that the spaces between the half-hewn poles were filled with cooking refuse. It was as much as your life was worth to try to walk on it without calked boots."

"Joe was always so dirty and greasy," says another, "that you couldn't hang onto him with a pair of sharp ice-tongs. One year—it was 1907—George Yates, a Newfoundlander, went up Paul Stream early in the fall to start a new camp operation, and he had to take Joe along with him as cook. Just after they had cut out their main roads, built their camp, and started to cut logs, Yates fired Joe because the crew were all kicking on the grub. Joe put his turkey on the end of a stick and walked down to the company office at Bloomfield, Vermont.

"It happened that George Van Dyke, the autocratic boss of the C.V.L., was there when he arrived. When George saw him, he lit into him like an angry God on a sick angel. When Joe tried to tell him that Yates had fired him, George wouldn't listen, and told him to get back up there. He explained to him, and to everyone else in Bloomfield who was not deaf, 'It takes a tub of lard and a half a barrel of flour to get one of you bastards greased up, and I'm not going to have to do it twice in one season!'

"Joe went back up Paul Stream but he went to another camp and cookeed until some other cook quit, and then he got back into the grease again."

Joe was not, however, devoid of wit. Many years after that he came down out of the woods and put up at Hinchey's Stewartstown Hotel, in West Stewartstown, New Hampshire. "You aren't lousy, are you Joe?" asked Hinchey before handing him the key.

"If I ain't now I will be by the time I come down from dat room of yours," retorted Joe.

The old cooks always had a tub of sourdough working behind the stove. From this ill-smelling stuff they would bake biscuits four inches tall and white as snow. But they had to be clever in judging the amount of soda to put in. Woodsmen used to say that the first three days in a new camp were starving days, until the tub of sourdough had soured.

Not all cooks had the light touch. I have heard of one who made doughnuts so heavy and soggy that one day when he threw his dough into the frying kettle the boss, who was present, asked sourly, "Aren't you going to buoy them up so you can recover them?"

Many woods cooks were fine and jolly people, but a goodly number —afflicted with corns, too much lemon extract, or other ills—became exceedingly temperamental, not to say downright misanthropic. Al Mac-Neill, a noted woods boss of the Great Northern, stopped one day for lunch at Red Brook camp, where such a cook presided. The cook told Al that if he wasn't in a hurry he should wait until after the men had eaten, and he would give him a decent lunch. Al asked what was the matter with the crew's lunch. The cook replied, "There's some of these sons of bitches who don't appear to like me, and I'm taming them." Al had that cook fired as soon as he could send in another cook. The worst of it was, that man could cook as well as anyone, when he wanted to.

Cookees usually became cooks, and after the turn of the century, more and more cooks were city dwellers to begin with. The city employment agencies would ship unqualified men up to the woods, just to get the head fee, and in addition, they would collect from the company, (which in turn subtracted the amount from the man's first wages), more or less padded charges for alleged room and board advanced to the future employee. This became quite a racket on both sides, for the men would desert and go to a camp other than the one to which they had been assigned. But at any rate, being unskilled woodsmen, about the only thing they could do was to swamp or to cookee.

Joe Bully was greasy, but strangely enough, there were woodsmen who like grease. Joe was just born too soon. Omar Sawyer, who for years had charge of timberlands on the upper Kennebec, once told me that a camp crew consisting chiefly of Finns protested loudly when their very greasy cook was replaced by a new one. "We need the grease!" they said.

Omar also recalled stopping into a camp one afternoon and being offered a dish of tea by the cook. Of course, a tea-pot was always boiling and sizzling on the stove, twenty-fours hours a day. But this tea tasted a little strong, even to Omar, who was used to black tea that would float an axe. Finally he got up and looked into the pot. An old sock, hung up over the stove to dry, had dropped into the pot and had never been fished out.

The New England woods cooks insisted on silence at table—and they got it. The reason for silence is obvious—the cook and his cookees had a lot of dishes to wash and cleaning up to do, and if the men talked instead of eating, they spent extra time at the table, holding up the work. Johnny Maxwell was a well-known cook for the International Paper Company. One winter he had to go down to Rumford Falls to get his teeth fixed, and his substitute let the men talk at table. Johnny eventually returned, and found that supper was prolonged. He ordered the men to shut up and eat, but they didn't pay him much attention. Presently, they asked for more biscuits. He brought them a panful, but as he got to the table he dropped them all over the floor.

"Sorry," he said, "I just stumbled over that big load of logs you fellers were hauling."

He had no more trouble.

In most logging camps it was the cook who wanted silence at table, who demanded it, and who got it. But Ave Henry, next to George Van Dyke the most celebrated lumber baron in New England (he was called the "Grand Duke" of his "Grand Duchy of Lincoln" in the public prints), spared neither himself nor his men, and did not propose that his lumberjacks and teamsters should waste his time in unnecessary talk. He posted conspicuously, in his camps in Zealand and later in Lincoln, "J. E. Henry & Sons Rules & Regulations," of which Rule 46 stated plainly, "Any person found throwing food or making unnecessary or loud talk at tables will be fined."

Ave made it stick, too. It was his duchy, and he ruled it autocratically, albeit paternally. He or his sons owned the whole town of Lincoln, except for one building, were postmasters, assessors, and judges, hired and fired the schoolteachers—and if anyone didn't like it, he could move out. Indeed, on the back of passes issued to workers by the Henry Company was printed: "Lincoln, N. H., is one mile from the town of North Woodstock on the Concord & Montreal Railroad. It is the headquarters of the J. E. Henry & Sons Lumber Co., one of the largest firms in the state. A good man can find work all year. A poor man better not go there, as such men are not wanted."

A favorite complaint against cooks in the old days was that they put soap into their batter to make it rise. That may be a canard, but it is a fact that one Penobscot cook used to stir his beans with a cant-dog, and another, named Larry Sharkey, was widely if not too favorably known for his curious custom of kneading his bread with his mittens on. He claimed it made his hands cold to put them into the cold dough.

Along with baked beans, and in Maine at least, baled codfish, another staple food was pea soup. Joe Bully's thick pea soup was famous. He was cooking for Charley Leighton in the winter of 1897 on Teapot Brook when the word arrived, just as the men were finishing supper, that twenty more men would come in from Paquetville in about half an hour, and would have to be fed. Apologetically, Leighton explained the situation to the cook. Old Joe was undisturbed. "Orrie!" he cried to the cookee. "T'row anodder pail of water on de soup!"

The steady menu of the logger consisted of pork and beans three times a day, with plenty of molasses and gingerbread, and lots of black tea. This was sometimes enlivened by meat and potatoes. Sugar and milk were unknown to him. The lumberjack thrived on this diet. Probably the molasses had a good deal to do with it. Fred Gilbert thought so. He always kept a sample bottle on his polished desk, and when he caught the company purchasing agent buying an inferior brand, he took the purchasing of that important article quite away from him, and bought it himself.

After about 1910 the kinds of food on a logging-camp table became much more numerous. The passage of various state laws had something to do with this change. The appearance of vegetables, condensed milk, sugar, lots of pies and cakes, and varieties of meats, became usual instead of unusual. Even before 1910, at least on drive, food had become much better. The C.V.L. had John Pattee, a North Stratford storekeeper, send a man down the river ahead of the wangan to buy fresh milk, eggs, and other goodies for the cook to use when he should arrive at the next camping place.

But pork and beans, baked in a beanhole, remained the logger's main dish. There's a good reason for it, namely, that there is nothing better in God's sweet world, when it is cooked right. The ample mess of fat pork, dissolved by the heat, is neither fried nor boiled, but becomes amalgamated with the beans and when the whole is well cooked it is a food that can't be beat for succulency of flavor and savory richness of nutrition. Such baked beans have staying power that is possessed by no other food.*

There is one more item, which no one much under ninety years old has ever seen, but which was toted by the barrelful into every woods camp in the North Country throughout most of the last century—cider-apple sass (sauce). A lumberman would no more think of running a camp without it than he would think of eliminating baked beans.

"My God!" said one very old man whom I asked about it, "I used to make it myself, but I haven't seen any since 1890 or thereabouts. I'd give five dollars for a plateful of it right now!"

Tears came into his aged eyes as he spoke.

After the era of cider-apple sass in the camps, came dried-apple sass. Windfall apples were peeled and quartered by the womenfolks and children in farm families. A long string attached to a darning-needle was drawn through the quarters, which were hung up behind the kitchen stove to dry. This work was done in the fall, and by the time the peeled apples were dried, the flies covered them. It used to be said that the farmer took his apples to the town market, and what he couldn't sell he took home and fed to the pigs; what the pigs wouldn't eat he ate himself; what he couldn't eat, he peeled and dried and sold to the lumber camps.

In the winter of 1918–19 Dan Kelliher was cooking for a hundred men in a camp on Scott Bog, which runs down from the Canadian border to Second Connecticut Lake. Here he prepared and the men consumed seventy-five to a hundred pounds of beef per day, a bushel of cookies, three bushels of potatoes, thirty pies—apples, mince, cherry, raisin, lemon, and prune—twenty one-pound cans of condensed milk, two gallons of tomatoes, three gallons of canned apples, sixteen to twenty big double loaves of bread, two hundred doughnuts, ten yeast cakes, forty pounds of sausage, twenty-five pounds of liver, two gallons of molasses, plus cabbages in the fall and turnips in the winter. It is hardly necessary to mention tea, coffee, oatmeal, and beans.

The humble prune deserves a special word. In later days it was very common, both stewed and in pies. As a French-Canadian cook, I think it was Joe Buckshot, once remarked, "For me, I'll take the prune. It makes even better apple pie than the peach."

* The old order changeth everywhere. Long logs have given way to four-foot pulpwood; horses have vanished from the woods, scared out by gasoline tractors; rivermen wear safety helmets and life-belts; and even the Bean, the luscious, potent, belly-filling Bean, has at last yielded to what we hopefully call Progress.

In the Littleton (New Hampshire) *Courier* of February 24, 1966, we read that "Prof. R. B. Pike [no relation to the author of this book] of the Agricultural Department of the University of New Hampshire recently discovered a 'bean that isn't mean.' His epochal discovery was heralded in newspapers across the country. Two days after the story appeared in Maine papers more than 200 letters poured in, and within two weeks more than 2,000 letters were received from all parts of the country. To date the total is nearly 3,000 and Pike has run out of seeds. One man wrote to Pike, 'Your gasless bean may be the only thing which can save my marriage.'"

13

The Camp Clerk

A CAMP CLERK could make or break a camp boss. An expert woodsman quite capable of doing every bit of woods work expertly, from estimating a stand of timber to shoeing a horse and breaking a dangerous log jam, was sometimes not good at figures, and a lazy or incompetent clerk could ruin him.

But a good clerk hardly ever got any credit, even when he richly deserved some. Since the clerk could read and write, he usually considered himself a bit superior to the horny-handed axemen and teamsters, who, in their turn, were inclined to esteem the man with the pencil about as hardy laborers everywhere are acustomed to esteem "eggheads."

Horace Frost, the gigantic walking-boss of the Brown Company, was once proceeding into the woods accompanied by a callow clerk, and one night they stopped at a camp where they bunked together. Horace had a disconcerting habit of gnashing his teeth in his sleep, which made the going pretty rough for the poor clerk to begin with, and when a mouse ran over the latter's face, he became quite unnerved. "Mr. Frost! Mr. Frost!" he cried out, "a mouse just ran across my face!"

"Shut your damn mouth, or he'll run in!" grunted the boss.

The men often took time on a rainy Sunday to write requests to the Ladies Aid Society of a nearby town for camping kits, which were supposed to contain thread, needles, bachelor buttons for those who could not sew, bandages, medicines, shaving soap, and what have you. The ladies often hopefully tucked in moral tracts to help the lumberjacks' morals, but probably without great success. Occasionally tobacco or candy were added, which really were appreciated.

This situation led to a mild racket which inspired one bright clerk on the Androscoggin to flood his neighborhood with misspelled letters of the sob variety to which he attached foreign names, thereby working up a considerable correspondence. By this nefarious means he kept himself in candy and tobacco all winter.

Men who couldn't write would enlist the aid of the clerk. I know of one clerk who was asked by an illiterate woodsman to write letters to his young wife. The clerk cheerfully complied, but inserted certain frolicsome remarks of his own; when he read out her replies to the fond husband he skipped over similar answering passages. There resulted quite a rumpus later on, both at home in the spring when the woodsman arrived there, and again at the camp in the fall when he returned.

Usually, in the old days, the camp boss (except at a depot camp) had no clerk, but kept his own time book and ran his own wangan, or company store, which was limited to tobacco, socks, mittens, and a few simple items like cough medicine and bandages. Other articles, such as boots, pants, and mackinaws, were sent up from the depot camp on request, or the men might go down to the depot camp on a Sunday and pick them up in person.

Later on, most camps had a camp clerk, and his duties entailed many things besides writing letters. He could be impressed to fight fires; he laid out corpses; he helped perform major and minor operations; he sold supplies from the wangan—tobacco, clothing, and the like—and he jotted down the charges, to be subtracted from the man's wages when he should be paid off at the break-up of the camp in the spring.

He had not only to sell supplies, he had also to check them in—chains, food, tools, hay and grain—and to keep track of everything else that had to do with accounts. If men were paid by the day or by the cord or by the board foot, he had to keep a record of each day's work for each man, and at the end of the season the walking-boss could figure up which of his camp foremen was delivering the most logs at the lowest cost.

Clerks are not machines, and, as in all professions, there were good and bad ones. On February 5, 1914, Mr. P. E. Whalen of the Great Northern put out the following circular:

Despite our previous warning it is deplorably true that many of our timekeepers have neglected to look after supplies and equipment in a way that shows they have the interest of the Company at heart. In a good many places that we know of equipment is scattered around and lost under the snow. Supplies get wet and frozen in the dingles, some of them covered up with other goods and lost track of; and good grain bags are laying around everywhere with no more attention paid to them than to the chips near the wood pile. We want every timekeeper to cultivate a memory for the following: That although keeping time and wangan accounts is an important duty and should be attended to properly and primarily there is another branch of his routine work, namely, the checking, recording, accounting, and care of every conceivable article of supplies and equipment that he must either attend to or get out, so we can put someone in who will. The usual April excuses will not be listened to hereafter no matter how well put.

Gambling and drinking, except on vacation, were often forbidden to camp clerks, but the rule was tranquilly broken. By gambling, especially. The foreman, the scaler, and the clerk, along with any other "long-eared" gentry handy, were accustomed to play poker, for small stakes, by the light of the old kerosene lamp. Coins would roll off the table and disappear through the cracks in the floor. When a logging operation was finished it used to be the custom to go around and burn the old buildings, lest they give shelter to irresponsible hikers who might set fire to the woods. Men given this job always poked around in the ashes of the office, and would find three or four dollars lying there.

Gambling was sometimes carried on in the ram-pasture, but as a general thing the lumberjacks didn't have much ready money until the custom arose of paying them by the week or by the month instead of at the end of the season. Then professional gamblers, disguised as woodsmen, sometimes wandered in long enough to make a killing and then leave. Sometimes they cheated, but if they got caught at it their victims might lose their temper. I am reminded of an old C.V.L. woodsman I worked with, named Will Bacon. He wasn't a big man, but he was very "cordy." One night in a bar-room on Cedar Stream a man who thought he looked easy picked a fight with him. They were slamming and biting each other something awful, and finally the fellow drew a knife and stabbed Will in the chest.

"You know, Mr. Pike," he told me, for he was a very polite man, "that made me lose my temper."

From what he then proceeded to do to his opponent it may be judged that it doesn't pay to make people like Will lose their temper.

A German nobleman named Justus Schmidel came to this country some sixty-five years ago and spent a good deal of time in logging camps, some of them in the east, but most of them in the state of Washington. In 1922 he published, in German, a rare and curious book about his life among the Americans. Because I am probably the only man who ever read the book, I think it is not malapropos to recount (in my translation) a story of his about a cheater he observed in a camp near Mount Baker, Washington.

The sun had gone down. It became perceptibly darker and colder. The long bunkhouse I had entered seemed almost empty. By the miserable light of the lamps hanging from the rafters I saw only a few men lying on the rough board bunks that rose up in four tiers along the walls. They were sleeping, or smoking corncob pipes.

At the long table in the middle of the room sat, as if alone, Jim Robertson, a man of gigantic stature, in the finest bloom of life. Apparently sunk deep in thought, he was mechanically shuffling a pack of cards. He was a stranger here. He had come to work in Elder's camp only a few days before. Although he did not differ from the other lumberjacks in his manner nor his clothing, yet an indefinable something in him had awakened my interest. And I had noticed something else about him. When he had taken off his shirt to wash, after work, the night before, I had noticed a scar on his back that seemed to have been made by a knife-stab.

In the upper darkness among the bunks a match suddenly flamed up. In the light I saw someone sit up on the bunk, light a pipe and look at the sitting lumberjack. The cards that the latter was shuffling seemed to make him restless. In a moment two heavy, spiked-booted feet swung over the edge of the bunk. The body followed. Then the man leaped down onto the floor, stepped up to the table, and sat down. For a good while he stared in silence at the cards that Jim Robertson was shuffling, suddenly reached inside his blue woolen shirt and took out of a wallet worn around his chest a handful of silver coins, dimes and quarters, which he counted carefully and laid on the table. On both sides there was motion in the bunks. Three or four men sat up. Slowly, as if against their will, they came to the table and sat down. Jim Robertson seemed to be unaware that others had joined him, that five pairs of eyes were looking greedily at the pack of cards, for he continued to shuffle quietly, without looking up. Suddenly, however, he yawned loudly, and, as if he were bored to death, threw the cards with a flourish onto the middle of the table.

"Jackpot!" said one of the men.

It was the only word spoken. Then each one drew a card and the poker game began.

At first bets were low, and no one seemed especially favored by luck. Then Jim Robertson pulled a full bottle of whiskey from his pocket, took a swallow from it, and passed it to his neighbor. The bottle passed from mouth to mouth. When it had gone around once, it was empty. The strong alcoholic drink did not fail to have its effect on the men. They grew more talkative. Their faces lighted up. From time to time someone even cracked a joke.

Jim Robertson seemed either to have good cards or be willing to bluff, for he suddenly bet five dollars. The gold-piece flew clinking onto the table. It lay there, shimmering yellowishly, among the pieces of silver, and tempted seductively.

"Raise you five!" called one of the players and covered the gold-piece with a ten-dollar bill.

Jim Robertson reached into his pocket and threw three gold-pieces onto the pile: "Raise you ten!"

As if shot from a pistol, came his opponent's answer: "I call you!" Quickly he added ten dollars to the rest of the money and triumphantly uncovered his cards.

"Four kings!"

Conscious of victory, he stretched out his hand for the money. But Jim Robertson, who had likewise uncovered his cards, called: "Not so fast! I have a straight flush!"

Slowly and thoughtfully he raked in the money, while a hot wave of blood suffused his opponent's face. The loss he had just experienced was considerable—twenty dollars. He had had to work a week for that.

Fortune didn't seem to want to leave Jim Robertson that evening. Three, four players had already stood up and climbed silently back into their bunks for they had no more money. Others, who had come from the other buildings into the bunkhouse had taken their places, without any better luck. Jim Robertson won. Then the saw-filer, Willy McCarty, an Irishman, came to the door, a heavy stone jug of whiskey in his hand, and approached the table.

Where had he found so much whiskey? God knows. The saw-filer in a logging camp can get himself a lot of things, for he earns fifteen or twenty dollars a day. He had probably become bored with drinking in his cabin alone.

So he had come into the bunkroom in the hope of finding company. The jug passed from mouth to mouth. It was gurgling down the throats of the men even as Willy McCarty sat down and picked up the cards so willingly dealt out to him. He had no luck. And since, in addition, he played foolishly, his fat wallet was very soon flat and empty. His carefully folded-up pay check that he had received only today he kept doubled up in his hand. I could see how hard it was for him to stop. Hesitatingly he stood up. Robertson, who was just dealing, apparently did not notice, for he dealt out five cards just the same. The temptation was too great. Half erect, the Irishman picked up the cards, and when he looked at them I noticed the expression of dejection on his face suddenly vanish. He must have got good cards. Quickly he sat down again, and when Robertson opened with ten dollars, he bet his whole pay check, almost five hundred dollars, against it. As if hypnotized, all eyes turned to the folded piece of paper that now covered the pile of gold and silver coins. In breathless tension I too followed the play. Five hundred dollars! Who would win?

Slowly and cautiously, without turning a hair, Robertson had added an equal sum, in gold and paper money, to the pile. Now he dealt his opponent the two cards he had asked for. To himself he gave one. When the two turned up their cards, it was so still in the bunkhouse that one could have heard a pin drop on the floor.

Jim Robertson won.

The filer stood up with an oath, while Robertson, with the most indifferent face in the world, reached out his hand for the money. But quite suddenly one of the onlookers who was standing behind him bent over the table and snatched the check. At the same moment, with his other hand he reached into the lucky player's sleeve and drew out a card that had been hidden there and threw it onto the table. It was an ace of hearts, from a different pack.

Robertson sprang up, his face contorted with rage. He was a head taller than the lumberjack who had dared to unmask him. With frightful force his huge fist smashed into the other's face. It sounded soft, dull, as if he had hit a lump of putty. The unfortunate fell to the floor without a sound.

Bewildered by what had happened, everybody, speechless and without moving, stared at the accusing cards. The filer was the first to come to life. With a mighty bound he leaped over the table and struck the cheater a blow on the neck that would have felled an ox. But the latter, who was busy trying to pry the check from the doubled-up fist of his victim lying there on the floor, paid the blow no attention. He merely shook himself a little. Then he straightened up to his almost superhuman height, seized the filer by the throat and hurled him backwards against the heavy table with such force that the table collapsed, with a crash.

The filer didn't seem to want to give up the unequal contest. He grabbed hold of his huge adversary's coat with both hands. As he fell he rolled his body together like a cat and drew his knees up to his chest. The inch-long pointed spikes on the soles of his boots shone like the teeth of a wild animal. Robertson, who was trying to tear himself loose, bent down over him. . . . The Irishman struck him in the belly with all his strength. The giant roared with pain. With a mighty effort he tore loose from his adversary, leaving a part of his coat in the latter's hands. His face was as pale as death. I thought he was going to fall to the floor, unconscious. But the color came back into his face. Raging, he was about to leap on the Irishman.

Before he could carry out his intention the lumberjacks had surrounded him. Cursing, they struck and kicked him and tried to bear him to the floor. Thrusting aside his opponents, who had jumped on him from behind, as if they were weak children, he sprang quickly back against the wall. There he stood, his back protected, a head taller than all the others, like a beast of prey surrounded by a pack of dogs, and awaited the lumberjacks' attack. There was nothing human in his face, distorted with rage and pain. Two strong men jumped at him. He picked them up off the floor, knocked their heads together so their skulls clunked hollowly, and hurled them back into the pile of his attackers. Suddenly a heavy stool whizzed through the air straight into his face.

The giant staggered. Blood spurted out of his mouth and nose. His arms struck aimlessly around in the air. Filled with rage, the lumberjacks leaped upon him. He collapsed under their blows and kicks. The knot of men, who had thrown themselves on him, rolled over him, stamping with their feet, striking with their fists, hurling him along the floor.

The sight reminded me of a beetle conquered by a lot of ants. When the knot of insects that cover him lets loose, there is nothing left but the wings and horny skin.

Through the bunkhouse door, out into the night, flew the bloody limp body of the cheater, thrown as you would a heavy sack.

It's all the same, whether he perishes miserably outside, or whether the raw night wind will bring him back to consciousness and he crawls off in the direction of Maple Falls. A professional card-cheat, who dresses himself up like a lumberjack, steals in among those rough men to cheat them of their hard-earned money. He has been thrown out of the camp. Nobody may take him in, care for his broken limbs. Such is the unwritten law. . . ."

Back in 1920 a young soldier named Joe Marceau, just back from France, applied to the Great Northern Paper Company for a job as camp clerk. He had excellent references and they were glad to hire him. In 1965 Joe retired. A reporter, Henry Milliken, came to visit him at his home in Greenville Junction, Maine, and wrote an interesting and informative account of his long career for the magazine section of the Lewiston (Maine) *Journal* for November 20, 1965. A good deal of the account is pertinent to this chapter, and I produce it verbatim:

. . . Joe Marceau can remember the days when the main staples on the "grub list" were potatoes, salt cod fish, salt pork, prunes, molasses, baked beans, cornmeal, carrots, turnips, beets, cabbage and occasionally a side of fresh beef.

As the years passed the number of items gradually increased. From 1928 to 1935, it became apparent to the superintendents of large woods operations that the woodsmen were following the best cooks as well as the best foremen into the logging camps. The company that supplied the best food boasted the most contented and hardest working crews.

"Back in the '30's, at some of the cutting camps, the cook was paid about a dollar a day less than the foreman," said Joe. "At the Depot Camp of a big operation, the cook's importance was even more pronounced; he received more than the foreman. But the old-time cooks, the ones we called 'sizzlers' or 'boilers,'" were replaced by men who were well versed in all phases of cooking. In other words, they were professionals, often backed with hotel and restaurant experience."

"What came first, better food or better cooks?" I asked Joe. . . .

"Both came with improved methods of transportation. For instance when horses were used to haul carts and sleds loaded with food supplies over narrow, rough woods roads, few perishable items could be handled. Few camps had eggs before 1927 or 1928. Later, say in 1933 or 1934, when motor trucks could be used to reach the Depot camps and often some of the surrounding cutting camps, a wider variety of food was shipped into the woods."

"The number of items sold to the woodsmen likewise increased," I said.

"Certainly, more and more shelves were built in every office to store and display the dozens of new items demanded by woodsmen. The contractors. called 'jobbers,' invariably figured that the profits derived from the sale of wangan items would pay for their clerks. Thus the office shelves were packed with cigarettes, smoking tobacco, chewing tobacco, snuff, aspirin, cough syrup, candy bars, chewing gum, shaving soap, razor blades, handkerchiefs, matches, bachelor buttons, safety pins, needles, thread, underwear, shoes, sox, pants, hats—plus other clothing items."

"How do sales today compare to those during 1940 or 1950?" I inquired.

"Don't drop your cup of coffee while I answer," Joe said. "From 1940 to 1950, or there-abouts, the initial purchase order of merchandise to be sold to the woodsmen to stock four or five cutting camps of a woods operation would total at least $10,000. Today, a sixty-man camp is stocked for less than $500."

"Unbelievable!" I exclaimed. "What are the most popular items now sold to the woodsmen?"

"Only three items are carried on the shelves of most camps—cigarettes, work gloves, and towels."

"Towels!" I muttered, "Don't kid me!"

"I'm not kidding," said Joe. "When a woodsman returns to camp after spending the weekend at home, he seldom has a clean towel among his belongings. Thus, each individual visits the office to purchase a few."

"Shades of John Ross!" I exclaimed. "The old-time woodsmen never thought of purchasing towels; they used roller towels furnished by the Company."

"Correct," admitted Joe. "Each morning and night, the woodsmen lined up in the room separating the bunkroom from the cookroom. One man would wash his face and hands and then step along and use one of the roller towels hanging on the wall; his companions would follow him. By the time the entire crew had washed up, the towels were in sad shape and had to be replaced by clean ones supplied by the Company and kept clean by the bullcook."

"Forty years ago the woodsmen didn't go down river every weekend."

"Most woodsmen stayed at a logging camp at least four months without going 'outside,' said Joe. "Many men had six to eight months 'hitches' and occasionally there would be an individual who would stay one or two years. Those days are long past. Woodsmen now work 40 or 50 hours during a week and then climb into their automobiles and go home to spend some time with their families." . . . Camp yards of today's modern logging camps have the appearance of parking lots. Joe said that if there were 60 men at camp, there are at least 40 cars in the yard. Every Saturday and Sunday the yard is almost deserted, there being perhaps only two or three men left at camp."

When Joe Marceau began his career as a woods clerk in 1920, there were from 80 to 100 woodsmen at many logging camps. These men would cut and haul anywhere from 6,000 to 10,000 cords of pulpwood. Today, a 60-man crew harvests from 15,000 to 20,000 cords. Chain saws, tractors, bull-dozers and other modern equipment have done much to change the production sheets.

While Joe and I were discussing various aspects of his career in the logging camps, we scanned some pulpwood operations reports regarding wages in the camps of long ago.

During the 1933–34 cutting and hauling seasons at Cooper Brook Operation, at one of the Company camps, the foreman was paid $4.75 per day; the assistant foreman, $3.75; cookee, $1.75; teamster, $2.25; feeder, $2.25; laborer, $1.75; blacksmith, $3.25; and timekeeper, $2.75.

We placed the reports to one side and picked up a newspaper with several large ads of three pulp-wood cutting concerns wanting woodsmen this Fall.

One ad stated that two-man crews were needed to cut and yard pulpwood, at $6.00 per cord, horses owned by the company, 40 hours per week, batch camps furnished.

Another company wanted 50 three-men crews to work with small tractors, 120 two-man crews to work with horses. Gasoline and oil furnished for power saws. This concern also wanted a cook at $1.45 per hour, 60 hour week; a cook's assistant at $1.40 per hour, 60 hour week, time and one half after 40 hours.

The third company was anxious to obtain woodsmen for an operation on two townships in Aroostook County. Besides the cutting and yarding crews, they needed the services of two bulldozer operators at $1.60 per hour, 50 hour week; two clerks at $1.25 per hour, 50 hour week; two crane or shovel operators, $1.50 per hour, 45 hour week; two scalers, a $1.75 per hour, 50 hour week; one woods mechanic, $1.45 per hour, 45 hour week.

14

Lumberjack Ballads

The music of our burnished axe shall make the woods re-
sound,
And many a lofty ancient pine will tumble to the ground;
At night round our shanty fire we'll sing while rude winds
blow,
O! we'll range the wild woods over while a-lumbering we
go.

A PRIME diversion in the evening around the old logging-camp stove was singing. The loggers were, for the most part, illiterate, and had the illiterate man's surprising ability to memorize stories, and songs. Nor were all the lumberjack singers "wailers," or else "bull roarers," as has been unfairly alleged. There was usually in a camp crew at least one man with a true, clear voice, who was always being called on to "sing us a song, George!"

Such a man was Baker Thurston, of Hanover, Maine. He and his three brothers were all Maine loggers. "Give us a song, Baker" the men would call out.

"Well, what do you want?"

"Oh, sing anything!"

"All right, here's 'anything!'" And the boss (for he was a camp boss for many years) would begin his favorite song, which must be very old:

You ask for me to sing a song
As through this world I jog along
I jog along through thick and thin
And I can sing most anything!

The song goes on through quite a few stanzas, some of them hardly fit for the Epworth League, and terminates:

And now my song it is complete,
I think it is your turn to treat;
My favorite drink's hot whiskey sling,
But I will drink most anything!

The oldest woods songs we have date from the first quarter of the nineteenth century, and originated in Maine. As Fannie Eckstorm says in her *Minstrelsy of Maine*, they can easily be distinguished from the later ones, for in them is no morbidness, no introspection, no sentimentality. They are about loggers as a class, not about individuals—songs of the white, snow-covered landscape, the tall, black pines, the red-shirted crews of lumbermen going in to lay them low. Vivid in color, Homeric in simplicity, here are the wild woods and the old Yankee woodsmen.

One of the most popular of the early songs is "Canaday-I-Oh," of which one segment goes:

> *Arriving at the shanty with wet and cold feet,*
> *We all pull off our shoes and socks and supper we must eat;*
> *Supper being over, we from the table go,*
> *Then all pick up their pipes and smoke till everything looks blue,*
> *At nine o'clock precisely into our bunks we climb.*

Many songs were known by heart by most of the crew, so the singer would sing the first few lines solo, and the entire crew would roar out the final lines of each stanza, as a chorus.

Most woodsmen's songs are mere doggerel, but there are some that are good, even very good, poetry. But whether good or bad, the songs the lumberjack preferred to sing and to listen to at least reveal what he was thinking about, and "as he thinketh in his heart, so is he." Your logger thought of Rum, of Love, of great deeds on drive, and of death in all its forms. And he loved to hear sentimental songs of home.

A number of pretty good woodsmen's songs came from Canada's Maritime Provinces, whence also came many of New England's best loggers. A good example is

THE LUMBERMAN IN TOWN

> *When the lumberman comes down,*
> *Ev'ry pocket bears a crown,*
> *And he wa-a-anders some pretty gal to find.*
> *If she's not too sly, with her dark and rolling eye,*
> *The lumberman is pleased in his mind,*
> *The lumberman is pleased in his mind.*

It goes on through six melancholy stanzas, relating how he is made welcome until his money gives out, but then is thrown out and returns to the woods. He works hard, forgets his previous bad experience, and goes on another spree. Finally:

> *And kind death will cut the tender threads of life,*
> *And kind death will cut the tender threads of life.*

Most famous of all lumberjack ballads is one called "The Jam on Gerry's Rock," with its chorus:

> *We'll break the jam on Gerry's Rock*
> *With our foreman, young Monroe.*

Mrs. Eckstorm notes its universal appeal to outdoorsmen everywhere, for it moved out onto the plains of the West and Southwest, where cowboys, rangers, soldiers, freighters, and homesteaders sang it. On the same tide of migration it threaded the Rocky Mountains to the very coast.

By far the favorite song of loggers in northern New Hampshire, and in adjacent areas of Maine and Vermont, was about a backwoodsman who lived on Perry Stream in Pittsburgh, New Hampshire. Dan Day was his name, and besides the numerous progeny mentioned in the song he had a set of triplets named Lum, Peen, and Lay. Their birth gave rise to a classic joke: "The Day 'Settlement' on Perry Stream is the only place in the world where they ever made three Days in one night."

A neighbor, Alonzo Perry, congratulated Dan on his begetting prowess. "Yas!" answered Dan, "and if my foot hadn't slipped I'd have had a whole basketful!"

OLD DAN DAY

> *There lives an old man in Pittsburg here*
> *Who sometimes drinks rum and sometimes beer*
> *Or a little cold water when rum ain't near.*

> *Every night when he goes to bed,*
> *He places a bottle under his head;*
> *And in the morning when he awakes,*
> *A jolly good dram this old man takes.*

CHORUS (to be repeated after each stanza):
I wish to God the time would come
When Old Dan Day won't drink no rum;
But you might as well wish for the day of his death,
For he'll drink rum as long as he draws breath.

> *He had a son, his name was Zeke,*
> *I've heard them say that the truth was he couldn't speak;*
> *But I know better, for I've heard him say*
> *He believed the very devil was in Old Dan Day.*

> *He had another and his name was Dan,*
> *If 'twa'n't for his failings he'd be quite a man;*
> *But you that know them know what they be,*
> *And if I don't tell you, why you can't blame me.*

> *He had another and his name was Kim,*
> *All the men in God's world couldn't beat him;*
> *He likes to be with the women alone,*
> *Other men's wives as well as his own.*
>
> *He had a daughter and her name was Sue,*
> *I don't know but what I'd kiss her if I wanted to spew;*
> *It's enough to gag the devil when she puckers up her mouth,*
> *I'd rather kiss a nigger from away down South.*
>
> *He had another and her name was Jane,*
> *I think that her character is deeply stained;*
> *With old Doctor Robbins she used to lay*
> *When her husband was far away.*
>
> *He had another and her name was Ab,*
> *Selden thought he'd got the first grab;*
> *But over to 'Lonzie's they say she went,*
> *To ride old Rob was her intent.*
>
> *There's one thing more that I do crave,*
> *That this old man sha'n't have no grave;*
> *Throw him into a watery hole,*
> *The sharks take his body and the devil take his soul.*
>
> *Now my song is at a close*
> *And that don't like it can turn up their nose;*
> *But those that do, in a smiling way,*
> *Give three rousing cheers for Old Dan Day!*

A more typical woods song that I have heard in camps all over the North Country is variously entitled "Peter Anderbell," "Peter Emberly," and "The Man Killed in the Woods," and doubtless originated in New Brunswick. It consists of the supposed last words of a young lumberjack killed by a falling tree, and its melancholy ending—an appeal for divine mercy on Judgment Day—apparently pleased the rugged loggers very much, for it is very common in lumberjacks' songs. It is now many years since I have heard anyone sing "Peter Anderbell," but I still recall a few of its haunting lines:

> *Little did my mother think*
> *When she sang sweet lullaby*
> *Of the lands that I would travel in*
> *Nor the death that I should die.*

Such bits stick like a burr in one's memory. There exists another woodsman's ditty of which I recall only two lines:

That you are a logger, full well I do know
For your muscle is hard from your head to your toe.

And another:

Oh she married George Chapple
Down by the river side;
'Twould have been a blessing to him
If he'd in his cradle died.

Composed much later, when new ballads were conceived not to be sung, but rather as "poems" (although many of these, too, *were* sung in the camps), is the following account of an event that took place in a camp on Cedar Stream, in northern New Hampshire. The protagonist was a woods boss from the Connecticut Lake country.

THE BALLAD OF ROARING BERT

Come all you honest lumberjacks,
A song to you I'll sing
Of how the famous Roaring Bert
Was licked by ancient Win.

Now Roaring Bert was walking boss
That winter on Cedar Stream,
A bigger, better walking-boss
I'll say I've never seen:
Full four axe-handles wide was he
And very strong and tall,
And he roared before the camp one night
That he could take and fall
A spruce tree quicker than any man
In all the North Countree
And slammed upon the deacon-seat
Ten bucks in good monee,
And dared the men to call his bluff,
If bluff they thought it was.
But all the men knew Roaring Bert
And you didn't hear a buzz
Out of all that crew of hardy lads—
Full thirty-five were there—
Until a chap in a corner dark
Where he sat in a barrel-chair,
Spoke up in a voice so soft and low
But full of amusement too:
"Now Mister Bert, I'll take that bet
And I'll win ten bucks from you.

I'll get a man from this North Countree
He'll be here tomorrow night,
And he will fall a big spruce tree
As quick as his axe can bite,
And he will beat you all to hell,
Or my name ain's William Blight!"

When Bert heard this, he roared aloud,
Like a he-wildcat in pain,
And he swore such a man could never be found
Though they went to the state of Maine
Where men are born with an axe in their hand
And a peavey 'twixt their teeth.
But William Blight did only smile
Until the roaring ceased.
And then in accents mild and calm
He spoke when Bert ceased to rave:
"The man who'll win your ten bucks for me
Is the ancient, decrepit Win Schoppe
Who has one foot in the grave."

Now six years had passed since men had seen
Old Win in the woods, you bet.
But the fame of his name was very green
Wherever woodsmen met.
And the thirty-five in the bar-room there
Set up a silent cheer
And waited with breathless eagerness
To see what they would hear.
They gazed at their boss, big Roaring Bert,
The best man in the land,
A man who'd never been licked in his life,
And a man chuck full of sand.

But this time Bert knew that he was done,
And though it greived him sore,
He stood up straight, full six foot two,
And cried in his famous roar:
"In forty years in lumber camps
I've held my own and more
And by the Roaring Jesus, I've never backed down before:
But here, Bill Blight, is your ten bucks,
You've earned 'em fair and free,
For even with one foot in the grave,
Win's a better man than me!"

Roaring Bert Ingersoll was said to be the best axeman in the North
Country, and as he says in the ballad, he had never backed down before.
But nobody ever thought less of him for doing so on this occasion, for it
was old Win Schoppe, then a very old man, who had taught Bert all he
knew. When he made his bet, Bert had forgotten that the old man was
still on earth, though "with one foot in the grave."

Down in Maine they sing an excellent little song about a Penobscot
cook named John LaRoche, of which a couple of lines go:

> *An' fer Judgment Day, fer dat final shout*
> *Dey've hired Old John to r-oo-lldem out!*

These refer to the cook's pre-dawn cry to the snoring lumberjacks: "Roll
out! R-oo-l-l *o-u-t!*"

Another catchy old number is "The Black Stream Drivers' Song,"
the chorus of which was howled by the whole crew. One stanza goes:

> *Who makes the big trees fall kerthrash*
> *And hit the ground a hell of a smash?*
> *'Tis Johnny Ross and Cyrus Hewes (repeat three times more)*
> *Who gives us pay for one big drunk*
> *When we hit Bangor, slam kerplunk!*
> *'Tis Johnny Ross and Cyrus Hewes.*

John Ross, a Bangor lumberman, was the most famous riverman in
the world, and appropriately there is a song about him, composed by an
old woodsman named Dan Golden:

> ### JOHN ROSS
> *O, the night that I was married, O,*
> *And laid on marriage bed,*
> *Up rose John Ross and Cyrus Hewes*
> *And stood at my bedhead.*
>
> *Saying, "Arise, young married man*
> *And go along with me*
> *To the lonesome hills of Suncook*
> *To swamp them logs for me"* . . .

The authors of the older songs are usually unknown, but we can
often identify the composers of the later ones. Joe Scott, a Maine
woodsman-poet who died in 1916, composed a good deal of doggerel
verse—for a couple of dollars he would make up a song about anybody
who wanted one—but at times he turned out some genuine poetry. I recall one song, too scabrous to print, that starts:

> *I hired with Sammy Golden and to the K.P. I was sent*
> *And with a bunch of Polacks up the Allagash I went.*
> *When we arrived in Patten, it was there we stopped for*
>   *chuck . . .*

Another of Joe's songs that was popular among the woodsmen sixty years ago is entitled "The Whore's Lament." It is a résumé of life in the area in which entertainment was found by the Bangor woodsmen (and others) whose morals were frowned upon by the "elite" of Bangor. The area's popularity was enhanced by the fact that at times the woodsmen encountered some of these elite there in a surreptitious search for the flesh-pots. The loggers used to say that such meetings were the only occasions they had to mingle with Bangor's leading citizens on an equal basis.

Best known of the lumberjack ballad-makers was Larry Gorman, who died in 1923. Professor Edward S. Ives has devoted an unusually good book to him. Here is a stanza of his long song "The Winter of Seventy-Three":

> *He shaved his jaws all roundabout, except a big moustache,*
> *And said when he was going out he meant to cut a dash.*
> *He took a stocking full of gum, the ladies' hearts to gain;*
> *But all the thanks he got from them, they said that he was green.*

A true Maineiac, though born in Nova Scotia, Gorman went over to Lincoln, New Hampshire, in the high White Mountains, one winter and worked in one of J. E. Henry's camps. He did not like the treatment he got there, and he made up a long poem about J. E., of a very critical nature, that became widely known and quite possibly kept a lot of good woodsmen from going there to work.

Probably the best poem in Gorman's hefty repertory is

THE HOBOES OF MAINE

> *All brother Hoboes, I pray come along,*
>   *I hope you will listen and join in my song;*
> *I would be delighted to have a thing righted,*
>   *Especially now, if there's anything wrong.*
> *I'm poor and neglected, I'm mean and dejected,*
>   *I never can visit my birthplace again,*
> *I've joined that great order, since I crossed the border,*
>   *So prominent now, called the Hoboes of Maine.*
>
> *There are many young men crossing over the line,*
>   *Who have not in their hearts a bad thought or design;*
> *They'll come in great hopes, for they know not the ropes,*
>   *And fear not the allurements of women or wine.*

They leave their dear mothers, their fathers or brothers,
  Their kind, loving sisters they'll ne'er see again;
As soon as they come here, they'll each find a chum here,
  And fall into line with the Hoboes of Maine.

They'll come by the hundreds, those hardy young bloods,
  All neatly attired in their own native goods,
In search of employment and earthly enjoyment,
  They'll find it no trouble to hire for the woods.
They'll send them upstream then, to chop and drive team then,
  In hope that their wages will all be clear gain.
But by those man traps they are all handicapped,
  And their names are enrolled with the Hoboes of Maine.

They'll come down in the spring and they'll hang around some
    dive;
  When their money is gone they will hire for the drive,
Their eyes with a glaze on, most painful to gaze on,
  Like bears in the winter, more dead than alive;
With calked boots and greaser, a long-neck apiece,
  They are marched to the station and shipped on the train;
I doubt if they wake till they reach Moosehead Lake,
  When they'll take the toe path with the Hoboes of Maine.

With boots on one shoulder and coat on one arm,
  Their destiny next is the Roach River Farm;
Their way they will take over mountain and lake,
  As the sceneries around them afford little charm;
They'll look tired and dreary, fatigued and leg weary,
  Each one of his lot will sorely complain,
Their toes and their ankles both blistered and rankled,
  A common complaint of the Hoboes of Maine.

With little regard for a room or a bed,
  They'll throw themselves down on a filthy old spread;
They'll lie there till morning, until given warning,
  When each will arise with his eyes crimson red.
They'll rise from their beds then, with awful swelled heads then,
  Prepare to resume their hard journey again,
O'er mountains and ridges and corduroy bridges,
  All cursing the fate of the Hoboes of Maine.

That night they will reach the camp where they drive,
  Where they are packed thicker than bees in a hive;
Both tired and half-drunk they roll into their bunk,
  As you'd think by their groans they'd never survive.

*They'll curse and they'll swear then, they'll vow and declare
    then,
    They'll never be seen on Roach River again,
That they'd rather go beg, with one arm and a leg,
    Than be caught on the drive with the Hoboes of Maine.*

*Then the City Police they plot and connive
    To snare those poor dupes coming off of the drive,
They'll hang round the station, in deep consultation,
    In watch of those victims before they arrive.
They'll joyfully hail them, all ready to jail them,
    And welcome them back to their city again;
Each man, as he'll walk up, is booked for the lock-up,
    To lie there and sweat with the Hoboes of Maine.*

*The man who resists them is used very rough,
    He is thrown on the pavement and quickly handcuffed;
You'd think by their twisters, their chains and cell-wristers
    They surely had captured some notable tough;
They'll pound and they'll bruise him and shamefully use him,
    They'll capture his money, his watch and his chain;
Likewise their design to collect a big fine,
    Or to keep out of jail with the Hoboes of Maine.*

*Next morning he's brought to his honor Judge Vose,
    Who sits there prepared to give him a dose,
As the victim acts silly from blows of the billy,
    His cuts and his scars he will scan very close;
He bids him to stand up and hold his right hand up,
    Saying, "They tell me young man, you've been drinking again;
A fine I must levy, exceedingly heavy,
    Or have you break stone with the Hoboes of Maine."*

*Now I have served out my thirty long days;
    Last night I slept in a cold alleyway;
I'm totally busted and cannot get trusted,
    Folks would know, if they'd trust me, I never should pay.
I'm shabby and bare now, and never would dare now
    To visit my own native country again:
They'd jeer me and boot me and threaten to shoot me,
    And bid me go back to the Hoboes of Maine.*

*I'll tell of a man who was given to roam,
    Being weary of tramping he thought he'd go home;
I mean not to name him, in case I'd defame him,
    But just for a nickname I'll call him Bill Vroam.*

He thought he could bluff them, and tried hard to stuff them,
He claimed he had served in the Cuban campaign;
But as soon as they spied him, they identified him;
They knew he belonged to the Hoboes of Maine.

But the Hoboes of Maine are still in great hope
That in some future day they will have further scope;
There's too much restriction, too much interdiction—
In some other states they've tasted the hope.
If those would-be rulers kept out of the coolers,
They'd soon become powerful and certain to reign
In the lowlands and highlands and Prince Edward Island,
Quebec, Nova Scotia, New Brunswick and Maine.

As Mrs. Eckstorm so acutely says of this song, the picture of the woodsmen, those "Hoboes of Maine," represents only too truly their condition as they congregated at the corner of Exchange and Washington streets, in Bangor, near the old European and North American depot, which stood on the site of the present railroad station. Here they are to the life, with their slickers to shed the spring rain, their calked boots hung on their shoulders, and the "long-necks," or bottles of whiskey. It is a grimy picture of the woodsmen—dazed, doped, half drunk after a brief carouse upon their winter's wages—being loaded in the early morning upon the up-river train at the old yellow depot, to be sent on the drives.

We need not accept the poet's closing prophecy of the proletariat supreme, nor acquit the woodsman of all responsibility for his condition; but Larry Gorman spoke like a poet and not a mere rhymester when, seeing so clearly the hard lot of the woodsmen of his own day, and painting it with the grim realism of that famous fifteenth-century poem "The Sailing of the Pilgrims from Sandwich Towards St. James of Compostella," he did not end with the portrayal of the tragedy of hopeless weakness, wickedness, and despair, but ardent and yearning, saw a vision and sang of what he saw as a glorious possibility for ruined men.

Another song once popular in the camps was composed by a woodsman named Ed Shallow, of Colebrook, New Hampshire. Ed was drunk and disorderly in Lancaster one day, and an influential citizen named Colby had him arrested. Judge Ossian Ray sentenced him to jail:

IT'S HARD TIMES
IN LANCASTER JAIL

A prisoner's fate let me tell you is hard,
The doors they are locked and the sills they are barred;
With bolts and with bars they will make you secure,
God damn'em to hell and they can't do no more.

CHORUS (to be repeated after each stanza):
And it's hard times in Lancaster jail,
And it's hard times I say.

The food that you have is a loaf of brown bread
As hard as a rock and as heavy as lead;
Or a pint of bean soup, and your meat it is stale,
You're bound to go hungry in Lancaster jail.

Oh the bed that you have is the dirty old rugs
And when you lie down you're all et up with bugs
For the bugs they swear they'll never give bail;
You're bound to get lousy in Lancaster jail.

There is old Colby, a very rich man
He spends all his time in loafing around.
Your boots he will raffle, your clothes he will sell,
Get drunk on the money, God damn him to hell.

Now there is young Ray, he's a dirty mean crew,
He'll look at his men as if looking them through,
To Lancaster jail he will send you to dwell;
For one pint of whiskey he'd send you to hell.

Now to conclude and finish my song,
I hope that I've sung nothing that's wrong,
May the Stars and the Stripes together prevail
In hell with Old Colby and Lancaster Jail.

The French-Canadian loggers brought their own songs with them: "Ma Boule Roulante," "Le Bastringue," "C'était une Jeune Fille," "A la Claire Fontaine," and dozens of others. They could sing "A la Claire Fontaine" in a way that would make tears come to the eyes of the listening lumberjacks, who were not exactly men who cried easily. They had a fine song entitled Les Raftsmen, and even one about the baked bean, *la bigne, la bigne, la jolie, jolie bigne,*" and its flatulent effect.

But except for the Canucks, no one sings in the logging camps today. Singing was driven out by the advent of the phonograph and radio, and helped toward its demise by the big influx after 1914 of men from northern and eastern Europe, and even from Italy. For these people, sent up to the woods by employment offices in Boston and Portland, did not speak English and could not memorize the old songs.

Today, college professors tour the back blocks seeking out the oldest inhabitants and taking down with tape-recorders their quavering renditions of "The Redlight Saloon," "The Little Brown Bulls," and other woods classics once known and sung in smoke-filled bunk-rooms from coast to coast.

Let us close this nostalgic chapter with an anonymous song entitled "When the Drive Comes Down," of which I can say what old Vern Davison said when he sang it to me nearly forty years ago—I like it as well as any lumberjack ballad I ever heard:

WHEN THE DRIVE COMES DOWN

Come all ye gallant shanty boys and listen while I sing,
*We've worked six months in cruel frosts but soon we'll take
    our fling.*
The ice is black and rotten and the rollways are piled high;
So boost upon your peavey sticks while I do tell you why:
*For it's break the rollways out, my boys, and let the big sticks
    slide!*
*And file you calks and grease your boots and start upon the
    drive.*
A hundred miles of water is the nearest way to town;
So tie into the tail of her and keep her hustling down!

When the drive starts down, when the drive starts down,
Oh, it's every lad in heaven he would swap his golden crown
For a peavey stick again and a soaking April rain,
And to birl a log beneath him as he drives the river down!

When the drive comes down, when the drive comes down,
*Oh, it's then we're paid our money and it's then we own the
    town!*
All the gutters run with whiskey when the shanty boys so frisky
Set their boot calks in the sidewalks when the drive is down!

There's some poor lads will never lift a peavey hook again,
*Nor hear the trees crack with the frost, nor feel a warm spring
    rain.*
'Twas falling timber, rolling logs, that handed them their time;
It was their luck to get it so—it may be yours or mine.

But break the rollways out, my lads, and let the big sticks slide,
*For one man killed within the woods, ten's drownded on the
    drive.*
So make your peace before you take the nearest way to town,
While the lads that are in heaven watch the drive go down!

What makes you lads so wistful-eyed as we draw near to town?
Other eyes is soft and bright, like the stars of a June night—
*Wives and sweethearts, praying, waiting, as we drive the river
    down.*
God bless the eyes that shine for us when we boil into town.

15

Logging Railroads

THE late years of the nineteenth century and the early years of the twentieth formed an era of expansion. New England was emerging from the period following the Civil War. Cities were being built, all of wood. Lumber was king. Trees had to be cut down and marketed. If they couldn't be profitably floated down rivers, then they had to come out some other way.

The logging railroad was the answer. In those early days the virgin forest came right down to the village limits, so the railroads were built out into the timber a little way and were gradually extended as the woods were cut back. They were all standard gauge—4 feet 8½ inches—and the lumber companies were helped very much by competing railroad companies: the Boston and Maine, the Maine Central, and the Grand Trunk expected to make money on freight receipts for hauling the lumber, so they cheerfully rented rails, switches, and other expensive track properties to the logging firms. Frequently other items of equipment, large and small, were thrown in gratis.

What is now known as standard gauge was by no means universally used on the early American railroads. This gauge of track came to us from England, and its origin is interesting. The distance between the wheels of the ancient Roman chariots happened to be 4 feet 8½ inches; English carts and wagons followed suit, and when the first railroad track in that country was laid, the "gauge" of the familiar horse-drawn vehicles was used for the new "highway."

For the first twenty years all the locomotives were wood-burners. If a crew ran short of fuel all they had to do was to stop and cut down a few trees and away they would go, shooting sparks in every direction and causing numerous forest fires, some of them very disastrous indeed. Later, coal was used, and fires decreased somewhat.

Most logging railroads operated only during the winter, when the ground was frozen hard, but others worked all the year round, and picked up small change in the summer by putting benches or chairs on the cars and running "excursions" into the wilds for tourists. In those days, summer visitors came by train or stage-coach and would spend the whole summer at one hotel, instead of staying only a short time as is the custom today. It was no trick to sign up a hundred or more young gentlemen and ladies on a fine Saturday afternoon, at North Woodstock, or Conway, New Hampshire, to take a bumpy but jolly ten-mile ride through magnificent scenery to some large logging camp where everyone was served pies, cakes, doughnuts, and tea cooked by doughty woods chefs.

Vermont never had more than half a dozen logging railroads. The Rich Lumber Company built the Lye Brook Hollow branch in Manchester, and in 1885 the Deerfield Valley Company built eleven miles of railway to reach its wood-pulp and sawmill plants at Readsboro. In 1892 this road was extended as far as Wilmington. There were one or two other short lines, but they were not primarily built to haul logs.

A genuine logging railroad was the single-track affair, twenty-five miles long, built up the East Branch of the Nulhegan in 1922 to take out hardwood logs to the New Hampshire Stave and Heading Company's mill in North Stratford, where sugar-barrels were manufactured. The company soon went bankrupt and was taken over by the C.V.L., which owned the stumpage on the East Branch. After many subsequent changes of ownership, the mill is now operating busily making veneer from logs brought in by truck. The tracks of the old railroad were removed many years ago, but the right-of-way is still used by hikers and hunters.

Then there was an interesting contraption one might call half a railroad. As we have mentioned, in the old days logging was done only in the winter, when snow made it possible to move logs less expensively. How essential the snow was, is shown by the experience of Tom Trudeau, of Bethlehem, New Hampshire, back in 1895. Tom was a veteran lumberman and had amassed quite a fortune when he was inveigled into taking a job over in Victory, Vermont.

The Victory area consists of 23,000 acres of swamp and one mountain, and probably more softwood has been cut there than anywhere else in New England. Men were logging there prior to 1840, and in 1940 the C.V.L. cut the last two lots of virgin spruce (on Umpire Mountain) left in the state. And the C.V.L. was still cutting spruce in Victory in 1966.

Anyway, Tom, with the wisdom of long experience, got together his crews, his axes, his peavies, his chains, his sleds, his provisions, his chewing-tobacco, and everything else needed for such an operation, and moved jauntily into the swamp. But the Lord forgot to make it snow in Victory that winter, and Tom's three score horses stood all winter in the hovel.

At least, they didn't draw any sleds. In desperation, the lumberman built a railroad track, using unpeeled spruce logs for rails, and getting flatcars that had flanged wheels which fitted over the logs; his horses drew the cars. But on a frosty morning the iron wheels chewed thick slabs two feet long out of the "rails," which then had to be replaced. Apparently the bark on the logs caused the chewing, but Tom started too late in the season to peel his logs, for it can't be done in the fall and winter. Also, the cars would go only on a straight track. They refused to turn on curves. Tom came out in the spring with his shirt, but poorer by a hundred thousand dollars.

About 1900 came the Victory Lumber Company, which bought stumpage and erected, at Damon's Crossing, a large steam mill capable of sawing out forty thousand feet of lumber a day, which was a very big capacity in those days.

Profiting from Tom's mistakes they built another railroad, using peeled spruce logs for rails, and instead of horses a steam locomotive. And their cars could turn on curves. We have a rare photograph of that odd track and of the odd locomotive used on it. The latter was not a Shay or a Baldwin. God alone knows what it was. It was invented by a Frenchman (he is shown in the photo) from up in Quebec. Perhaps some old railroad buff can tell more about it.

In 1904 the company leased the mill and sold stumpage to the Moose River Lumber Company, an outfit owned by Johnson and Stebbins. By that time the wooden rails had been replaced by steel ones, on a different road-bed, and a twenty-three-ton Lima Shay locomotive was used for hauling. The operation closed in 1907, the rails were taken up, and the mill was taken down, but aerial photographs still show the course of the old railroad.

A few miles farther up the Moose River, in the town of Granby, the Moccasin (Stevens) mill had a logging railroad that went five miles back into the woods up the West Branch, but it used conventional iron rails and a Shay engine. The railroad has long since vanished, and so has the mill, but enormous piles of sawdust still mark the site.

Maine, too, had only half a dozen logging railroads. The Bangor and Piscataquis Canal and Railroad Company might be called one. It was built in 1836, and in 1854 General Samuel Veazie bought it and used it exclusively for hauling lumber from the Old Town mills to Bangor.

In 1911, Hollingsworth and Whitney built a thirteen-mile line to Bald Mountain Town. They leased rails from the Maine Central, and when they finished logging in that region in 1922 the rails were taken up. The construction work was done by Italian laborers and cost five thousand dollars a mile. It is interesting to note that the Italians were paid a dollar a day and boarded themselves.

Between 1919 and 1927 the Great Northern Paper Company built an eighteen-mile-long railroad known as the Seboomook Lake and St. John, which was to be used to bring pulpwood from the headwaters of the St.

John River. Apparently there was some question from the beginning about the feasibility of the whole project. Not one stick of pulpwood and not a single log was ever hauled over it, and by 1929 those opposed had won out and the rails were taken up. Gravel roads and trucks were found more useful. (In 1941 the Great Northern dug a canal a mile and a half long enabling them to float wood down the Penobscot.)

Probably the very last of the old-fashioned Maine loggers of great stature was King Ed Lacroix, whose home range was the St. John, but who was willing to go wherever he could make good money by cutting down trees. For many years he did a lot of business with the Great Northern, and in 1926 he built, way off in the deep woods, a remarkable logging railroad that he called the Eagle Lake and West Branch Railroad. It was thirteen miles long, and he operated it from 1927 through 1933, transporting nearly a million cords of pulpwood on it. He is probably the only man who ever drove a river in two directions at once, for he sent his saw-logs down the St. John while his pulpwood went up the St. John watershed and over into the Penobscot (with a useful assist, it is true, from his railroad).

The building of that railroad was a gigantic undertaking. Lacroix brought in his men, his supplies, and his equipment fifty miles through the forest from Lac Frontière, on the Quebec border, on iced tote-roads and across frozen lakes, using enormous sleds to transport sixty flatcars and a ninety-ton oil-burning steam locomotive. His terminus was Eagle Lake. There he built three conveyors, each of them 225 feet long, that raised the pulpwood twenty-five feet up out of the lake and onto his cars. The conveyors were run by diesel engines and would deliver a cord of wood from the water to the car in one and a half minutes, so that it took eighteen minutes to load a car. The cars were thirty-two feet long and each took about twelve and a half cords of wood. They were provided with high rack sides, one which was hinged at the top, and the car floors had a twelve-inch slope.

After a little experimenting the railroad went on a schedule that first year of three twelve-car trains a day, moving wood from Eagle Lake down to Umbazookaskus. Here a trestle six hundred feet long had been built out into the lake, and on it the track sloped six inches toward the water. With the twelve-inch slope on the car floor, Ed had eighteen inches to help him unload when he unfastened the lower edge of his racks and let them hang by the hinges on top. Thus when the side was released, the wood slipped very quickly out of the car and into the water. It took about an hour to empty a whole train, the men working with hooks and poles to unload what did not fall out by gravity.

It took about three hours to make the trip, because they had to run slowly around the many curves across the numerous trestles, one of which, over Allagash Stream, was 1,500 feet long.

By 1933 Ed had cut all the timber, so he moved elsewhere, leaving his railroad, rolling stock, and other equipment behind him. All that is left are the rusting rails on the right-of-way, and here and there a rotting flatcar. Allagash canoodlers stop and stare in disbelief at the ninety-ton locomotive, still standing there, way to hell and gone off in the woods, and wonder what kind of men brought it there, and why.

New Hampshire, especially deep in the White Mountains, and sometimes out in the foot-hills, saw quite a few picturesque logging railroads, built by equally picturesque loggers. The subject has been studied very thoroughly by E. Francis Belcher in various issues of *Appalachia* since December, 1959. He notes that the greatest of the old-time lumber barons ("about any one of whom a book could be written"), George Van Dyke, never built but one road, the seven-mile Little River Railroad, just west of Zealand. He dwells with nostalgia on the East Branch and Lincoln road, built by J. E. Henry in the 1890's. He traces the history of the Blanchard and Twitchell road that operated from 1894 to 1907 in Success township. He tells us about the oldest one of all, the John's River Railroad (1870–1902) in Whitefield, and of others on both the eastern and western slopes of the White Mountains, each chapter replete with entertaining and informative anecdotes, and each one a monument to prodigious research. About the only one he leaves out is the seven-mile road at Millsfield Pond, which began nowhere and ended nowhere, and for which, as for Lacroix's Eagle Lake road, all the equipment, the locomotive, and so on, had to be hauled in on sleds. But while Ed operated in flat country, the Millsfield area is very steep indeed. The locomotive was a temperamental creature named Rosy, and was later sold to the Conway Lumber Company.

Practically all of northern New Hampshire, including the White Mountain area, was covered with virgin forest as late as 1867. That year the governor decided to sell off all that public domain as fast as he could, and he proceeded to do so, at prices ranging from twenty cents to a dollar an acre. City slickers (and some country ones) who knew a good thing when they saw it found means and ways to purchase those lands. An official report shows that by 1904 the timberlands of the state were owned almost entirely by seven large companies. And they were all cutting fast and furiously.

During his career George Van Dyke drove over a billion feet of logs down the Connecticut. Over on the Androscoggin the Brown Company between 1860 and 1964 handled twice as much. The small rivers in the heart of the mountains were too rough, crooked, and mill-infested to permit successful driving, and the need for railroads there is obvious.

No account of logging in New Hampshire would dare omit mention of George B. James, head of the New Hampshire Land Company. George and his company never did any logging, but they were the chief speculators in New Hampshire timberlands. Belcher tells us that James was directly connected with land sales and mortgages involving eleven out of the seventeen White Mountain logging railroads. And while he was doing his utmost to despoil the hillsides, he was going around lecturing on timber conservation!

J. Willcox Brown, in an article in *Appalachia* (December, 1958) entitled "The Forest History of Mount Moosilauke," has an interesting account of how James used to acquire title to timber lots:

Working for James as land agent was a certain Oren James (not related), whose job was to bring in the lots "by hook or crook," and it would seem that full use was made of both methods. The New Hampshire Land Company's formal embrace of a lot to which the claims of others were vague consisted of running and blazing a line around it, thus establishing a sort of ownership by possession. Alaric Demeritt, an old local surveyor, ran lines for the Land Company with a remarkable staff compass which had a tendency to deflect around a good clump of spruce but always ended up on the corner. Mr. George Gordon told the writer that A. E. Moxie, in surveying the lands about to be acquired by the National Forest, found the corners to be satisfactory, but the lines afflicted with kinks and bulges.

In this connection we might mention a remarkable deed on file in the registry of deeds office at the Grafton County court house. It is dated July 19, 1902, and conveys a property owned by George B. James of Boston, to the approximate value of three and a half million dollars to the White Mountain Paper Company. The property has a total area of about four hundred thousand acres. The deed conveying it was further made legal by the attachment of revenue stamps to the amount of $1,700 as required by law. The document is composed of sixty-three pages of typewritten matter and is neatly underscored with red ink where necessary. The revenue stamps are headed by a thousand-dollar stamp, followed by seventy ten-dollar stamps.

The property was located in the New Hampshire towns of Woodstock, Thornton, Hatch & Chase's Grant, Waterville, Campton, Ellsworth, Rumney, Warren, Wentworth, Benton, Piermont, Groton, Holderness, Franconia, Lincoln, Livermore, South Raymond, and Grant. The deed of transfer includes a budget of papers from other parties to the White Mountain Paper Company.

Those old boys were as slick at selling land as they were at buying it. J. Willcox Brown relates how George L. Johnson—the notable lumberman we have mentioned as reputedly so crooked he could hide behind a corkscrew, and the builder, among other enterprises, of a profitable logging railroad in the Lost River country—sold hardwood stumpage to an unsophisticated purchaser:

Johnson's parting touch was the sale of the hardwood stumpage on the tract [Lost River country] which he considered of little or no value, to the Mattson Manufacturing Company of Pennsylvania. Mattson, who was esteemed as a fine but foolish sort in Woodstock, moved his concern into the North country in the fall of 1910 to show the New Hampshire folk how to log hardwoods. He and his men were taken on a grand tour by Johnson's agent, a certain sly Jim Ward. From every angle they were marched around and over certain select knolls until the end of the long day, when tired, but convinced of the vast extent of the remaining timber resources, they returned to close the deal. Mattson bought the Lost River mill, built a chute running two miles onto the high shoulders of Waternomee, constructed a storehouse at Lost River, and established a whole settlement called "Little Canada" halfway to Johnson P.O. where a dry kiln and flooring mill were raised. Johnson hauled Mattson's lumber to the flooring mill on his railroad, and Mattson settled back to absorb a severe financial drubbing. With the timber running far short of expectations in both quantity and quality, he hung on grimly until his mill burned, and then moved back to Pennsylvania.

J. E. Henry, who built the East Branch and Lincoln logging railroad, started from nothing in Littleton, New Hampshire, in 1831 and died in Lincoln in 1912, worth some ten million dollars, all of which he had earned himself. It is recorded that in his old age he once said, speaking of the days of his boyhood, when he had to go to school barefoot and the other boys stepped on his toes, blue with frost, "I licked 'em when I could, and when I couldn't I set my teeth and said, 'You hain't agoin' to step on my toes always,' an', by God, they hain't!"

Henry had previously built in Zealand the crookedest and steepest logging railroad in New England, but in Lincoln he did a first-class job, as is evident to this day. All his operations in Lincoln showed care, forethought, and thrift. Most of the bridges, trestles, and road-beds of his East Branch and Lincoln Railroad were built by a fat Canuck named Pork-Barrel Dumas, whose only transit was in his head, but who was a great construction boss, even if he could barely read and write. Some of his long, high trestles stand today, to the wonder of the passer-by.

A logging railroad was built up a main valley, and if the timber warranted it, spur-lines were built up side-valleys. Horses twitched or sledded the logs from the stump to landings beside the track. The main landings were at the camp clearings, and many of them stand today, easily recognized by their elevated crib-work. On the East Branch and Lincoln, landings were built of peeled hardwood logs and normally accommodated from four to six cars, with storage capacity of ten thousand board feet or more. Each had an upper and a lower section, to sort the pulp (for Henry built a paper mill along with his sawmill at Lincoln) and timber logs.

A train normally hauled about three or four thousand feet of logs, though after 1910 this was doubled. The longest load ever brought down at once was twenty-eight carloads, behind a thirty-five-ton Baldwin engine, but that was very long indeed.

The major problem of the engines was not how to haul their trains, but how to brake their heavy loads on the down-hill run to the mill. The only air brakes were on the engine, with individual handbrakes on the trucks for the brakemen to set tighter on a whistle from the engineer. It was a unique operation, says Belcher, and doubtless many engineers offered prayers that their long loads weren't too long for the many short curves between the landings and home. When the hogger whistled his crew for more brakes for the steep grade ahead, woe betide the brakeman who wasn't careful going over the grinding, twisting log-serpent, often wet and icy, in daylight or after dark. In an official report concerning the accident of a log-train brakeman in 1900 the New Hampshire Railroad Commissioners stated: ". . . for it is to be said that the business in which he is engaged is an extra hazardous one, that the machinery and methods in use in moving logs appear to be primitive and crude, and to afford little chance of even the most prudent brakeman to do the work in safety . . . we must expect similar casualties in which the best of men lose their lives."

Harl Pike, in 1966 living in Littleton, New Hampshire, and ninety-one years old, was a fireman on the White Mountain Division of the Boston and Maine in January, 1903. He and his engineer, Ted Nourse, were shunting a train of cars loaded with long logs at Jefferson Junction. A big, handsome young man named Fred Ray Stuart, from Woodsville, who was about to get married, was working as brakeman on the loaded flat-cars. He had been doing the job for months, and was well used to it, but that afternoon he either got careless or just had bad luck, for he slipped.

As the locomotive backed slowly up, pushing the train, Harl looked out the window of his cab and saw Stuart lying beside the track, on his back. He thought he was doing it for a joke.

"Anything I can do for you, Ray?" he called down.

"Yes," said the other. "You can knock me in the head."

They stopped the train in an instant and Harl jumped out. He wasn't a big man, and Stuart weighed fully twenty-five pounds more than he did.

"I don't know how I ever did it," he told me, "but I picked him up and carried him in my arms. His right leg and thigh had been cut off three times but his overalls held the pieces together. He was bleeding like a stuck pig. I was soaked with his blood, but I lugged him up into the cab and we went down to the hospital in Whitefield as fast as the wheels would turn, but it was no use. He died that night. The next day we were shunting past the same place and I looked down and there were all the toes of his right foot, standing together, beside the track. 'Stop,' I said to Nourse, 'I'm going to bury those toes. I don't want to go by here every day looking at them.' I got out and scraped a little dirt and a little snow over them, but I can see them now, more than sixty years afterwards. . . ."

Yes, that kind of logging was man's work, all the way from the stump to the millpond.

16

The Steam Log-Hauler

IT IS NOT given to many men to move the earth, but Alvin O. Lombard, of Waterville, Maine, did it. Alvin was born in 1856, a farmer's son, and he turned out to be a mechanical genius whose inventions are still being used around the world.

Of them all, the lag tractor tread, which moves today's bulldozers and a host of other machines, is the most important. The "Lombard Steam Log Hauler," in which this tread was first used, was patented on May 21, 1901. Lumbermen and inventors had been attempting for years to find some mechanical means which could replace the four-horse team in moving heavy sled-loads of logs. The problem was to find a powerful form of traction that would adapt itself to snow roads full of irregularities and steep pitches and grades, and not turn over or blow up.

Many odd inventions had been tried out before Lombard came along, but for one reason or another had been found impractical. One was a steam engine with huge roller drums for wheels, another was supposed to kick itself along like a grasshopper, and a third had revolving elephant feet which were supposed to step over small obstructions, but when tried out suddenly lost traction in a hole.

Lombard invented a machine that looked like an ordinary locomotive except that in the place of the driving wheels a broad band of lags, which furnished traction, revolved around an oval frame on rollers driven by sprocket wheels inside, connected to the engine. The water tank was placed directly under the boiler and had a capacity of ten barrels, providing steam which would run the contraption about five miles. At first, wood was used for fuel, and although it would not keep so even a temperature as coal, and there was always danger of ramming out a boiler plug when stoking up, at least the use of wood made the hauler independent. Later, most of the wood-burners were converted to coal, which of course was always the fuel on large operations.

Although at its zenith the steam Lombard hauled as many as twenty-four sleds loaded with long logs, making a train 1650 feet long, that was a record. Back in 1904, three sleds were the maximum, and they were held apart by reaches, a reach being a plank used between the sleds. Cross chains between the sleds enabled them to track each other.

But sleds will slew, just as an old pung sleigh would slew, and over-turn. The mishap wasn't the fault of the horse hauling the pung, nor was it the fault of the log-hauler, although it was popular to ascribe accidents to the infernal machine itself. A crew consisted of four men—an engineer, a fireman, a conductor who would connect and inspect each sled to see that it was properly loaded and secured, and the steersman, the most important of the four, who was a hardy and intrepid soul, quite unaccustomed to fear.

There were no brakes on a log-hauler. Close to the rear, the conductor rode the logs, communicating with the cab by a bell-rope which ran along the sled stakes. Should one of the wooden reaches break going around a curve, the unhitched sleds would head for the brush, and the conductor had to jump for his life. From his cab, the engineer worked the throttle, watched the lags turning underneath him, and swore at the fireman. The fireman swore back and kept poised to jump.

And all alone, far up front, huddled the steerer. Directly behind and above him loomed the smokestack, and when the wind was right it belched smoke that blinded him and sparks that set his clothes on fire. So there he sat, grasping mightily a heavy iron wheel, steering for his life, and hoping every time he came to a steep down-grade that he would survive long enough to find some other way to earn a living. Sometimes the foreman put a road monkey at the steep grades, to shake hay over the road as the log-hauler approached, and sometimes, though rarely, hay-sheds were built in such places, so the bare ground would act as a brake.

Going down was bad enough with a four-horse team, with the pole horses sliding back onto their haunches in the breeching, but the steam log-hauler didn't have even that much brakage, though there was a way an artful engineer could reverse the engine and gingerly cracking on enough steam to "pillow" the pistons, could help a bare trifle. The fireman, too, in a real extremity, might shovel out coal to help trig the following sled runners, but usually the fireman, never as brave as the steersman, had already jumped. Only the intrepid steersman, wrapped grotesquely in a blanket to ward off the often 30-below-zero frost, stuck like grim death to his iron steering wheel until the very last moment. "Stay with her!" was his motto, and by God! he usually stayed. The stories of his feats were often discussed along the deacon-seat.

Lombard had originally used a horse, or even a pair of horses, hitched in front of the hauler, to do the steering. Even after the solid steering wheel was added to the machine, some loggers continued to use a horse. And from time to time a crude shelter from the icy winds was added to the steersman's seat, a sort of box to keep the sparks off his clothes and whiskers, and some of the cold air out.

Also, since the machines, unlike horses, were not subject to fatigue, and didn't have to stop and eat, people who bought log-haulers were prone to use them day and night, by working two shifts. Blazing acetylene headlights were fixed to the front, and on a cold winter night, black as velvet, or perhaps shot through with frozen stars, when a Lombard, thudding on its lags, rocking to and fro, belching fire and smoke, came slewing and twisting down a woods road, wakening the echoes, throwing sparks to the tree-tops, blowing and snorting as it dragged its long serpent's tail of loaded sleds around the curves, it was an awesome sight.

The Lombard really was practical. It could maintain a speed of four miles an hour, it could haul a heavy load over the slight rises in the road that horses could negotiate, it could go back up the hills at the same speed it came down them, and it never contracted a fatal disease, though it often got mechanically sick. Instead of two turns in a twelve-hour day with a four-horse team to land two loads, a maximum of six turns in twenty-four hours for one engine was achieved on a four-to-six-mile haul, to land eighteen loads, or the work of nine times four horses—theoretically.

But as a matter of fact, as the Brown Company found out when they bought three of them in 1904 to log Stetson town in northwestern Maine, a comparatively flat region, theory didn't equal practice. One had to own three haulers in order to keep one running all the time, so frequent were breakdowns. And anyone who went out to repair a stranded log-hauler could appreciate Dante's lowest circle in hell. Crews were often forced to build bonfires along both sides of the engine to thaw out parts and keep themselves from freezing, and in those days, when there were no set specifications for iron, cast-iron parts would often snap like a pipestem on a frosty morning. After crawling around in the dark with jacks and blocks, handling ponderous, ice-cold chunks of iron, one yearned for the smell of sweaty horses and hot manure.

It was discovered that the initial cost of building the main road was about doubled because stronger bridges had to be built to bear the weight of the haulers and greater care had to be taken in side-skidding the curves to prevent sleds from leaving the road. Sharp curves had to be avoided if possible because of difficulty in making the train of sleds track properly. Grades of over 5 per cent had to be eliminated, and particularly steep pitches. If the pitches could not be avoided, they had to be properly sanded because the majority of accidents occurred on the down-grades as the sleds were apt to forge ahead, jack-knife, and turn out of the road.

Larger and stronger sleds had to be used not only because each sled carried a heavier load, but because there was a greater strain in starting and stopping. After a good deal of experimentation it was learned that hardwood poles served better than reach and cross chains, for they facilitated the tracking of the sleds. Also the best width for the sleds was four feet, so that they would track on the surface made smooth by the lag chains of the tractor.

A number of other useful tricks were discovered by the process of trial and error. For example, a log-hauler operated at its maximum efficiency when no time was lost. To make this possible, three sets of sleds had to be used, one loading at the skidways, one hauling on the road, and one unloading at the landing. Also, it was desirable to have sufficient skidways and rollways, placed about six feet apart to make the uncoupling of sleds unnecessary, and to have each end of the road form a loop so that the hauler could place round the top of the loop the sleds just brought in, pick up the waiting sleds, and always be headed in the right direction.

Finally, an essential feature in the operation of a steam hauler was the handling and care of the machine itself. A first-class man was needed to operate it, and it required a daily overhaul and greasing.

The cost of all those requirements, and of a telephone line strung along the tree-trunks beside the main road, a dispatcher and a host of other roustabouts, and repairs, delays, and capital depreciation, was so great that while Brown's three haulers had done the work of sixty horses, the company actually lost money. So they abandoned the log-hauler scheme and the old sleds were scattered all along the east bank of the Kennebago from Oquossoc to Kennebago Lake. Frank King, who had charge of the Cupsuptic storehouse, and his men spent almost an entire summer burning the combustible parts and carrying the iron into the woods out of sight because "Bobby" Brown, as the old-timers called W. R. Brown, the company's woods manager, said that fishing parties on their way to Grant's sporting camp were criticizing the company for leaving all that "valuable" equipment to rot in the woods.

Lombard, however, kept on improving his product, and steam log-haulers were used almost everywhere in the woods until 1930, when their era practically closed. Today they are museum pieces, or would be, if those still available weren't hidden in such far-off places as Churchill Depot, in Maine, where they have been roosting for a generation. The year 1928 saw the last big operation using them, on Cooper Brook, a tributary of the Penobscot. The Great Northern hauled more than nine hundred tons of coal into the woods there for their twenty-ton Lombards, they built one trestle 1,250 feet long, and they removed 42,000 cubic yards of dirt and rock to ease the grades. Go-back roads were used to route the returning empties, so as to give the loaded sleds a clear run. Once a train was started it was better for it not to stop; the runners of loaded sleds had a way of freezing in.

Lombard ceased to manufacture steam haulers in 1917, though he continued to build parts for several years. But he had foreseen that the steam-driven machine was proving too expensive for operators, and that it would eventually be supplanted by gasoline tractors. So he went to work and developed a gasoline tractor, in fact, two—the "Lombard Standard 6" and the "Lombard Big 6." Both of these caught on immediately and everybody bought them. Unlike the steam hauler, they required only one man to operate; they had greater maneuverability, and fuel cost less.

By this time, long logs had given way to four-foot pulpwood. A gasoline tractor could haul between fifteen and twenty-five sleds, depending on the terrain, or a payload of up to one hundred and fifty cords, representing nearly two hundred tons. The Lombard gas tractor held its own until 1937, when it was driven out of business by the more powerful and cheaper Caterpillar tractor. Gasoline tractors were regularly employed by all companies on long flat hauls until trucks were designed that would go practically everywhere to the stump for pulpwood.

Liars will figure, but figures don't lie. In 1915 the Great Northern Paper Company, the largest pulpwood operator in New England, had 1,200 horses in the woods. In 1965 it had only 125. But the old lag tractor, patented by Alvin Lombard in 1901, is still going strong. The last thing I read about it was that a firm out in Ohio had completed one twenty stories high, weighing fourteen million pounds, for use in open-pit mining. What can horses do against a monster like that?

17

The Sawmill

When the buzz-saw hums,
Look out for your thumbs.

THE earliest way of sawing lumber was by the whip-saw in a saw-pit, and the earliest sawmills consisted simply of a whip-saw connected to a drive-shaft and moved by water-power instead of by hand. These mills appeared in medieval times, and underwent no development of importance until the nineteenth century.

The first sawmill in New England was built in York (then called Agamenticus), Maine, in 1623. Like its primitive successors it contained one saw, that strolled up and down in a very leisurely manner, cutting only on the down stroke. Its power was furnished by an overshot waterwheel.

In the town of Bow, New Hampshire, in 1936, I saw one of those old slow-motion saws in action. It was probably the last one of its kind in the United States, but it had been sawing logs every spring since 1801.* As the saying goes, the saw "went up today and down tomorrow," and it is a fact that a man could sit on the log and eat his lunch while a single board was being cut off. But the process was a lot pleasanter than sawing in a pit.

In such mills the saw did not travel to the end of the log. Consequently, as there was always a split end on the old boards, there arose the practice of allowing four extra inches on the log. The regular process was to take off a slab first and then proceed to the sawing of boards. The rough boards were next piled and edged together, or the sawyer might put each board on top of the log to edge it as the log ran through the next cut. The sawyer would sit on top, to keep it straight.

About 1825 the edging saw and the edging table came into use. These freed the main saw to do more work, with a consequent increase in total output. The edging saw was a small circular saw, and the boards were moved to it over "dead" rolls, the motive power being furnished by a man strong in the back.

* Some years ago George Woodbury, of Goffstown, New Hampshire, restored the Colonial mill of Colonel Goffe to working order, and it may still be going.

The old up-and-down saw produced about four thousand board feet of lumber a day, although a few cut more, and a great many cut less.

Yankee ingenuity, aided by the desire to make two honest dollars where only one had grown before, brought on the "gang" saw. The gang mill consisted of a massive iron frame, rectangular in shape, in which several up-and-down saws, up to thirty in number, were arranged vertically, and were given a rapid reciprocating motion. Logs fastened, or "dogged," securely on wheeled carriages were drawn against the thrust of the saws. The entire log passed through the saw-laden frame, yielding two-inch pine boards or two- and three-inch spruce boards. The frame was equalized with four boxes of the sliding type, one on each corner, which were designed to move up and down on heavy, smooth-surfaced iron rods. The boxes were of lignum vitae and to reduce friction were lubricated with mutton or beef tallow. Sometimes a vigorous "gang-man" had the entire apparatus surrounded by flames and smoke. Often things got so hot that all the machinery had to be shut off for a short time. Fires were frequent, but with luck and a good head of water, thirty thousand feet of pine or hemlock boards and even more of spruce could be turned out in a day.

Speaking of flames and smoke, practically every sawmill in the United States, in the nineteenth century, burned down or burned up at least once. And the workmen, with no safety devices or guards, suffered more casualties than civilians in a modern war. You could always tell a shingle-mill worker by his few fingers, or by the peculiar way those few had been cut. Men were sawed in two; legs were sawed off; hands, arms, and heads were sawed off. A fourteen-year-old girl named Florence Kelley was scalped at Waterford, Vermont, when her long yellow hair got caught in a circular saw where she had gone to take her father his lunch. One of the most effective devices of an enemy was to drive a heavy spike into a saw-log, which could not then be run into the saw without endangering the lives of the sawyers. Not infrequent was loss of life from the explosion of a steam boiler, and flying pieces of wood thrown from a saw caused painful injuries. What old-timer can remember without a shudder the ominous sound of a whirling saw suddenly hitting a knot? In 1880 a Wisconsin law made five years in prison the punishment for driving spikes into logs, and in the 1890's a law was finally passed requiring safety guards on circular saws.

The circular, or rotary, saw had been patented in England in 1777 and again in the United States in 1814, but though it was soon used for light work in sawmills it did not become popular for sawing big logs until after 1860. It had teeth all around its circumference and spun like a huge wheel, slicing the logs that were held against it. With it came a new carriage which made possible the sawing of the entire length of the log, including those last four inches, which had not been reached by earlier saws. A very wide saw was necessary for the great pines of those days, and to achieve sufficient rigidity the saw was at first made very thick. It left a kerf half an inch wide! That made the woods scale less than the mill scale, of course, and when the millman bought logs, an adjustment was accordingly made in the purchase price. This "adjustment," in the mill-man's favor, was continued for years after new improvements had made the kerf no wider than a knife-blade, and it did not make the logger happy.

The sawmill worker's profession was as hard as the logger's, perhaps even more dangerous to life and limb, and they were both connected with lumbering, but you had only to see a sawmill man and a riverman side by side to tell which was which, even if they were both dressed in their Sunday clothes. As Senator Isaac Stephenson, who knew the business from *A* to Z, once remarked: "In sawing, which is essentially a matter of mechanical equipment and arrangement, conditions are everywhere equal and no mill enjoys an advantage over competing mills, but in logging there is a wider field for the expenditure of individual effort and exercise of skill and it is in this that the profits are made or losses of operations sustained."

It was precisely that expenditure of individual effort and exercise of skill that made the millman and the riverman look different. Yet, to both, lumbering was more than a business or a job. It was a subtle, hypnotic essence, always persuasive, often seductive. The attitude, or feeling, of the riverman is well expressed in a woodsman's song we have already quoted:

> *Oh, it's every lad in heaven he would swap his golden crown*
> *For a peavey stick again and a soaking April rain,*
> *And to birl a log beneath him as he drives the river down!*

It is expressed again by a sawmill artist of doggerel who envisions what he will do when he reaches heaven:

> *I'll stand by the gate and keep watching for those*
> *Who come with the smell of the pine on their clo'es.*
> *For even in heaven I'll want it, I will,*
> *The smell of the sawdust that comes from the mill.*

Even after 1900, every little stream in northern New England that came tumbling down from the mountains furnished power to dozens of mills, often less than a hundred yards apart. The burbling outlet of Hall's Pond in Concord, Vermont, which empties into the Connecticut, was typical. There, in three miles, one passed a sawmill, a carding mill, a starch factory, another sawmill, a grist-mill, two more sawmills, a tannery, and a rifle shop. And if one drove up the main river one passed a sawmill at every brook, with its fragrant smell of fresh sawdust and freshly "stuck" boards, and its screeching saw. Today, the whole length of the Connecticut, there are perhaps three, and those, of course, are not driven by water-power.

Farm boys adored sawmills. They liked to play on the logs in the millpond, they liked to watch the millman pike-pole a log along to the slip and hitch the bull-chain onto it, and then they would follow the dripping monster as it came onto the carriage and would watch wide-eyed as the whirling circular saw ate into it. They shuddered when the saw hit a knot and screeched like a he-wildcat in pain, and inevitably they tried to hold their fingers as close as they could without having them cut off.

The blower that sent the sawdust out through a long, wooden pipe to a pile that grew and grew was another interesting sight. When the blower wasn't working it was an adventure to climb to the peak of the huge pile and flap one's arms and crow like a rooster, and "caves" could easily be dug in its soft sides.

Sawdust was much used in those days by farmers—to pack ice, as bedding for livestock, and for other purposes—and they were always coming to fill long "wagon-bodies" with the stuff and take it away. As they always dug out of the same place, away from the blower, a great overhang developed, which froze solid in the winter, and no one could tell when it might cave in. This happened sometimes when men were shoveling inside, but I never heard of a man being injured by such a collapse.

The early overshot water-wheels depended, for the amount of power developed, on the direct drive from the axle, and thus power was in proportion to the size of the wheel. Though individual wheels were sometimes as much as thirty-six feet in diameter, the average size was twelve to fifteen feet. The undershot wheel was a later invention, not so powerful, but more compact. Even in 1965 there is one water-driven sawmill being operated in New England. It is owned by Harold Alden, in Lost Nation, New Hampshire, and has run every year since 1856. Unfortunately the big wheel is covered over, which is a disappointment to sight-seers.

A curious incident occurred at the Jackman sawmill, at Dodge Pond, in Lyman, New Hampshire, in 1920. One day everything suddenly slowed down. The machinery indeed continued to clank, but oh, so listlessly! The engineer ran frantically about with his monkey-wrench and oil-can, but to no avail. At last, one of the workmen, wise in his generation, spat tobacco-juice on the floor and suggested he look at the water-wheel. So they took the box off the water-wheel—and found thirty eels, many of them five feet long, wrapped around it!

About 1860 the iron turbine wheel, much smaller and much more efficient than the old wooden wheels, came in. This turbine wheel, in one form or another, has lasted down to the present day. Where water conditions are right, mills still find it advantageous to use this wheel rather than to change over to steam or hydro-electricity.

In 1863 a test showed that a circular saw could cut four thousand feet of unedged boards in an hour, even if it did waste a lot of lumber with its half-inch kerf. Today a circular saw will cut up a hundred thousand feet a day. Steam power is what makes the difference. Steam also accounted for the introduction of "live" rollers—that is, rollers revolving by mechanical power and not merely turned by the movement of the boards across them—to propel the boards from one saw to another. After 1860 other ingenious devices were invented to speed up production and get the boards out of the mill faster. Greatest among these was the "nigger," as it is called today from coast to coast. Down South the mill owners had used Negroes to turn the log on the carriage. When someone invented a simple arm that came up through the floor beside the carriage and by means of iron teeth turned a heavy log over into the desired position, it straightway was called a "nigger." It was the greatest invention in the sawmill industry in thirty years.

The old gang saw was set in the morning and had to stay set all day, which frequently resulted in much waste. Steam changed this. Steam changed the method of using haul-up (or "bull") chains from the pond; steam permitted steam loaders (onto the carriage); steam jump-saws for trimming boards saved on sawdust. Later on, electric power was substituted for steam. The old, slow carriage was speeded up: at first it was drawn back and forth by a cable, and finally, a steam piston was introduced that hurtled it across the mill like a bobbin in a shuttle. The sawyer, on whose keen eye and experienced judgment depends the amount of merchantable boards to be gotten out of each log, sits on an iron seat, like that of a mowing-machine, and hurtles with it. He is the highest-paid man in the mill, and he deserves to be, for seven years of that jerking back and forth is all he can stand. After that he has no kidneys left.

There is another type of saw, called the "muley," probably from the German *Mühlsäge*, meaning "mill saw." This is a straight vertical saw with teeth on one edge. It is not stretched in a gate or a sash, but has a rapid reciprocating motion—three hundred strokes to the minute—and has guide carriages above and below. It has certain advantages, but it does waste lumber. It is notable that lumber produced by a vertical saw is superior to that made by a circular saw. The latter tends to be "washboardy."

About 1894 a new great invention appeared in the sawmill. This was the perfected band saw. The principle of the band saw had been known for many years, but it had not been possible to apply it to sawing big logs. This type of saw consists of an endless, belt-like blade of steel, toothed on one or both edges. Its introduction once more greatly increased the amount of lumber that could be sawed in a given time.

By 1900 the large mills in the Northeast were using a single-cut band saw instead of a rotary, and were working two shifts—an eleven-hour day and a thirteen-hour night. It is an interesting fact that the shorter day shift produced very nearly as much as the longer night shift, for men slow down after midnight.

Until about 1900, sawing was still done only between April and December. The rest of the year the mills shut down for lack of water to float logs into the mill, the ponds being frozen with several feet of ice. If a millman did want to work in the winter, he had to have his logs hauled out of the pond and piled on the bank before freeze-up, and they were dragged from the pile to the mill by horses. The frozen surface of those wet logs impeded sawing and reduced production, and much dirt and grit made plenty of work for the filers.

In 1900 W. R. Brown had charge of the Brown Company's sawmill in Berlin, New Hampshire. Being a notionable man, he figured out a way to increase production in the winter. The frozen, dirt-caked logs dragged into the mill by horses, he had dumped into a big tank where they were thawed out by the exhaust steam from the furnace, then they came up the bull-chain clean and steaming. The scheme worked so well that other mill-owners adopted it. Today, where the millpond is still, air can be pumped to the bottom to bring up warmer air with it and overcome the freezing.

If you have ever worked in sawmills, or with other men who have worked in them, you have heard any number of entertaining and informative stories. On September 8, 1900, W. R. Brown, having made all preparations, selected his logs, got his crew into the proper mood, and so on, set a world's record of 221,319 board feet sawed out with a single-cut band saw between 7 A.M. and 6 P.M. The record still stands. They sawed 714 logs, mostly fifty-six-foot spruce, into planks two and three feet wide and two, four, and six inches thick, to be shipped to Argentina.

It was quite a day—once the bull-chain broke from the unusual overload, but a red-hot link was all ready, and a man was there with a peavey to catch the broken chain before it slid down into the pond, where half an hour would have been lost in fishing it out. Once a band saw had to be changed. The too-eager sawyer started sawing before the saw got to whirling at its maximum speed of three thousand feet a minute, and it broke into pieces, coiling about like a snake. But the millwright was right there, and replaced it, and then stood behind the sawyer with a wrench, threatening to brain him if he started too quickly again.

Handling the heavy timbers the men worked like demons, hour after hour, until they were in a daze, out on their feet, blood running from the ends of their fingers—but when the whistle blew at six o'clock they had established a record that has stood for more than sixty-five years and probably is good for another sixty-five. (I ask you, where could you find 714 fifty-six-foot spruces three feet in diameter in New England today?)

In the winter of 1888, Arthur Gordon, of Lisbon, New Hampshire, then eighteen years old, was working in the woods as an axeman for the I. B. Andrews Company. One Sunday he was out digging spruce gum when an Indian who was also working in the camp, and who had taken a liking to him, came wandering by. The red man sat down on a spruce log about fifty feet long, and the following conversation took place:

GORDON: *Nice log.*
INDIAN :   Looks good.
GORDON: *It is good.*
INDIAN :   Maybe. No tell.
GORDON: *What's the matter with it?*
INDIAN :   No tell. No put to test.
GORDON: *What do you mean?*
INDIAN :   You go small end. Put ear close.
           You hear anything?
GORDON: *Yes, I hear a sound like scratching.*
INDIAN :   Listen again. You hear anything?
GORDON: *Yes, I can hear that sound even better.*
INDIAN :   The log is good.

Because he liked the young paleface, the Indian told him the secret of how to listen to test the soundness of a log, and Gordon promised not to tell anyone.

Years later, while Art was working in a sawmill in Easton, New Hampshire, for Charles Young, an order came in for a piece of sound timber, 2 by 12 inches and forty feet long, for the foundation of the casino at Bethlehem. The boss told Gordon to save such a specimen of timber when he found it. The next day among a pile of logs one such piece turned up, with the right dimensions and the appearance of soundness.

Several workmen were called to pass judgment upon the soundness of the log, and all were in favor of using it. Then Gordon offered to try the Indian test. With Young at the listening end, he started the mysterious maneuver. Young could hear nothing, but without divulging his secret, Gordon declared that in his opinion the log was unsound.

The boss then ordered the men to saw it. About six feet from the butt they came onto a two-foot piece of rotten wood in the heart of the log.

Seventy-five years ago there were 160 big sawmills on the Kennebec River. Today there aren't three. Bangor was once the lumber capital of the world. Today in Bangor if you want to build a house or a pigpen you have to import boards from Puget Sound. It's the same all over the North Country. Of course, the obvious reason is that local spruce goes into pulpwood, which is more profitable than other forms of lumber. People assure me that there is more timber growing in New England than there was sixty years ago. One big paper-company executive in Maine tells me the trees are growing faster than the company can possibly cut them. Another, an even bigger executive, of an even bigger firm, asserted some years ago that their great problem was too much timber.

I hope he's right.

18

Forest Fires

FOREST fires are caused by lightning, by disgruntled poachers who have been thrown off lumber-company lands for stealing timber, by coal-burning railroad locomotives, by brush burners, and above all by cigarette-smokers. A cigarette fiend, accustomed at home to throwing his burning coffin-nail onto the nearest piano, carpet, or bedspread, has no compunctions about throwing it into a pile of dry leaves.

Then there are a number of minor miscellaneous causes of forest fires, among which we might mention artillery fire, which in 1926 caused a conflagration in Sidney, Maine.

Wood-burning and later coal-burning railroad locomotives, especially in mountainous country, puffing up steep grades, were always throwing off sparks. In 1912, in New Hampshire, there were 730 forest fires caused by locomotives. In 1903, George Van Dyke sued the Grand Trunk Railroad for $300,000 for damages resulting from locomotive sparks to his timberlands along the Nulhegan in northeastern Vermont.

In 1761 and again in 1762 fires set by settlers desiring to steal the King's mast trees swept across parts of New Hampshire and Maine. A single fire in Maine, in 1825, destroyed 5 per cent of the total forested area of that state—1,300 square miles, or 832,000 acres. Indeed, Maine has had so many immense forest fires that it would be tedious to enumerate them. In 1837 150,000 acres of fine pine timber around Patten went up in smoke. This fire started from the burning of haystacks along the Seboois River, and, curiously, had been ordered by the state land agent himself. He thought that the destruction of the hay, which had been cut and stacked by timber stealers on state land to serve as feed for the oxen they used in transporting the logs, would stop the rascals from cutting, so he told a man named Chase to burn the hay. Chase barely escaped with his life. The only good resulting was that the burned-over area was largely reseeded into white birch, a valuable tree.

In 1884 there was a fire ten miles long in Washington County, Maine, and hundreds of men sweated and dug trenches to contain it. It is mentioned here only because its origin is interesting. It was set by a couple of gents for the purpose of promoting blueberry growth!

Vermont has had some bad fires, but nothing like New Hampshire and Maine. In 1912 there were 1,118 forest fires in the Green Mountain State. The most extensive fire on record covered 350 acres in Groton in 1912.

The year 1903 was bad for fires all over northern New England. Vermont, New Hampshire, and Maine all suffered. In Maine, more than 267,000 acres were destroyed. The frequency of fires in 1908, another bad year, finally roused Maine and New Hampshire to pass their first protective laws of any consequence (though in 1855, the Maine legislature had passed a law forbidding persons to kindle fires upon lands not their own, an exception being made only for rivermen, who were, however, held responsible for any damages). The first forest-fire protection laws in Vermont date from 1903. The last really bad fire was 1947. In Maine that year people were burned up, houses were burned down, and the city of Bar Harbor alone suffered damage of more than eleven million dollars.

"Slash" (tops and branches left from logging operations) burns with special fervor and of course constitutes a terrible fire hazard. The question of compelling lumber companies to burn all their slash carefully, under strict supervision, has been much debated. In earlier days there would have been some point in adopting such a plan, but in 1922 the Brown Company, after considerable experimentation, reported that the cost of burning slash would be greater in a given period than the cost of all damage by fire (which had been reduced by the new state fire laws) and would, when added to the other costs of producing pulpwood, make it unprofitable for a company to log at all.

In the old days, slash was a real menace. On July 8, 1886, began the great Zealand Notch fire in New Hampshire, just south of Mount Washington. J. E. Henry was logging in that region, and the fire burned up three of his camps, many animals, and a vast amount of logs and sawn lumber, besides a good part of his logging railroad. Twelve thousand acres were burned to a crisp.

In 1892, Henry pulled out and moved to Lincoln, but George Van Dyke continued to maintain a big mill there, and in fact a whole village called "Zealand," which in May, 1897, was totally destroyed. The camp was one of the largest in the North Country, and the fire left over a hundred people homeless, with little besides the clothing they were wearing. The fire originated in a peculiar manner: a pulley in the box shop had become loose and its friction set on fire a quantity of shavings. The alarm was sounded immediately, but in less time than it takes to relate it, a strong wind fanned the flames and they spread from house to house and mill to mill until the whole village was ablaze. Fifty million feet of logs and two million feet of sawn lumber were destroyed. In the dry year of 1903, ten thousand more acres in the Zealand valley were swept by fire.

In that year alone, 200,000 acres were burned in New Hampshire, 84,000 of them in the White Mountains.

The most amazing thing in the whole busines is the present aspect of Zealand Notch. A visitor writing after the great fire of 1886 said: "Zealand is today a dull-brown waste of lifeless, fire-eaten soil and stark white boulders. All about lie the great blackened stumps and tangled roots of what were once majestic trees. It is as if the contents of some vast cemetery had been unearthed in that little valley."

Nobody thought the valley would ever be green again. Yet, by 1960 the Notch presented a remarkable and outstanding testimony to the infinite healing powers of Nature. Nowhere does New England offer a better example of regeneration after disaster, unless it is in the once fire-desolated Kilkenny Range above York Pond, in New Hampshire. The valley is green again; trees are growing again; fish are in the streams again. Old men who saw it then and who see it now just can't believe it.

The railroads were always being bitterly sued by timber owners for damage caused by their locomotive sparks, and they philosophically considered such payments part of their operating overhead. But about 1912 it was finally brought home to them that it would be cheaper to do something about fire prevention than to pay damages, when they were shown a map of all railroad fires that had occurred in the state of New Hampshire during the preceding ten years, each fire on either side of the track being marked by a red dot. In many places the map was almost solid red. The Grand Trunk, the Boston and Maine, and the Central Vermont sent for their records to see what they had paid out in damage claims, and they were convinced. They installed spark arresters on all locomotives, and they delayed the usual spring burning of old ties that had been replaced by new ones until late fall, when the fire hazard had passed. Portable sawmills, too, were required to use spark arresters.

Not until 1900 were there any fire towers, or lookouts, in the North Country. The first ones were simply made from four tall trees standing close together on top of a mountain. The tops were lopped off, a shaky platform built across the bare poles, a set of cleats nailed onto one of them, and the agile and intrepid firewarden clambered up to his perch. Later towers were made of steel, with a glassed-in room on top, equipment to locate the fires spotted, and a set of stairs with a hand-rail. Even later, airplanes were used to patrol vast areas.

Different firewardens had different ways of treating fire violators. Jack Haley, a noted woodsman of the North Country who died in 1958 at Island Pond, Vermont, aged 87, passed many summers as firewarden at a solitary camp on Aziscoos (pronounced "Escohos") Lake, in northwestern Maine. A good number of hikers passed through his yard, many of whom were smoking cigarettes. It was said of Jack, whose ability as a pistol-shot was as legendary as some of the stories about him, that he would shoot the offensive thing from the hiker's startled mouth, accompanying the removal with a profane injuction to go and sin no more. It is on record that the incidence of forest fires in Jack's bailiwick was very small.

It is as hard for a person who has not been close to a forest fire to imagine what it is like as it is for the ordinary American civilian to imagine what aerial bombing is really like. Many ex-soldiers, who know, say it is too bad the Americans didn't undergo some bombing in the last war—the experience would have made us more pacific, they say.

The Reverend Duncan M'Coll, describing a Maine fire in 1821, says: "The woods in this neighborhood caught fire this afternoon; everything being uncommonly burnt up with drought . . . cattle are heard roaring and burning, crops are destroyed in the fields and miles of fence are consumed and exposing what remains to cattle. Some houses are consumed. The woods are destroyed, the soil on the top of the ground ruined for miles."

Fred Beals describes a New Hampshire fire in 1912:

A cloud of thick white smoke hovered over the center of the conflagration and large tributary curls could be seen twisting up from dozens of places. . . . [Next he reaches an area where fire-fighters have just subdued the fire.] The smoldering logs and charred trees even then, when fanned by the wind, glowed and smoked. A gentle gust turned an apparently dead stump into a bed of live coals, from which a tongue of flame shot six feet into the air. We heard a rustling and snapping almost above us; it was a blazing clump of little poplars, which until now had somehow escaped the flames. Now, however, this isolated little clump, an oasis in the black desert, was roaring and blazing. Crash! down came some of the outer ones and at length the remainder, with undermined and fire-gnawed roots, thundered to the ground, falling almost across the road a few feet ahead.

In the great Maine fire of 1825, flames roared like thunder and could be heard a dozen miles away. The smoke was so thick that the Penobscot ferrymen were compelled to use compasses, and so heavy that images were reflected like mirages. Contemporaries tell of sparks as big as bushel-baskets being carried for miles, of great pitch-filled pines, exploding like enormous fire-crackers, of deer with their hooves burned off, of the blackened bodies of women and children, of streams dried up, of dead fish and oxen. . . .

The most memorable account, oral or printed, of a forest fire that I know of is in the German book by Justus Schmidel, previously quoted in the chapter on the camp clerk. One day Schmidel found himself at a rail-head camp beyond Maple Falls, close to Mount Baker:

No smoke was rising from the chimnies, no laughter, no ringing of cash-registers sounded from the saloons. The clanking of chains, the puffing and panting of the locomotives were silent. The steam-shovels, the arms of the cranes above the long rows of trucks that had ceased to creak forward, hung motionless. Today, Mount Baker, veiled by smoke and haze, was invisible.

In the western sky, the dirty gray veil of the smoke that hung above the ground like thick fog, stood the evening sun, gigantic, almost touchable, a pale yellow disk. Fear brooded in the oppressive hot smoky air, clutched the heart as if a frightful catastrophe was being prepared that threatened to destroy every living thing. The smoke, the fine wood-ash dust, that was everywhere, made breathing difficult.

I was standing on a hand-car that powerful human arms had lifted in mad haste onto the rails. Now it was gliding toward Maple Falls. Twelve Italian section-hands in two rows of six men each were working the two handles. Up and down flew their bodies. They worked as if it were a question of life and death, as indeed it was.

I knelt on the narrow platform of the machine beside two men who were writhing with pain. Their clothes were blackened, full of burnt holes, their hair singed, the leather of their boots white, hard, and cracked. Their faces were covered with rags soaked in glycerine. No more help than that could they receive until they should reach Maple Falls. They were two lumberjacks who had been working somewhere in the bush. The fire that had suddenly started up in the forest and had spread so fast because of the drought had surprised them. Only with the utmost exertion had they succeeded in saving themselves.

The last buildings of the construction camp strewn here and there among the boulders and knotty giant tree-trunks, whizzed past us. Faster and faster the hand-car shot down the steep road. Now we plunged into the gloomy tunnel of the virgin forest that stood on both sides of the track. Here came a smoking field on which nothing green remained, a little clearing made by the lumberjacks, through which we raced. The ground was black as in a coal-seam, Black were the huge tree-stumps and the trunks lying criss-crossed every which way. The crowns and branches of the fallen trees had vanished, devoured by the fire. The fire had eaten far into the virgin timber and had destroyed the underbrush between the trees. The trunks of the mighty cedars and the giant firs rose up fantastically black. The flames must have licked clear to their tops, for the crowns were singed and yellow like hard faggot-wood.

We had attained a mad tempo. At express train speed we whizzed past the clearing in which the fire had raged so destructively. The Italians could barely hang onto the handles as they flew up and down. It seemed to me that they had lost control of the machine, as if their arms would be torn off if they should fail to bend up and down in time with the handles.

Gradually the twilight set in. The sun, tired and heavy, had plunged down deep into the dirty gray veil of smoke that hung over the trees. Blue smoke haze hovered over the rails ahead of us. Then I saw ahead, to the right, on the cut-over strip that ran parallel to the rails, a fire flame up. Already we were whizzing past. It looked like a campfire kindled by weary hikers wanting to spend the night at the edge of the forest. Fanned by no breath of wind, it crackled softly and peacefully and fed itself on little pieces of wood, bark and dry branches that were lying around everywhere on the ground. A bit farther, at a spot where wild raspberry bushes grew among the tree-stumps, the ground was burnt black all around. There the fire had gone out, probably because it had found no more nourishment.

Only light smoke was still curling above the terrain. We glided past a second fire, similar to the first. Over to the left at the forest edge a third one was burning. And as we rounded a curve I saw fire after fire lining up ahead of us on either side. It seemed to me that we were gliding through an enchanted forest. The countless fires seemed kindled by invisible woods-spirits like will o' the wisps. With such uncanny softness did the flames break out and crackle in the approaching darkness, veiled by the silence of the primitive forest.

One couldn't see the road too far ahead, for directly in front of us a dirty gray mass of smoke was billowing over the rails. The hand-car sped at it like an arrow and before I was aware we were in the middle of it. I felt an unpleasant irritation in my throat, my eyes began to water. Here the fire must have eaten into the green virgin forest, but I could perceive no gleam of flames. A hissing and singing and a frequent loud cracking came from the invisible steaming cloud of smoke that was rolling through the underbrush. It must have been boiling hot.

Black and white and sulphur-yellow colors churned and turned in it. Then it looked as if blackened rags were being slung aloft. A witches' kettle there in the gloomy firs, bubbling and hissing. At one spot where the smoke was rolling thickest among the giant tree-trunks, a pale-yellow tongue of flame suddenly shot up and hurled a blackened mass of some animal into the air. It was if there was a crater there in the forest. Hidden by charred, sulphurous smoke, the flame darted forth again. The smoke that rolled forward was coal-black. But already the site of the fire lay far behind us. Green and untouched was the virgin forest past which we were gliding. Only the fires on both sides of the tracks refused to cease. Then I saw, just ahead, new clouds of smoke rolling over the tracks from right to left. As we approached it with the speed of the wind I heard a loud cracking in the forest as if a herd of wild animals was crashing through the brush.

In a peculiar manner it began to howl softly. In the black smoke that was rolling among the fir trees ahead of us there suddenly appeared a pale-yellow glow. It plunged at us blood-red and frightful—a lambent, flickering, raging mass of flames—like a hydra waving its heads to and fro on swollen necks, feeling in every direction, and seeking its stinging, death-dealing road. Lengthening monstrously, crackling and roaring suddenly with frightful power and speed, the flames shot up the trunk of a 300-foot fir, dripping with pitch, so fast that the eye could scarcely follow them. The roar of the greedy flames had grown to a horrible bellow as if a hundred bloody lions were raging round the tree.

In an instant the flames were high overhead, leaped through the tree-top and spread out up there in a wild fiery sea. One could clearly perceive how the branches, the fir needles and the adjoining trees caught on fire, shriveled up and seemed to melt away as if they were made of wax. Great pieces of burning bark, whole boughs, were hurled high into the air from the raging fiery sea and flew above the tree tops, driven by the wind like fiery comets with steaming tails. Somewhere in the woods, or wherever they fell outside, they must have caused a new conflagration.

Mortal terror was printed deep on the faces of the Italians who the whole time had been looking stupidly straight ahead. Now suddenly they all began to talk excitedly in their native language, and set their strength against the up and down flying handles.

In front, at the brake, stood the section-boss. The whole time, without a single word, he had kept his gaze to the front. Now he turned around and measured his subjects with a glance as hard as steel. Quickly he snatched up a heavy iron monkey-wrench from the platform and threatened to split their skulls if they did not stop bearing down on the handles to stop the car. Dully the wrench came down on the shoulder of one of the rebellious men, who howled with pain. The others said nothing more but bent obediently over the handles. From time to time they cast a glance at the boss like a lot of dogs—reproachful, fearful, imploring. The fear that gripped them no longer seemed to be so much of the fire in the woods but of the man there in front, who raged as if mad, cursing them and swearing by all the saints they knew that he would send them all to hell together.

In the face of the all-power of nature, which was revealed here, of the roaring fire in the forest, of the giant trees, everything that makes men tick seemed to me so unreal, so puny. It suddenly seemed to me that I was sitting in a puppet show somewhere far from the earth, out in the universe, and was watching a game that the gods had invented for their amusement. A toy that whizzes obliquely over the stage, rattling on miniature rails. I could see the end of the rails,—there, where the station buildings, the red doll-houses with their white-painted window-sills were standing,—so near and yet so far from the little men with their rear-furrowed brown faces and comical moustaches, loud red neckerchiefs and grotesqe slouch-hats, who were flying up and down at the handles.

Ahead, at the brake, the raging boss was Punch dressed as a robber chieftain, and the burning forest was the scenery invented by the gods, probably to frighten the little men. How would the play end? Perhaps the hand-car would skid off the rails from the speed with which it was going, to be hurled in a wide arc into the burning forest. Then the wheels of the overturned machine would still whir for a while. —But no, lifeless dolls are not what the gods fashion for their amusement. Invented by Divine Mind, called into existence, they bear forever after something divine in themselves, like the divinity that had fashioned them—something stronger in one man than in another—the will and the power to master matter. In this struggle, to be allowed to play with the raging passion of the fire that Divinity had willed—to cry, to bellow, to pump strength and courage into those dull everyday people to whom spirit was lacking—to conquer. How the blood raced through the arteries and how the heart hammered. —Life as stakes—it was cheap.

"Three miles to the bridge!" bellowed the boss, just as we shot past the burning tree. "Everybody pump! Pour the leather to her!"

The air that blew over the hand-car was glowing hot. In the smoke one's breath came in coughing gasps. The sinews on the brown arms of the Italians stood out like ropes. They were using all their strength; for they knew that the only salvation lay in getting out of the burning forest and over the bridge as quickly as possible. It was impossible to go back. And it seemed it was impossible to go forward.

From behind us, ahead of us, on both sides of the track, the flames were assaulting the great trees. Between them there was a hissing, a chattering, a crackling as if a thousand rifles were being fired at once. Sparks, blazing burning pieces of bark and fir branches which came flying from the forest along the road dropped upon the platform of the hand-car. They smoked like pitch-torches. We trod on them, kicked them off the platform. With wet sacks we protected the bodies of the two lumberjacks for whose sake we had undertaken the trip to Maple Falls.

Suddenly the hat of one of the Italians began to burn. A spark must have fallen onto it. In an instant the boss, who now was swinging a wet sack instead of his iron wrench, tore it from the man's head and nipped the fire in the bud. It got worse and worse. Instead of oxygen one was breathing a hellish fiery smoke into his lungs. The railroad ties ahead of us began to smoke, to burn. Then the first Italian, overcome by the smoke, collapsed onto the platform. — Ahead of us, around the bend, had to be the bridge.—

"Hang on!" roared the boss with hoarser voice. I heard it as from a great distance, as if he were speaking through a peculiarly woven thick veil. I saw a burning fir branch fall onto the platform; I know that I stepped on it, kicked it off. Our pain was horrible. Wasn't I continually breathing smoking fire? My lungs were burning, spongy dumplings that pierced and stung. They seemed to be swelling up, and everything inside me seemed about to burst.

What happened next, as we came over the bridge out of the flaming forest, none of us knows.

The first thing that I could remember was a feeling as if a heavy flabby sack were lying on me which threatened to strangle me, which stank disagreeably of charred rags, —and then the noise of wheels turning on iron beneath me. The terror that went through me brought me back to complete consciousness.

I was sliding downhill at a dizzying speed on a masterless machine. It was a miracle that it had not yet gone off the track and broken into a thousand pieces. Painfully I freed myself from the unconscious Italian who was lying on top of me, crawled slowly forward and pulled the brake-lever back. Then I sank down onto the platform exhausted, and breathed in the fresh air—one lungful after another. Air that no longer was burning and stank.

Thus did it happen that a hand-car came to a halt at the Maple Falls station on which twelve wild-looking Italians were working the handles. Their faces were blackened; their clothes and slouch hats bore burnt holes, but not one of them wore a complaining face. They all looked with pleased grins at the station agent who regarded them in astonishment.

Thus did it happen also on the same day that the two lumberjacks could be cared for in a hospital and that in the evening something happened that had never happened before so long as Maple Falls had been there. In one bar or another you could see broad-shouldered, gigantic lumberjacks standing at the bar with a despised Dago, and in comradely fashion drinking one glass of whiskey after another with him, while the courteously smiling bartender stuck one cigar after another into his pockets, paid for by the lumberjacks, or with the compliments of the house.

W. R. Brown tells how, accompanied by several prominent politicians, he once scaled a mountain by a back trail and came to a fire tower. In this tower the ancient heliograph (which sent signals by reflecting the sun's rays) had been replaced by a telephone, which was on a party line. The firewarden was not to be seen. The visitors had not been born yesterday. They cranked the number of the firetower. Straightway a voice answered: "Warden So-and-So speaking!"

"Oh! Where are you, warden?"

"Right here in my tower, sir! What can I do for you?"

"Any fires in sight?"

"No sir, I haven't noticed any."

"I've heard there's smoke over to the northeast. Take a look and tell me what you see."

Pause. "Yes, now I see it. I'll report it right away."

Meantime the gentlemen in the tower could detect the sound of girlish giggles at the other end of the line. As they had suspected, the warden was down at the foot of the mountain calling on a settler's daughter.

"By the way, warden, do you know who is talking?"

"Who are you?"

He was informed.

"And do you know where we are?"

"Where are you?"

"We are up in your fire tower."

The young man never showed up again.

19

The Riverman

*For something about them, and the idea of them, smote
my American heart, and I have never forgotten it, nor
ever shall, as long as I live. In their flesh our natural passions
rant tumultuous; but in their spirit sat hidden a true no-
bility, and often beneath its unexpected shining their figures took on heroic stature.*

—OWEN WISTER, "THE VIRGINIAN"

THE lumberjack was a special breed of man, but the riverman was *very* special. Like the cowboy, he was a product of his environment; now that the environment has passed, he no longer exists. He
started in the Northeast, where countless streams and rivers came tumbling down from remote and tangled mountains where there were no
roads. The lumber was there, but the only way to get it out was by
water, and the water was not suitable for the navigation of lumber
schooners or for rafting. So the logs came down loose, and they had to
come in the spring, when the melting snows provided a brief period of
high water. Two phrases coined from river-driving that remain in the
popular language are "come hell or high water" and "as easy as falling off
a log."

It is very easy to fall off a log, even a large one, as you can prove to
yourself by trying it, but the rivermen not only rode logs through rapids
of considerable force and volume, treading with squirrel-like swiftness as
their footing rolled, but also used the slippery, unstable logs as a place
from which to work.

Pushing stranded logs out of bushes, heaving, lifting, doing everything that the heavy labor of moving logs demanded, they made their ad-
justments unconsciously, while they devoted their whole attention to
their work—treading now one way, now another, as the supporting log
rolled, automatically shifting their feet as the pressure on it became too
great for its buoyancy. Laymen would watch them working for hours at
a time, fascinated.

Good rivermen were born, not made. Or at least they had to start
early. When they were small boys of eight or so they spent their time

trying to walk the booms at the mills, and were fished out of the river a hundred times. At an early age they took naturally to the pike-pole and the peavey, working first on the still waters of the mill-booms, later on the drive. Such men developed an inarticulate love for the river. The work was hard and dangerous, the food was not of the best, there were no women, wages were low—and yet the call of the river drew them just as the call of the sea draws the deep-water sailor.

Probably most basic was the challenge the dangerous work offered to the rivermen's pride, for pride they had, an unvoiced, usually unrealized, but deep pride that was a very vital factor in their lives—and often in their deaths.

When the logs had been rolled into the stream, and the drive had reached the swift water, then the river-hogs' latent skills came into action. There the men were separated from the boys; there each man's courage and experience showed at their best in contention with the might of the great logs as they raced down the river.

It was the ever-present danger that gave zest to the work. The river men would work and heave and pry on a tall jam for hours—and there was nothing more fascinating to watch than the "hauling" of such a jam. All at once the apparently solid surface would begin to creak and settle. The men would zig-zag rapidly to shore. A crash and a spout of water marked where the first tier of logs was already toppling into the current. The front would melt like sugar. A vast, formidable movement would agitate the brown tangles as far as one could see. And then with another sudden and mighty crash that could be heard for miles, the whole river would burst into a torrent of motion.

If everything had gone well, the men were all safe ashore, leaning on their peavies, but ready at any instant to hasten out for the purpose of discouraging, by quick, hard work, any tendency to plug on the part of the moving timbers. And just as the logs broke loose one would see men, out of sheer bravado, jump from the breast of the jam to logs floating ahead, thus to be carried into the sweep and rush far down the river. A single slip meant death. It may have been foolish, but it was magnificent just the same.

The fascination of conquering the jumping logs as they twisted and turned like bucking broncos called to the woodsman every spring with inexplicable power. Once felt, this power never wholly left him. It was like the thrill of the Alpine climber conquering a mountain, or the control of great speed. "I want to go back to my little river," Dan Bosse, the great riverman of the Androscoggin, lamented to me in his old age. Life had not been kind to Dan, but that was his only complaint.

The business of the riverman was to guide ("drive") the logs from where they had been piled in rollways during the winter by the lumberjacks, down to the screeching sawmills of civilization. The drive might last three weeks, or it might last two years, if water was low and the logs became stranded on the dry ledges.

Contrary to popular belief, the riverman did not spend most of his time nonchalantly riding a surging log. Far more often he was lugging and prying and lifting the heavy, inert timbers from where they were jammed against the bank, and shoving them out into flowing water.

His constant heavy lifting made him as strong as a horse and as hard as nails, while the demand for quick action as he balanced on the rolling, slippery logs, or as he worked from an unstable bateau or on treacherous jams, kept him from getting muscle-bound.

He had to be as agile as a panther and as sure-footed as a mountain goat, merely to survive. Small wonder that one could always spot a riverman among other workingmen. His stagged kersey trousers marked him, to be sure; his little black felt hat and his red shirt, the plug of Climax ("the Grand Old Chew") in his hip pocket, and of course, his spiked boots, armed with three-and-sixty case-hardened spikes from one-quarter to three-quarters of an inch in length.

Those calked (pronounced "cork" by the rivermen) boots were their distinctive badge. Everywhere in the river-towns you could see the trace of the calks—the wooden sidewalks were picked into fine splinters; the floors of stores and saloons were pockmarked by them.

But the spiked boots and other paraphernalia were only external marks of the riverman. Anyone with money could buy them. Impossible to buy, however, were the riverman's walk, which had a little swagger in it, the devil-may-care swing to his shoulders, and the good-humored, reckless gleam in his steady eyes. Those were acquired not for money, but from much peavey work, many days of balancing on unstable footing, and the cheerful facing of danger.

From the moment the men began to break out the frozen rollways till the day, sometimes six months later, that the drive was safe in the booms hundreds of miles downstream, the riverman flirted with death a dozen times a day. The heavy, slippery logs that he had to roll, pry, and lift would fly back at him and knock him literally to kingdom come, or he himself would slip and a whole rollway would pass over him. He was afraid of nothing that walked, or crawled, or swam, or flew. I have known a riverman to go into a blacked-out shed stacked with dynamite, knowing that a full-grown wildcat was in it, loose, and come out lugging the wildcat.*

Your riverman had, first of all, to know how to ride a log, and that

---

* Old loggers assert that this story was common in camps from New Brunswick to Michigan. Myself, I have heard the protagonist named as Albert (Jigger) Johnson, of the C.V.L., with the encounter taking place at the railroad station at the foot of Gorham (New Hampshire) Hill. One thing is certain: Jigger could and would have done it.

did not mean just standing on it without falling off, nor being able to ride it in quiet water. As a matter of fact, riding a log in quiet water and riding it in fast water require entirely different sets of muscles and reflexes. A journey downstream was a very simple matter—he merely stepped onto a log, stuck his peavey into it, and leaned on the handle, while the current swept him along. If the water was rough, he used the peavey as a balancing pole, and if another log came along to roll his under, he just stepped onto the new log and continued on his way.

To ferry from one side of a stream to another was more difficult, but it could be done. There were various ways of propelling a log across the current. Of course, one could always paddle with a peavey, or push one's way across with a pike-pole, if the water wasn't too deep. But that was slow and commonplace. If the stream was narrow, the riverman would take a violent running jump and land with both feet on the rear end of the timber. The bow thereupon rose in a flurry of foam, the rear was depressed, and the log was forced violently ahead. At the proper moment to avoid upset the riverman ran forward to the center. If scattering logs were adrift, progress could often be compelled by seizing on these with the peavey and pushing and pulling them back. One of the prettiest ways was to work your log sideways by rolling it under you.

Skill of this sort was presupposed, just as a cowboy's skill in horsemanship is assumed. Without it a man was useless. And just as a cowboy likes to show off or compete in a kind of horsemanship that can have no practical application to his trade, so did the riverman have his little tricks. Some Bangor Tigers would do a handstand on their peavey stuck into a floating log; others could perform a somersault; most any riverman could lie down at full length while floating with the current—a riverman has been known to float twelve miles downstream on a log he could pick up and carry across his shoulders. Dan Bosse could go out onto a big four-foot stick of pulpwood and play with it until he had it standing on end in the water, and then he would stand on top of it.

A favorite amusement of the riverman was log-rolling, or "birling." Two men got on the same log. Each tried to throw the other into the river, but without touching him in any way. If one was quite superior to the other he did this quite simply by rotating the log, as a squirrel does his cage, faster and faster until the other man could no longer keep pace. But when the opponents were evenly matched, more strategy was employed. The log whirled one way, stopped abruptly, started the other way, checked again, blurred into foam, and stiffened into immobility. Professional birlers at woodsmen's jubilees would have looked rather wan and pale if pitted against some of your old-time river-hogs.

It is evident that the riverman's specialized skill required and developed an extraordinary quickness, a remarkable control of equilibrium, the power to make instantaneous decisions, and a high degree of what might be called physical judgment. In the spring of 1915 the Brown Company was driving the Little Magalloway River, a tributary of the Androscoggin. Foreman George Anderson had a crew of fifty or sixty men up there breaking out rollways. They were rolling the logs down into the river over a steep bank ten or twelve feet high. The water was high and fast, of course, but below one rollway was an eddy that kept the logs inshore instead of letting them float down with the current. The logs got piled up pretty deep there, so George told the men to wait while he took two men and went down to pole them out into the river.

They were working away and had got them pretty well cleared out when the men on the bank let out a yell. George and his crew looked up and saw that all the logs on that rollway had got loose and were starting to roll down on top of them. They turned and ran over the floating logs for the middle of the river. The two men made it safely, but George didn't.

With his first jump he landed on his left foot on a big spruce, but before he could bring up his right foot, another log bobbed out of the water and his foot was caught between the two logs. He jabbed his peavey into the log and pulled for all he was worth, but he was stuck there as if he were in a bear-trap. The falling logs had just reached the edge of the bank, and old George's time had come. He knew it too, but just then a miracle happened. Or at least a mighty good example of what I mean by instantaneous decisions and physical judgment: Dan Bosse was working up on that rollway, and the instant he saw the fix George was in, even before the logs came thundering down off the skids, he ran out and jumped ten feet straight down; he landed on the log holding George's foot and drove one end of it deep into the water. The foot was free then, and George sailed out of there one second before that rollway landed kerplunk where he had been standing, filling the river ten feet deep with logs. Dan was right behind him on the same big spruce.

Another stirring incident that illustrates the riverman's quickness took place at Upper Dam, which is below Mooselookmeguntic Lake, one of the Rangeleys, down in Maine. Ten boom sticks, held together by toggle chains, had been carefully worked around lengthwise into the current above the dam, to be sluiced through for use below. The boat's crew doing the work rowed hard to straighten out the boom before the powerful suction at the gate seized the forward end and drew the line through with the speed of an express train. The last few logs, however, drew in upon one side of a narrow platform built as a V-shaped guide to the logs going through the sluice. Upon this platform four men were standing with pike-poles to keep the logs running and straightened out. Suddenly a stray branch of dead wood caught between the toggle chains of the running boom, twisted out of water, and swept down upon the men about knee-high. Not a second was given for reflection; it meant death to be thrown into the whirling maelstorm that sucked through the gates. The first man saw the danger, gave a cry of warning, turned and hurdled the flying stick, and came down catlike in his place. Instinctively, each of the others in succession did the same, not one losing his balance, all coming down right side up and unhurt.

All these qualities of balance, judgment, and quickness, along with tough endurance and physical strength, constituted the essential equipment of the cheapest man who would go on drive. But there was, in addition, a deep "log sense" that came only with experience, and to some men more than to others. The tendencies of currents, the effects of different volumes of water moving at various speeds, the places where jams were likely to form, the reasons for them, and ways to avoid them, the places where jams would break, the probable situation of the key-log, methods of rollway breaking and dam running, and a thousand other technical details—knowledge of these things was what distinguished the riverman who rose to the top of his profession.

In a rough-and-tumble fight, the riverman was probably the best man with his hands in the world, and the riverman loved to fight. Like most outdoorsmen, he was, unless drunk or provoked, a modest and soft-spoken man, but his robust virtues were equaled by his robust vices. When the riverman hit town—especially at the end of the drive, with the logs in the booms and his pay in his pocket, with the memory of months of hardships, of back-breaking work and narrow escapes from death behind him—he figured it was his duty to rip the town apart. It might take from three days to three weeks for one great and glorious bust, while God-fearing citizens locked their doors and the local police looked the other way, before the riverman had thrown away all his money, and broke, sore, and sober, headed back to the tall timber.

The riverman fought with his fists and his head and his spiked boots, but never with guns or knives. A favorite trick was to turn away from a foe as if abandoning the fight and then lash back at the man's face with a calked shoe. Or again, as quick and skillful with his feet as with his hands, the riverman would hurl himself through the air feet first at an opponent, raking his face and chest with his terrible spikes.

Dan Bosse had a trick of coming at an enemy while turning a handspring. The other man, bemused at the sight of his charging foeman suddenly putting both hands on the floor, usually hadn't time to recover before Dan's two feet had struck him in some sensitive spot.

Your riverman was a hard man to lick. Nobody ever heard of a riverman being killed in a fight, though he might lose an eye or have an ear chewed off.

Albert Johnson, from Fryeburg, Maine, was known throughout all the North Country as Jigger. For years he was a woods boss for the lumber company that owned all of northern New Hampshire, and one spring he had charge of the Connecticut River drive when it reached Beecher Falls, where New Hampshire, Vermont, and Canada come together. Here, astride the international boundary, stood the "Line House," a notorious drinking place, called a hell-hole by righteous citizens, but highly favored by rivermen and lumberjacks.

Jigger profanely and explicitly told his crew of forty men to keep away from that place and continue working while he went off to West Stewartstown, a mile below, to scare up more drivers. But it was dark and the men were cold. Heedless of Jigger's orders, a good many of them dropped their pike-poles and peavies and went down to the Line House and started to tank up. When Jigger came back and found them gone he knew where to look.

Ever a believer in direct action, he stormed into the big bar-room, grabbed the two men nearest the door, and ran them outside, telling them to get back to work. He went back inside, snatched from the wall a short length of peavey-handle used by the bouncer in case of emergency, and waded into the crowd, swinging with all his might, and Jigger was no puny lad. Men fell; men ran outside into the night. Out from a corner came the Line House bouncer, a big Canuck named LaPointe, who fell onto the smaller man (Jigger was only five foot six), knocking him to the floor. Then he jumped up into the air and began to stamp him with his spiked boots.

Jigger gathered the stamping legs in a bear-hug and upended the bouncer onto the bar-room stove. Unable to find a purchase to get loose, the unhappy Canuck screamed like a banshee, and the spectators could smell rump-steak frying. Paying no heed to LaPointe's entreaties in two languages to let him go, Jigger held him there for a good minute. Then he jumped back. He leaped onto the bar, grabbed hold of the big reflector lamp that hung from the ceiling, and yanked it out, frame and all.

With the whole rigging in his hands, Jigger jumped full two feet off the floor and brought the frame down over LaPointe's head, hanging it around his neck like a ruff. The kerosene started to leak and it flared up. Jigger picked up the peavey-handle he'd dropped and started for the bouncer, chasing him out into the yard, where someone threw a blanket over the poor man to douse the fire. The pockmarks Jigger got from his opponent's spiked boots, and a good many others, he always referred to as logger's smallpox.

Another riverman was named Dave Walker. Dave had gone peacefully out to see the county fair, and six men who had a grudge against him, and had heard he was at the fair, hired a rig and drove out, boasting to everyone that they intended to kill him.

They came upon their victim as he was standing beside a little peanut stand, and without wasting words, leaped at him. Dave jumped over the plank that formed the counter of the stand, pulled two of the men after him, and hit each one of them one blow on the face. Those men were taken to the hospital, where the attending physician reported that the bones of their faces were literally smashed in. The riverman then leaped back over the counter and attacked the other four, and inside a minute had put three of them to flight. He sent the fourth to join his companions at the hospital. To whip six full-grown men, using no other weapon than two fists, and to send three to the hospital, is certainly distinguished prowess. One is tempted to call it Epic.

The saw-log was to the riverman what the horse was to the cowboy —except that the log would take him downstream but wouldn't take him back up. Instead, the river hog, long after dark, tired and cold, stumbled back to camp, frogging his way through the mud and brush, and not infrequently falling into a deep and wide hole that had filled up with water when the gates of a dam up above had been opened during the day for sluicing logs. Dressed in wet and sodden clothing he rolled into wet and sodden blankets, and slept like a baby, untroubled by the melancholy howls of the wolves and the owls in the surrounding forest.

Many people who saw the riverman only in his worst moments—that is, in town after the drive was in, unkempt, drunk, roaring, and fighting —forgot or never knew that those moments of violent relaxation formed only three weeks out of fifty-two in the man's hard life. It was pretty apparent that a riverman was strong in the back, but most people thought he must be weak in the head.

That was not true. Many of them blew their hard-earned pay on a wild spree, but many more, when they got paid off, went home to some New England farm to help with the haying. I have known others who went to Boston or Portland and passed the summer in studying. And some rose all the way to the top. It may be remembered that Fred Noad, who ended up as a Deputy Minister in Ontario, and George Van Dyke, who acquired great wealth in lumbering, both began as rivermen.

But the rivermen—especially the bosses, all of whom had risen from the ranks—were constantly faced with problems that demanded not only quick physical reflexes, but also shrewd figuring based on sound judgment, and without any book education, they met and resolved those problems.

I have said that the riverman was proud. It was pride in his work that sustained him from daylight to dark, in the rain and often in the snow and the slush-ice. His feet were wet all the time. Camp was made in a different place every night. Blankets were often soaked beyond any possibility of drying out until the sun reappeared. The rear crew might be sacking stranded logs while rotten ice was still running in the current. The men worked immersed to the waist in what was—literally—ice water. Once in a while, if it got *too* cold, they would build a little fire to thaw themselves out, but usually they did not even think of it, as they were carried along by the intensity of their interest and their pride in knowing that their brilliant individual work was taking the whole drive down.

20

Dam It All!

VERY important in the riverman's cosmos was the Dam. And if the reader thinks, in the manner of Gertrude Stein, that a dam is a dam is a dam, he is dam wrong! Without introducing boring technicalities, we might name the flash dam, the horse dam, the run dam, the splash dam, the squirt dam, and the roll dam.

There were big ones and small ones, cheap ones and costly ones, but in the old days each dam was made by hand, usually of large and solid hardwood logs felled close at hand, with a superstructure, if it was a proper driving dam, of timbers squared with a broad-axe. The days of drives are almost over now, but still on many North Country headwater streams one can find those distinctly American landmarks, the driving dams—graying, moss-covered, almost always with a good trout pool below them, and surrounded with an indescribable aura of haunting loneliness.

The driving dams were so called because they were equipped with a plank gate in the middle, which was raised vertically in order to let logs be driven through. This operation was known as sluicing. The gateway, along with the attendant log apron below, was called the sluice. On drive, when the last logs were being sluiced through a dam, there were always half a dozen dare-devils who would jump onto logs and ride them down through the sluice and the white, rock-toothed water below, while yelling like fiends. It was always dangerous, it was sometimes fatal, but it was magnificent to look at.

Dan Bosse was tending out below Errol dam one day when a New York tourist and his wife stopped to watch. "How can you ever stand on a log like that!" marveled the lady.

"Oh!" said Dan, "that ain't anything!" and just to show off, he went up above the dam and rode a log down through the sluice. It struck a rock head-on and for a few moments Dan was running up and down that log as if he had a swarm of bees in his pants. But he didn't fall off.

"My God!" said the woman. "What are you—some kind of a squirrel?"

The raising of a gate on a driving dam after it had stayed in position

for some months was a task requiring a lot of muscle, weight, and color-
ful language. When a dam is in frequent use in driving season, the gate is
kept greased so it will slide up and down more easily.

In the early 1900's the Brown Company became convinced that margarine was more nutritious than butter, and bought tons of the stuff,
which was duly toted into the camps. Jack Lary, then a camp boss, despised
the new product. He had a camp on the Kennebago River at that time,
and he was responsible for raising and lowering a gate on a small dam near
his camp. So he purloined as much margarine as he could from the supplies and used it to keep the runways of the gate greased.

His deed might never have been discovered, but a couple of trappers
in his district began, quite illegally, to use strychnine on their bait. One
day, W. R. Brown came around inspecting, and as Jack and Mr. Brown
walked up the wood's road to the dam they came upon a dead fox lying in
the road. As Mr. Brown had never seen a dead fox lying in a road before,
he was curious. He picked up the animal and looked it over, but found no
marks. He handed it to Jack, who opened the critter's mouth and looked
down its throat, lifted its tail and examined that end of its anatomy, and
finally rendered a profane opinion:

"Mr. Brown, the fox licked some of the goddamned margarine off the
gate posts and it killed him!"

The driving dam at Long Lake, in the St. John waters, cost fifty
thousand dollars, and had a sluice twenty-two feet wide that would
handle twelve million feet of logs in a day.

A roll dam was a smaller affair without gates. A dam was built without gates, when a sufficient head of water could be obtained in the swell
of the river's surface. The logs floated up an inclined plane and down the
other side, thus causing the roll after which the dam took its name.

Rivermen rode logs through sluices, and they loved to row a bateau
over a dam. Even cook-rafts of considerable size, bearing all the wangan
and equipment, were commonly run over the tops of pretty high dams.
But on the Connecticut River drive, below Woodsville, the dams were so
high that the men had to take the horse rafts and the cook-raft apart and
reassemble them again when they had passed the dams. They did not like
to do it. On the other hand, in many seasons the mills had to shut down in
order to give the log-drivers water enough to sluice with. This resulted in
loss of money and of time; sometimes the mills would be shut down
three weeks at Bellows Falls and Turners Falls, and the mill-owners did
not like that. One spring a millman at Bellows Falls swore that no matter
what the others did, he was going to keep his wheels turning in order to
get out an important order. George Van Dyke, who was in charge of the
drive, told him he would give him twelve hours to shut down his mill.
After that, he assured him, he would blow up his goddamned dam! The

millman's wheels stopped.

In Maine, in the good old days, a stream couldn't be blocked by a dam unless a suitable means was provided for letting saw-logs through it. When the Aziscoos Dam, then a notable piece of construction, was built across the Magalloway River in 1913, flowing out the two Metallak ponds and making a lake more than twenty miles long, they had to build a plank sluice, or flume, in which logs and pulpwood could be sent over the dam and several hundred feet downstream. This rig, now falling into disrepair, still stands just below the dam where the road from Wilsons Mills to Rangeley crosses the river. Tourists stop and look at it curiously and wonder what prevented logs from jumping out and off. The answer is, nothing prevented them. When the rivermen were sluicing there, it was a healthy idea to keep a long ways back from that sluice.

In an office camp near Millsfield Pond one night I asked the boss what was the strangest thing he had ever seen in the woods. He was a quiet, gray-browed man, past middle age, and he thought over his answer carefully. Then, quite oblivious to the large printed sign above the table that in five languages forbade him to spit, he spat tobacco-juice against the hot box-stove, where it sizzed like a wet fire-cracker. Then he gazed upon us—there were four other men present, a scaler, a stumpage inspector, a clerk, and a bob-cat hunter—from beneath his thin gray eyebrows and deposed as follows: "The most unusual thing I ever saw was a dam that blew upstream."

At this terrible lie, the smoking ceased for a moment, but though all those present knew that no dam ever did or ever could blow upstream, they prudently refrained from saying so, for the boss was a man of uncertain temper. But by their loud silence they condemned him. I too thought he was prevaricating, but I wanted the story, so I asked innocently, "Is that so unusual?"

Then the men released their disapproval of the boss in a burst of laughter at my ignorance, and informed me that a good dam-builder's boast is that his dams never "blow"—that is, spring a leak, resulting in the dam being torn away by the stream, always *down*stream.

"There are many good dam-builders in the North Country," said the gray-haired boss, "and most of them will tell you they never built a dam that blew—and most of them are liars. I never knew but one man, and I have known them all, who could make that boast and make it good."

"And that," said one of the older men promptly, "was Grinner Schoppe."

"Aye," said the boss. "It was old Win."

And so he sat for a space, his mind busy with memories of other days, until I ventured to ask him how it was that the dam had blown upstream. Then he grinned a little with his thin, smooth-shaven lips, and eyed the men he knew believed he was telling a lie, and said, "Have any of you ever been to Success Pond?"

And several of us had, though it is a pond miles in the woods, and at the foot of Goose-High, and no road leads to it.

"There is a beaver dam there," I said, "the largest beaver dam ever found in the North Country, across the outlet of that pond."

The boss looked at me with interest. "Are you sure?"

"Quite sure."

"I'm glad to know it," he said. "I've been in the woods all my life and I've seen hundreds of beaver dams, but it never occurred to me that that embarkment had been put up by beaver. I remembered we wondered how it came there. Why, it's three-quarters of a mile long and you could make a two-sled road on top of it. Now I can understand some things I couldn't understand before.

"You see, one year we decided to build a dam across the outlet, Chickwolnopy Stream. The part of the beaver dam right at the outlet had gone out, but the rest of the embankment was still there, so all we had to do was to build a piece to fit in the hole, which we did. Now there's a stream called Silver Brook comes down the mountain and flows along beside the foot of the embankment and empties into the outlet just below our new piece of dam, and it comes in at such an angle that it's headed right toward the dam.

"We were driving Silver Brook the next spring, and the first time a head of water was let loose from our driving dams it came smashing down there so fast that it swept right up against our new section of dam and pushed it way back into the lake—*upstream!* We got some bateaux and towed it back, the whole damn thing, all in one piece, and made it more solid, and it's there today, and half of you fellows have seen it. But she blew upstream, just as I said."

He looked around the room from beneath his gray eyebrows, the shadow of a grin on his thin lips. The men nodded their heads solemnly.

A hoary story of dams was told to me one summer by an octogenarian woodsman. He said that when the Brown Company was repairing the dam at Kennebago Lake in 1912, the beaver took a notion that they wanted to use it. The crew worked every day in an effort to install new parts for the gates, and the beaver came every night and piled in wood and mud. The next morning the crew would clean it all out again, and then again the beaver would come on for the night shift.

The men used to watch them sometimes at night, so they got to know them. Finally, one of the beaver failed to show up, and they missed him, but in a few days he returned with an old, gray-haired companion.

Harry Foster, who had worked in New Brunswick, said he recognized the old fellow by a scar on the side of his head. He said that that old beaver was known all over the St. John as well as in the Miramichi country as an expert dam-builder, and he—Foster—allowed as how the young Kennebago beaver had been sent to get the old beaver to come and help build their Kennebago dam.

When the old beaver got his crew going, the sticks and stones and mud began to fly, and the crew boss telephoned to W. R. Brown to get permission to trap the beaver, but Bobby wouldn't permit that. He told the boss to put on a couple of men to keep the beaver away at night. Thus they finally got their job finished.

Not long after that, my informant went off to World War I, and when he returned, in 1919, he went to work for the Great Northern Paper Company. There several men from New Brunswick told him that the old beaver was still acting in a "consultative" capacity, but the condition of his teeth was such that he cut only the smaller logs himself.

21

River-Driving in Vermont

IN THE early days, the rafting of logs, as well as of hewn timber, was tried out on many New England rivers, from the St. John to the Connecticut, but it was usually found to be less practical than driving loose logs, and so was eventually abandoned.

Quite a little rafting was done on the lower Connecticut, below Bellows Falls, even up to the time of the Civil War. The old raftsmen were a hard-working, hard-drinking, self-reliant race of men who ran log rafts over the dams and poled loaded scows back up-stream. They were known locally and even state-wide as "river-gods," and it is a pity our information about them and their deeds is so scanty. The most noted of them was probably "Sol" Caswell, of Gill, Massachusetts.

In 1851 enterprising citizens on opposite sides of the Connecticut at North Stratford, New Hampshire, and Bloomfield, Vermont, built a raft of pine logs and hopefully headed for Hartford. According to the *History of Coos County* (1888), the only place that this bold and unique feat is recorded, the raft successfully passed through the canal around the Fifteen-Mile Falls and arrived at its destination. We do not doubt the whole story, but we do know that there never was a canal of any kind anywhere on those Falls.

Rafting was, however, extremely popular over on Lake Champlain, whose outlet, the Richelieu River, flows into the St. Lawrence. Mast pines were being cut at Shelburne, Vermont, as early as 1766 and rafted to St. John for the European market, and countless rafts of oak timber went the same route. No details are available, but inasmuch as hardwood logs tend to sink rather than float, presumably the boys on Lake Champlain used the same method as the boys over on the St. John in Maine, where they managed to raft huge square-hewn birch timbers with spruce "floaters." Forty feet of birch weighed about a ton. Two big spruce-log "floaters" were used for every two and a half tons of birch to assure the necessary buoyancy. The same system was used many years later by a firm at Bemis, Maine, which floated white birch logs across Mooselookmeguntic to use at their mill. Even today the method is used on Moosehead Lake by the Atlas Plywood Company.

It may surprise the reader to learn that after the opening of the Champlain Canal in 1822, the city of Burlington, Vermont, became the lumber capital of the world, a position it held until it was outstripped by Bangor.

That the early raftsmen were as turbulent as their successors, the rivermen, appears from a little international incident occurring in 1808, when Congress laid an embargo on all trade with Canada—a restriction which bore heavily on the Vermont loggers. That summer a huge timber raft, a quarter of a mile long, lay off Isle la Motte, waiting for a favorable wind to carry it over the Line.

A United States revenue agent, supported by a company of militia, was watching it, but rivermen, whether raftsmen or log-drivers, were never much impressed by military display. Quite undaunted, as soon as a breeze sprang up they pushed on to the north, while the militia floundered along beside them through the cat-tails. There was a brief exchange of musketry and rifle-shots, in which no one was injured, and then the raft crossed the line and proceeded on its way without further hindrance.

Loose logs were driven out of Victory and down the Moose and the Passumpsic rivers to mills on the Connecticut as early as 1830, and for many years Vermont's longest river, the White, had a sizable and lively log drive every spring, even up to World War I. To the northward, the Black river, debouching at Newport, often boasted of five different drives in one season, and at one time or another saw-timber was probably floated down every stream in Vermont large enough to hold a log.

The numerous branches of the Nulhegan, which drains an immense area in the northeastern part of the state, have been driven for more years than any man can remember. Men of wide experience have told me that the most spectacular river-driving they ever saw was the 1908 drive down the Nulhegan's East Branch.

The conditions that governed the driving of the East Branch that year were never duplicated, before or since, on any other stream in New England. They were unique. For a number of years previously, the East Branch had been handled in much the same manner as other streams: where several branches of such streams were logged simultaneously, no branch became overloaded with one season's cut. Log-landing areas were adequate and water was usually abundant. But with the cleaning up of the lower branches, the entire situation changed. Now, on the East Branch, where for the previous two or three years the lower and less steep areas had all been cut over, operating was confined to the higher, steeper, and rougher areas.

To continue to operate in those higher areas with the methods then customary and to land logs where adequate landing sites and water were available, would have involved long hauls with repeated snubbing, that, among other difficulties, would have made a go-back road almost impossible because the region is rough, steep, and precipitous.

Just who instigated the plan that was finally decided upon is hard to say, but a number of first-class loggers who worked for Van Dyke—'Phonse Roby, Dave Dillman, Will Fuller, Bill Smart, and Tom Graham, men who could do anything in a logging operation except cut a stick of timber twenty-five feet long and have only one end on it—all had a hand in it.

The plan was to space small log-landings at convenient places along the stream so that when the drive started the load could be strung over as great a distance along the banks as possible, with sagacious calculations to determine proper hauling distance, the best approach to the problem of snubbing, and above all the easiest possible go-back roads for the horses.

During the summer, several squirt dams were constructed and some other stream improvements were made, and we must notice that while the work had to be effective, it was necessary, because of the limited period for which the stream would be used, and because of the capital charge against the volume of timber that would ultimately be driven, to maintain tight control over costs.

The steepness of the valley was such that the amount of water that could be held by each of the squirt dams was limited. The success of the proposed scheme depended on the correct spacing of the squirt dams, the number of logs landed at each point, the amount of water available at each dam, and the ability of the men who had to get into that lovely cold water, fresh from the mountains above, to ease the logs around every rock, bend, or other obstruction.

Nowhere would a man be able to ride a log, for the stream became converted into a glorified, hellroarious flume with rock sides and bottom. Altogether it was an outstanding piece of engineering by a group of woodsmen without instruments, many of whom could barely write their own names.

To use the project after it had been constructed required no less ingenuity than was employed in conceiving it. In landing the logs, thought had to be taken to prevent the stream from becoming plugged, and to maintain a clearance so that when the water began to run, just enough logs would be released to assure that they would not jam. At the same time, the release of logs at each landing had to be co-ordinated in such a way that the water would not be wasted, but would carry every log with which it could safely be loaded.

At first there were indeed a few minor difficulties, but after things got organized and each man learned to do what he was supposed to do at the right moment, the logs flowed like a train of cars. However, tending out before daybreak up at that elevation was no picnic. A cold, white mist hid the gurgling river as the tired rivermen unbent their stiff and creaking joints to the cook's loud bellow to *r-o-ollo-u-t!* A dim lantern hung before their spectral white tent dispelled the gloom a little, and they stumbled over to the fire, where the cook had a number of iron kettles, short ones and tall ones, boiling and simmering. The kettles hung from S-shaped hooks depending from a stout pole which rested on two crotched stakes. On both sides of the fire stood tin bakers filled with browning pans, containing biscuits.

Each man picked up a tin plate and a tin pannikin for his tea and moved up to the fire, in the time-honored chow-line. A cookee with a vast tea-pot filled each pannikin.

They downed the food and scalding tea, and somewhat heartened, took their peavies or pike-poles and headed for the stream.

"That nice cool ice-water won't hurt ye!" called their boss, Tom Graham. "Just think, when the drive is over you'll be paying good money to a bartender to serve it to you with a *little* whiskey in it!"

Of course, once they got the drive down to the lower stretch of the stream, where they could operate in a normal way, driving the logs was a mere matter of routine: wading hip-deep in the mud and water of an alder swamp and coaxing logs out of a tangle of bushes, or rolling crooked logs off a gravel bar—God only knew why crooked logs were always most prone to ram themselves onto the bars. Of course, when a large bunch of logs, on a full head of water, came sailing down where the banks of the stream were low, tending out became a joke. It was impossible to divert those logs from their self-determined way.

Another thing that made that drive unique and showed the intelligence of the rivermen in charge was the way in which they coped with the problem of pulpwood competing for the same water. That spring John Hinman of North Stratford had been cutting four-foot pulpwood on one of the tributaries of the East Branch, and he proposed to drive his wood down the Nulhegan and the Connecticut to the paper mill at Fitzdale. Whether it is four-foot pulpwood or long logs, the timber has to go when there is water—that is, as soon as the ice goes out in the spring.

When Van Dyke heard that Hinman intended to drive that small stuff at the same time he was going to drive his long logs, he swore very picturesquely.

Charlie Roby had charge of Van Dyke's drive, and he had to see to it that the two kinds of wood didn't get mixed. Of course, in theory Hinman would keep his pulpwood boomed at the mouth of his tributary until the long logs had passed, but *he* needed that water, too, and it just happened that sometimes the boom got loose. Roby put crews to work stringing booms just as soon as the pulp started to pull, and held most of it, in spite of the possibility that it would be hung later by lack of water.

He strung double-plugged booms at strategic points where the current was weak enough so they wouldn't be carried away, and anchored rafts above, where logs could be diverted away from the wood. He had men in bateaux breaking up large bunches of pulpwood so that they would be directed into some of the booms. Some of the pulpwood did get away, probably ending up in Long Island Sounds, but the loss was not great. Roby really did a magnificent job.

In 1949 the Brown Company had a woodsmen's jubilee at Berlin and woodsmen came from all over New England to compete in the various trials of strength and skill. One of these was to stand on a saw-log and scull oneself across the pond with a pike-pole. Full of pep and ginger several youthful woodsmen lined up, stamping their calked boots determinedly. They looked pityingly at a big, white-haired old man who suddenly stepped forth from the crowd of spectators. He was chewing tobacco, he was evidently well over seventy years old, he was in his stockinged feet, apparently having just taken off his shoes, and now he was shucking off his coat. He asked for a pole.

"Give him one," quoth John Locke, from Canaan, Vermont, one of the three judges.

"He's too old," protested the youngest of the three. "He might have heart-failure out there, and we don't want to spoil the fun with a funeral."

John Locke, who had once been general manager of the C.V.L., grinned a little.

"I'll bet you ten dollars he'll win the match," he offered affably.

Miffed, his young colleague consented.

The oldster in his stocking-feet won by half a length, and going away. He was Tom Graham, Van Dyke's former boss from the Nulhegan.

22

River-Driving in Maine

LOG-DRIVING began in Maine on the Saco River early in the eighteenth century and progressed eastward. The fame of the Penobscot has overshadowed that of many other Maine rivers of great worth, both as producers of timber and as producers of men. Any of them —including the Saco, where long-log driving continued until 1947—could furnish material for a rousing book.

We have spoken here and there of the St. Croix, a notable stream along the Canadian border. Of even greater importance is the St. John, which starts in Maine but terminates in New Brunswick. One can easily see there the possibilities of conflicts between log-hungry Maineites and log-hungry New Brunswickers.

Tributary waters of the St. John were the scene of the Telos Cut War, on the Allagash, in 1841, and also of the Aroostook War, on the Aroostook, in 1838–39, when Maine carted a couple of brass cannon up north to shoot at Canadians allegedly stealing Maine timber. Governor Kent's militia built a blockhouse, Fort Kent, and there was a popular slogan everyone was singing that started:

> Maine went
> Hell bent
> For Governor Kent.

The land agent of Maine was arrested and put in jail in New Brunswick, and the head man of the opposing forces was held in durance in Bangor for a while, but although a lot of fist-fights took place, nary a cannon-shot was fired. As a matter of fact, the international boundary was not settled until the Webster-Ashburton treaty in 1842, but after that things calmed down.

The Madawaska Driving Company on the St. John, which functioned from 1904 to 1924, handled a billion and a half board feet of lumber in that time. The volume of their spring drive sometimes went as high as 127,000,000 feet, and they had 1,500 men on drive at once, which must be a world's record. The Driving Company folded up in 1924, driven out by the advent of railroads, the proliferation of portable sawmills, and by the stark fact that the timber had become too small to drive profitably.

At the headwaters of the Androscoggin in northeastern New Hampshire and adjacent Maine is an area with a wonderful network of lakes and streams, half a million acres of it owned by the Brown Company. Logs were cut and landed on Wiggle Brook, then driven down through a channel blasted in the ice of Little Kennebago Lake, on down the Kennebago River to Cupsuptic Lake, where they were caught in giant booms and towed across Cupsuptic and Mooklookmeguntic by a big towboat called the *Berlin*. The *Berlin* has been beached lo, these many years in the woods at the head of Cupsuptic, just below the site of the old company storehouse, where it rears up through the brush like a huge dinosaur. At the foot of Mooselookmeguntic the logs were let out of the booms and sluiced through Upper Dam, a tremendous affair 1,500 feet long, driven down the river into Mollychunkamunk Lake, boomed across Mollychunkamunk and Welokennibacook (Upper and Lower Richardson lakes), and sluiced through Middle Dam, then boomed across Pond-in-the-River and sluiced through Lower Dam into Rapid River—which really is rapid—and into Lake Umbagog, where they were towed another eight miles to the outlet, the Androscoggin River. They were driven down the Androscoggin, sluiced through Errol dam, and then driven on down through the Thirteen-Mile Woods, sluiced through Pontook dam, and so to Berlin, and points south by east, such as Rumford Falls and Lewiston. The Androscoggin is a fast river and a crooked river and a dangerous river, full of rocks and rapids and passionate falls, and just as it debouches from Lake Umbagog, there falls into it the Magalloway, famed in song and story, whose headwaters are the Little Magalloway River and Lake Parmachenee, for which was named the Parmachenee Belle troutfly. The principal tributaries of the Magalloway are the two Diamonds, the Swift and the Dead, which join just before they burst through the Diamond Peaks to empty into the Magalloway above the Brown Farm.

On the Dead Diamond are located the 27,000 acres of the Dartmouth College Grant, the only one left of the numerous land-grants given long ago by the state to various schools and colleges. Far up on the East Branch of the Dead is Garfield Falls, where the stream comes boiling down a deep gorge and falls forty feet into a pool; there it makes a sharp right-angle turn and goes roaring on between rocky cliffs.

In the spring, when the rollways were broken out and the fifty-six-foot logs came charging down, they would shoot clear across the lip of the falls and thud against the rock wall opposite, before dropping into the pool. Jams often formed on the rocks in the gorge below, piling up like a keg of board-nails dumped on a floor, and rivermen were lowered by a rope around the waist to cut the key-log and break the jam. No man was ever ordered down into that maelstrom, but volunteers were never lacking. Sometimes they were yanked up in time, when the jam hauled. Sometimes they weren't. Usually the dead men were found later on, several miles downstream, always stripped of all their clothing except their spiked boots. These, as was the custom, their mates hung on the nearest tree, a mute monument to a man who had died by his creed: Get the logs out!

The booming of logs across a lake was a special part of river-driving and in the old days it was always performed by an infernal man-killing device known as a headworks. These contraptions were used on First Connecticut Lake and they were used on Moosehead and the Rangeleys, and they still tow booms, though not propelled by man-power, on the headwaters of the Penobscot.

Logs will float down a river, but they won't float down a lake. When it was necessary to transport them across a lake, from two to five million feet of logs at a time, covering acres in extent, were enclosed in booms. The booms consisted of big logs, some thirty-two feet long, firmly fastened end to end by chains attached to ropes passed through holes bored by an auger. Before iron became common in the woods, when everything had to be done with an axe, the boom logs were held together by thoroughshot pins. In 1917, Sam Parks, who for years had charge of the West Branch drive, gave young Lud Moorehead an ancient thoroughshot complete with cotter-pin that he had picked from the bottom of Telos Lake. Lud still has it, and although he has offered a five-dollar reward to any man who can tell what it is, he still has his five dollars.

Once the boom had been closed around the logs, it was attached to the headworks by a short warp. The headworks was a raft of hewn log one log long and about fourteen wide, the logs being piled crosswise in three layers and stoutly treenailed together. (If the boomful of logs was small, the headworks raft could be much smaller and simpler.)

Upon the headworks was set the capstan, a great spool made of a single log, revolving around a central shaft, and pierced around the top for eight capstan bars. There were no pawls at the bottom, as on ship capstans, to prevent its surging back, but a number of small sticks slanting upward toward the barrel kept the warp from fouling under the spool. An anchor, weighing two or three hundred pounds, attached to a thousand feet of inch-and-a-half hawser, was used in a warping boom. Twelve to fifteen men were needed to coil such a rope and transport it across the carry.

The headworks was accompanied by a boat. The anchor was put into the boat, the boat was rowed out ahead, and the anchor was dropped; then the boat returned and all hands manned the capstan bars, two men to a bar, and began to spool up the warp. When the anchor was under foot, the boom was left to drift with the headway already gained; twelve of the men raised the anchor and rowed it out again while the other four fed off the warp from the spool. Then once more the boat came back, and the men tumbled upon the headworks and threw themselves upon the capstan bars, to begin their tramping around and around and around, as they wound up the straining warp. Thus, inch by inch, the boom was drawn across the lake, a mile or two a day being about all a full crew could accomplish.

The Maine lakes are anywhere from one to twenty miles long, and the old man-powered headworks, which, after 1850, gave way here and there to steamboats, and in recent years to gasoline-powered launches, could not be navigated when there was a wind blowing, especially a head wind. Then the whole vast circle of logs was forced to tie up at the shore and wait until the wind had died down. If it was caught well out in the lake, it might be blown all the way back to the starting point, resulting in loss of time and labor. Or, if the pressure became too great, logs would roll out from under the boom and never be recovered, or, worst of all, the boom would break and the immense collection of logs would go dancing over the billows, to land eventually in the dry-kye.

There was no work in the woods more laborious, less rewarding, and cursed so heartily as toiling on a headworks. But the men did it, working both day and night—indeed, warping a boom across a lake, as well as sluicing logs through a dam, was done best at night, when the wind was more likely to be quiet.

The work often made the men literally sick, and when the weather was cold and raw, the frozen hawser cut and split their hands. Sometimes a man would stumble in the coils of rope, and go overboard. If the water was cold he might well die there, tough though he was, and that night the cook would break out all the lemon extract he had on hand and the men would hold a proper wake for their dead comrade.

The men went round and round. They fell asleep and still walked around and around, stepping a little higher each time around as the warp rose with each revolution. In the Maine woods they still tell a story about Milton Shaw, a famous old-time lumberman of the Moosehead Lake region. It was in the early 1870's. Shaw had started a boom of logs from behind Sugar Island and was warping it down to East Outlet. The wind was wrong and the water was rough. Shaw, like all the ring-tailed old slave-drivers, never asked a man to do what he would not do himself. He was one of the crew on the headworks, marching around the capstan. To make progress it was necessary to work day and night when the weather permitted. There had been an extended calm, and the men had worked continuously for many hours and had finally gone to sleep.

About midnight, being asleep on his feet, Shaw caught his toe on the anchor line and pitched headlong into the icy water. His foreman, James

Bowley, opened his own eyes just in time to see him struggling in the water, and reached over to give him a hand.

"If you'd been attending to your own business," sputtered Shaw as he scrambled aboard, "you wouldn't have seen me!"

For many years the booms of logs were towed across the Richardsons and Pond-in-the-River by headworks, but later on the company provided an "alligator," an odd contraption that old rivermen insist was the greatest invention in river-driving since the peavey. An alligator is a flat-bottomed scow used as a warping-tug. It is provided with a capstan, and is run by steam or by gasoline. The alligator can "float on a heavy dew," and can even travel over land, "walking," on the ends of its paddle-wheels. It can also be used to pull single logs off the shore and out of the bushes.

"We had a boom tied to the shore one time on Pond-in-the-River," Jack Haley told me, "and we had half a dozen men living in a tent on the shore, watching the boom. One night we came down in a big motor launch to bring them some fresh milk. We had two ten-quart pails full.

"The wind was blowing something desperate and our boat was tossing like a chip. We couldn't get close to shore, but we eased up alongside the boom and Dan Bosse came out to see what we wanted. Christ! I wouldn't have walked out on that boom for fifty dollars!

"'We brought you some milk!' we hollered at him, 'but you can't ever carry it ashore, so go on back!'

"'Give me the milk!' says Dan, and he took the two pails, one in each hand. I've worked in the woods and on the river all my life, and I've seen some mighty good men on logs, and Dan was one of the best, but I swear I never thought he'd make it. We turned away in a big circle and went back up the Pond and I looked back. I'll never forget Dan walking ashore with those pails full of milk. The boom logs were jumping and slapping and rolling half-over, and Dan was going up in the air and down like a cork, but he made it—God damn him, but he made it!"

Rivermen are so used to performing and seeing their comrades perform incredible feats of courage and agility that they take most of them quite as a matter of course. Only something really extraordinary will arouse their enthusiasm and stick in their memory. One day Vern Davison was in the Brown Company railroad yards at Berlin. They were building a pulphauler to take the pulpwood out of the river. They had put up a forty-five-foot spruce pole, two feet and a half through at the base. The pole stood straight up in the air, and Dan Bosse hung onto the hook of the derrick and let them hoist him up onto the top of that pole, and he stood there with a sledge-hammer in both hands and drove bolts into the pole beneath his feet.

"There was a man named Haines working the yard office," Vern tells

me, "and when he saw him up there he just laid right down on the ground
and clawed at the grass with both hands."

"One summer," says Ralph Sawyer, "the company sent Dan up to
Windigo on the St. Maurice to drive team. They'd just strung an inch-
and-a-half cable across the river. It was four hundred and two feet long,
and of course it sagged in the middle. We used to amuse ourselves trying
to walk across it.

"With a pike-pole to balance us we could get half-way across, but
when we started up the other slope we always fell in. It wasn't because of
the upward incline but because a peculiar sway got into the cable then
and we couldn't keep our balance. One Sunday after Dan arrived, we got
him to walk the cable. Half a dozen of us tried it and we all fell in. Dan
tried it, and he got within ten feet of the other side and he fell in. He
swam back across the river and took off all his clothes, except his underwear and socks. Then he walked across that cable, turned around, and
walked all the way back!"

The outlet of Moosehead Lake is the Kennebec River. A little below
the outlet is The Forks, and here is Moxie Stream, with Moxie Falls, a
hundred feet high. They say that when pulpwood was driven down the
Moxie it would often jam back clear over the top of the Falls.

Like New Hampshire and Vermont, Maine was occasionally chosen
by Hollywood movie firms as the location for an "epic of the timber."
One outfit came wandering up the Kennebec some years ago and when
they heard that rivermen used to ride logs through the sluiceways of
dams, they were all hot to have a picture of such a rare sight. Since their
own hero and stunt man refused to do it, they sought out a native son.
They located Spider Ellis, one of the Kennebec's cattiest men on a log,
and offered him five dollars to do the trick. Two days' pay for two minutes of pure fun, even if a slip might cost him his life, seemed attractive,
and Spider obliged.

The movie magnate then offered him ten more to ride another log
through and fall off it down in the white water. Having received his
money in advance, Spider again embarked. Again he made the dangerous
journey, but he failed to fall off. Questioned by the movie man, he explained, "You see, I've never fallen off a log in my life. I find I just can't
fall off one for less than twenty-five dollars!"

One of the worst log jams in the history of New England logging
took place on the Kennebec early in March, 1896. The drive was in the
river above Augusta, but the ice below had not yet gone out. Came a
freshet, and what a freshet! Not only on the Kennebec but on the
Androscoggin, and on the distant Merrimack and Connecticut, raged
such floods as had not been seen in thirty years. Every bridge on the
Androscoggin below Rumford Falls was swept away.

On the Kennebec, the ice went out, bridges went out, roads and railroads were gulled out, houses were upended, trees torn loose. Mills and factories were knocked awry, traffic was disrupted, even the United States mail didn't go through. . . . Augusta streets were full of canoes and rowboats. The road below Gardiner was piled high with logs.

Ice crashed against the long, covered bridge at Gardiner, logs jumped over it, the raging water tore at it like a living thing, and the poor old bridge seemed to be fighting for its life against them all. At two o'clock in the morning of Tuesday, March 3, snow began to fall, and it fell thick and fast all day long; then came a gale that lasted two days. By Saturday, for seven miles above Swan Island, the Kennebec was a mass of logs, lumber, houses, bridges, trees, wreckage, all packed solidly together. In Hallowell many houses had water up to their second-story windows. At Augusta, three men were seen getting into a rowboat and casting out into the river. Evidently they were drunk. As the bemused spectators watched them they began to fight, and the boat overturned. One of the three, a man named Thomas, climbed onto the boat and was washed ashore. The other two climbed onto a great floating ice floe that came along, where they resumed their fist-fight with the greatest abandon. It was weeks before dynamite and a blessed thaw got rid of the ice and things returned to almost normal.

In Maine, as elsewhere, rafting was tried in the early days. A passage in A. Loring's *History of Piscataquis County* (1880) gives us an interesting glimpse of this brief but vivid phase of river-driving on the Penobscot:

In the spring of 1811 a raft was put together, below the Foxcroft Dam, and in a high pitch of water Thomas Chase and Benjamin Spaulding ran it safely over those falls. This was regarded as a superior display of raftsmanship. Chase was distinguished for this. Though for want of coolness he would sometimes break down in some fearful crisis. Guy Carleton Esq. once employed him to run a raft of lumber to Bangor. As they neared the "Schoodic Rock," in Medford, a very difficult pass on account of the set of the current, "Uncle Thomas' " courage failed him; he ceased all effort and cried out, "'Tis no use, 'tis no use, the set of water, let her run, let her run!" The raft did run upon the ledge, and lay there, a pile of wrecked and injured lumber, causing a severe loss to its owner. This was no uncommon event in their rafting adventures. As an incident connected with this mishap, we mentioned that Mr. Carleton had packed such valuables as he expected to need, in his leather saddle bags. In the crash they went down the river. Several weeks afterwards, they were picked up on the banks of the Penobscot, in the town of Hampden, and he recovered them. They had drifted some 60 miles down these rivers, and floated in the tide waters, and finally lodged on the shore.

The rafting business was full of wild adventures, and of great risk to owners and raftsmen. There was so much of exposure, that rum was regarded as an absolute necessity. No one could be trusted as a pilot, unless he was thoroughly acquainted with the best channels, the numerous falls, the dangerous rocks, the set of the currents and eddies, existing through the whole length of the streams, and could remember their locations. When dams were built across these rivers, a broad, sloping platform was attached to the lower side of the dam, called a slip, upon which the rushing water would glide the raft over, if it entered favorably. To run these sluices was a pleasant excitement to the raftsmen, and a fine entertainment to the spectators. In early times, lumber was rafted from Brownsville, Sebec, and Milo, and all the towns on the Piscataquis, as far up as Blanchard. But the multiplying of dams made it more expensive than hauling it with teams, and this branch of business was abandoned.

After driving long logs had supplanted rafting, sawn lumber was still rafted down the Penobscot. Some of the rafts were half a mile long. Bangor, with 410 sawmills in and above it, became the lumber capital of the world. The Penobscot was a lumberman's dream, a paradise. There were two and a half million acres of the finest pine forest in the world, not to mention the spruce, and all of it, through a vast network of lakes and streams could be funneled down the West and East branches of the Penobscot to the countless sawmills in Bangor and the towns just above it—Veazie, Orono, Old Town, and so on.

The waste from these numerous sawmills created a real problem. An enormous quantity of sawdust, edgings, and slabs was allowed to go into the river, and blocked ship traffic to such an extent that the United States Government had to dredge it out, while the individual millmen had long and bitter lawsuits over it. Typical was the case between General Samuel Veazie, one of the most rugged of the early lumbermen, who owned fifty-two sawmills along the river, and Rufus Dwinel, an equally rusty character, who had armed his loggers with butcher-knives a few years before and started the Telos Cut War. Dwinel sued Veazie, claiming that waste from Veazie's mill, thrown into the Penobscot, flooded the waters back to interfere with the wheels of *his* mill. The Maine Supreme Court in 1861 awarded damages to the plaintiff. If the proceedings were faithfully transcribed, they ought to make good reading, with those two salty gentlemen testifying.

Sam, who had a town named after him, and who, when he wasn't feuding with his peers, was busy getting legislation passed that would promote his benevolent schemes, merits an M.A. thesis from some young man at Orono. One of Sam's tricks was to have men on his company pay-roll appointed as tax assessors in townships where he owned property.

The city of Bangor stood "like a star on the edge of night, still hewing at the forest of which it is built," wrote Henry Thoreau in 1846. The city, like the river on which it stands, bears an imperishable name in the history of American lumbering. Later on, in the Lake States, and on the West Coast, there were far bigger logs and far bigger drives and far bigger jams, and cities far more gone in "sin"—but not one of them ever aroused the nostalgia, the pride, of the Maine article.

At its zenith, in 1860, Bangor was shipping 250,000,000 board feet of long lumber a year. During the same year, more than three thousand ships arrived and cast anchor in the river, lying there so thick that a man could walk across their decks from Bangor to Brewer on the other bank. Ships went forth to all the world—England, Australia, China—but especially to the West Indies, and in return for the lumber, the ships brought back rum and molasses, which were lapped down by the loggers, a perfect exchange that satisfied both parties.

It is hardly worth while to dwell on the saloons and whore-houses that lined the plank sidewalks of the Queen City. With sailors from three thousand ships coming up the river, and log-drivers from two million acres of wild forest coming down the river, there was naturally a demand for fun and relaxation, and where there is a demand, there springs up a supply. Reveling in work that permitted him to display his splendid strength and skill, the riverman also liked to throw himself into wild and boisterous play. Perhaps an office clerk who pushed a pen all day would be content to put on a wing collar and drink a modest glass of Madeira, but the red shirt and the tasseled sash of the riverman did not mark a man of such shy and retiring manners. The songs he roared out as he strode boldly from one Haymarket Square dive to another, or as he approached Fan Jones' noted Skyblue House of pleasure on Harlow Street, were not of the Sunday School type. There is a story of a logger whom a bar maid introduced to what she called "squirrel" whiskey.

"Why do you call it that?" he asked, after downing a glassful of the awful stuff.

"Because," she explained sweetly, "it will make a lumberjack run up one side of a tree and down another, just like a squirrel."

The logger came into Bangor for a good time, and he had it. True, he often woke up in jail with a splitting headache and bruises on his noggin, but after he had paid or worked off his fine he put a final bottle or two of the squirrel into his turkey and headed back up the river. There the passage of months and frequent re-telling to his colleagues made his Bangor adventures take on the aura of a wonderful time, and by the time spring had rolled around again he was ready and anxious to repeat the voluptuous experience.

The reasons for Bangor's pre-eminence are several: Bangor was the beginning—the first town devoted entirely to manufacturing and shipping lumber and entertaining loggers. Bangor men invented the peavey, which revolutionized the logging industry; the Bangor snubber, which slowed down sled-loads of logs on steep hills; the Peavey hoist, for pulling stumps and raising the gates of dams; the haypress, by which loose hay could be packed into small, tight bales, for transportation to the logging camps; the sorting boom; the log-branding hammer. All those things were universally used, and still are today, from coast to coast.

No wonder, then, that as the lumbermen moved ever westward they founded no less than ten towns named Bangor after the mother-city on the Penobscot.

And chiefest reason of all were the rivermen themselves. The "double-twisted Penobscot boys," the Bangor Tigers, were the last word, the *nonpareils*, the *ne plus ultras* of the river-drivers. They knew it, and many of them died, cheerfully, merely to live up to their name. "Proud" is the proper word—and they had a right to be proud. Joseph De Laittre, a prominent Minnesota lumberman, noted a nimble young man on the logs one day, and asked him where he came from. "He took a plug of tobacco from his hip pocket, bit off another chaw, and answered, 'From the Penobscot, b'God!'"

Bangor rivermen were imported for other river drives in New England, and drew top wages. Maine lumbermen who had moved to Pennsylvania, Michigan, and points west, were always making quick trips back home to pick up a few dozen Bangor Tigers to come west and show the boys out there how to do it. Thus the fame of the Penobscot and of Bangor grew and grew, so that when men speak or write of logging in the United States today they never fail to mention those two magic names.

Prior to 1825, every lumberman who had been cutting up-river drove his own logs down the Penobscot to Old Town, Bangor, and the like at the spring break-up of the ice. Since there were many mills and many lumbermen, there were many separate drives all trying to come down on the same freshet, and it was a hell of a job to sort them out from each other at the places they were destined for. Crews and boats were out night and day, and huge bonfires were built on the shores to make light upon the water so that they could see the logs as they went floating by in the darkness.

This situation led, in 1825, to the formation of the Penobscot Boom Corporation. The state legislature granted a charter to interested parties to build a boom across the Penobscot at Costigan Island, above Old Town, and as the years went by the charter was amended to permit certain side or extra booms. At the booms the mixed-up logs could be stopped and sorted. Presently the whole thing was purchased by Rufus Dwinel, who charged thirty-eight cents per thousand board feet upon lumber boomed, rafted, and secured, including the warps and wedges. In 1833 Dwinel sold out to General Veazie, who built another boom, at Argyle. At the end there were three sorting booms—the Argyle, the Nebraska, and the Pea Cove—consisting of numerous rock-filled crib-work piers strung along the river for more than three miles.

Here, as the logs came floating along, they were sorted by agile rivermen whose job was to read the stamps denoting the owners and to propel the logs into the right channels, where rafting crews made them into rafts containing about thirty logs each. Logs for the Bangor mills were not rafted until they came to the Bangor boom, much farther down the river. After delivering a raft to the mill, the scullers would take their long oars back up-river by rail or by hired wagon for another raft.

In 1846 the dog-eat-dog rugged individuals who lumbered on the river saw the benefits of co-operation and formed the Penobscot Log Driving Company (always known as the P.L.D.), which lasted until 1903. In that year the Great Northern Paper Company after a hard-fought court battle with the P.L.D., recorded with melancholy contempt by Fannie Eckstorm in her classic book *The Penobscot Man*—emerged the victor; it now owns practically all that territory.

The P.L.D. brought down all the logs from the north each spring. The company let the job out to the lowest bidder, and if nobody bid low enough the company appointed a "master," who attended to the job. John Ross, who held that post for many years, is unquestionably the most famous riverman who ever lived. It is to him that the Bangor Tigers owe much of their well-earned reputation. His name is associated especially with the West Branch (of the Penobscot) drive, and it is his genius that took a piebald lot of Old Town Indians, Canucks, Province men, Irish, and native Yankees and welded them into a body of log-driving bear-cats whose skill with pike-pole and peavey, with calked boot and driving bateau, has never been surpassed.

Especially, and above all, he made of those untamed individualists a close-knit unit possessed of a remarkable *esprit de corps*, with a fierce pride in their ability and what they stood for. Their job was to get out the logs, and that they did, come hell or high water. They never doubted that with John Ross to lead them they could accomplish the impossible —which incidentally they often did, as bears witness the famous Connecticut River drive of 1876, the Centennial Year. The rather young Connecticut River Lumber Company hired Ross and his whole crew of 150 Bangor Tigers to come over with their big Maynard bateaux and take the drive down to Hartford from First Connecticut Lake.

The task became impossible; 1876 was a famous year because the Connecticut had both the highest and the lowest water ever recorded, and Ross's men broke their hearts lugging the stranded logs off the bare ledges of the Fifteen-Mile Falls. But they did it; they brought the drive in, using dynamite to blast water out of the very rock. Worn to a frazzle, too exhausted at the end even to get drunk, they would have died rather than let John Ross down, and the honor of their name. As Jack Haley would say, "God damn them, they did it!"

But the West Branch master driver had to know a great deal more than merely how to handle men. He had to know the habits of scores of tributary streams, he had to know that logs will float faster than water—because the bed of the stream does not hold them back. That is why when a head of water was let through a dam it had to go on for a few minutes before logs were permitted to sluice through.

The master driver had to know the capacities of many driving dams, how much water they would discharge in a given time and how long it would take them to fill up again.

The master had to know when the ice would break up, when to set his crew to overhauling, calking, and soaking tight the double-ended bateaux. He had to know where to station his rivermen to tend out, (to keep the logs moving where jams might form). He had to arrange for communications. He had to understand the rate of progress of a saw-log—about two miles an hour in an ordinary flowing current—and he had to figure on a ten-per-cent loss by sinkage.

As late as 1955 there was an odd revival of the drive on the main Penobscot. Using diving equipment, two young men from Brewer worked at recovering logs from the bottom of the river. The logs had been thoroughly preserved by their complete immersion although many of them had been in the water for a hundred years, and bore the log marks of owners long since dead. The quality of the logs was excellent. They were found generally near the shore rather than in mid-channel. The divers were much handicapped by the water's becoming roiled with the fine silt of the bottom.

There was never river-driving before or since to equal what was seen on the West Branch. And its success stemmed in large part from two tools invented on the Penobscot—the peavey and the Maynard bateau. About 1860 these bateaux succeeded previous boats that were direct descendants of the army bateaux used in the French and Indian War. They were perfected at Old Town and Bangor. The "great Maynards," as they were called, were daringly conceived for daring work, says John Gardner in "Death Rides the River" (*Outdoor Maine*, October, 1960):

They had to be incredibly quick and responsive to paddle and setting-pole in dodging boulders, logs, and sunken ledges. So the bottom was made short to spin on a dime, and quite narrow. The long, ranking overhang of the boat, some seven feet in a thirty-two foot, was contrived to slide over obstructions, as were the widely flaring sides. The big Maynard was as quick as a cat and as slippery as an eel. It would scrape and careen past rocks that would sink an ordinary boat.

The unusually wide flare of the sides served another purpose also. It gave great additional displacement with very little increase in draught. These bateaux had to float heavy loads of men and driving gear in very shallow water. Size and great sheer were required to prevent swamping in the rapids. It is said that Jack Mann, a legendary bow-man on the Drive, called for an axe to chop arm-holes when the first high-bowed Maynard appeared.

The big Maynards made it possible to run rapids hitherto considered impassable, but the West Branch with its white water dashing through precipitous gorges, pitches, whirlpools and eddies all the way from Chesuncook dam beyond Katahdin down to its junction with the East Branch still had falls and pitches that could not be run, requiring that the boats be carried around. Some of these portages were three miles long, as the one at Ripogenus. The one at Ambajackomus was half a mile.

Lugging boat over blow-downs and boulders, across gullies and cradle-knolls for rods and miles in summer heat was something to gall the shoulders and drain the soul out of a man. The great Maynards weighed between eight and nine hundred pounds, even if that weight is light for a boat thirty-two feet long, nearly seven feet across, with better than two feet of sheer forward.

Penobscot men were the best bateau and canoe men in the world. Their ability to work wing or center jams from a bateau was proverbial. Only one who has himself worked a jam, or at least seen it done, can understand how difficult and how dangerous it is. More men were killed on drive from overturned bateaux than from any other cause. The constant practice of the Penobscot bateau men was of course a great help in attaining their excellence.

Finest of all the many stirring stories of the riverman's pride is Fannie Eckstorm's account of how Big Sebattis Mitchell ran the Sourdnahunk Falls. It was in 1870, and two bateau crews—six men in each—had just finished the painful carry around the falls. The day was hot and they were weary to death, and suffering from the galled shoulders and barked shins they had just received while lugging the heavy boats over the forty-rod portage. So they were glad to sprawl on the gravelly shore below the falls and wait for a third boat, manned by two Indians, one of whom was the legendary Big Sebat. Sebat was called Big because he weighed 260 pounds, and he was one of the best boatmen on the river; he was very strong, and a great believer in the conservation of energy.

So the two weary crews smoked and talked and waited for Sebat's yell to bring them up to help him lug the boat, for no man in the history of the world had ever run the Sourdnahunk Falls—they simply couldn't be run.

But Big Sebat, who had thrust the nose of his bateau up onto the shore above the falls, out of sight of the men, had determined that it might be done, and he persuaded his Indian bowman that they were the men to do it. Besides, knowing that two boat crews were waiting down below, who would report the deed, doubtless added to the attractiveness of his mad idea. So the two rivermen calmly talked over their chances of dying in the next five minutes, and then they shoved the boat out into the current.

The men lying on the gravel at the foot of the carry looked up just as the bateau shot over the first of the double falls, and they froze in amazement, their mouths open. Sebat and his companion, by a miracle of luck and good boatmanship, brought the bateau safely through, avoiding rocks and logs and whirlpools and sudden death, and surged out of sight around the first bend. The other rivermen came to their feet and ran down through the brush.

The two bateaumen, whose boat was nearly full of water, had vigorously used their paddles as brooms to get their craft nearly empty. They left a few pailfuls to make it look good, and when the other men came running up they found the two Indians standing on the shore, leaning impassively on their peavies, entirely at ease.

The men looked at the boat, they saw how little water had been shipped, they turned it over and saw that it had not been sprung on the rocks, they turned without a word and walked back to their own two boats, and they looked each other in the eyes, and still without a word they hoisted those huge Maynard bateaux onto their galled shoulders and marched with them back forty rods to the head of the carry, which they had just descended so painfully.

So they put in again, six men to a boat, and they pushed out into the current and they ran the falls. But both bateaux were swamped, battered to kindling wood, and the twelve men were thrown into the water and pounded and swashed about among logs and rocks. By swimming, or with the aid of Sebattis and his boat, eleven of them got ashore. The twelfth man drowned.

Why all this? Because in his own esteem a Penobscot man would not stand second to any other man. They would not have it said that Sebattis Mitchell was the only man of them who had tried to run Sourdnahunk Falls.

You may call this attitude foolish, or quixotic, or something else, depending on your temperament and on how you were brought up, but it shows the pride of the riverman, and explains why a man would say, "From the Penobscot, b'God!" when asked where he came from.

In the early days on drive, the men up above sluicing logs through the dam might keep them coming because they were unaware that a jam had formed at some bad spot farther down, and the logs would pile up. Various devices to signal back to the dam workers were tried out, depending on the terrain and the inventiveness of the boss. Men were stationed within sight of each other, all the way back, and would wave their arms in a certain manner, to indicate when to stop sluicing or when to resume. Sometimes flags of different colors were run up poles, or simply waved by the signaling men. The showing of a red flag meant, Danger! Stop logs. Black meant, Shut off water. White, displayed once, meant, Let water come; displayed twice, it meant, Let logs come. Finally came the telephone, working on one wire strung along the trees. Many woodsmen were afraid of the "talking box" that hung on a tree beside the stream. Others could not resist "rubbering," or listening in, whenever they heard the thing ring. The first telephone ever used in the Maine woods for river-driving purposes was installed by Fred A. Gilbert in the early 1890's from Canada Falls dam to Pittston Farm, a distance of four miles.

In the June, 1926, issue of *The Northern,* Jim Dubay speaks of this telephone:

It worked fairly well that first spring, considering the material they used to have in those days. On nice sunny days it worked first rate but during the heavy rains and winds, trees would often fall across the line and ground it. I believe Mr. Gilbert used it two or three springs for driving purposes and then gave it up. He still had faith in the telephone, however, and when he took over the management of the Spruce Wood Department he strung a line from Ripogenus Dam to the Lower Lakes, a distance of twenty-four miles.

To most of the river men in those days a telephone was a novelty, an object of great curiosity. I think it would be safe to say that not more than two men out of a hundred had ever used a telephone before that spring. I was at Sourdnahunk Falls in charge of a crew of fifteen river drivers. There was a telephone box at every falls between Rip Dam and the Lower Lakes. Usually the box was nailed to a convenient tree, so that the cook could answer the calls as they came in.

Owing to its being such a novelty, there was naturally a great deal of listening in. Every time the telephone rang, everyone along the line would take up their receiver and listen. This often bothered the parties who were speaking. Mr. Gilbert did not like this habit any more than anyone else and tried to put a stop to it. He even threatened to discharge anyone whom he might find listening in when it wasn't his call. One day he came down from the head of 'Suncook to Rip Dam and called the Lower Lakes. We were just coming in to second lunch. In my crew was a man named David Lavoi, a very good river driver, well known to Mr. Gilbert. Owing to his constant exposure to the sun, he was as black as an Indian. Lavoi picked up the receiver, intending to listen in, but just as he did so, "F. A." sang out, "Hang up that receiver, you black rascal!"

He dropped the receiver as if he were shot and ran to hide behind a big hemlock some twenty-five feet distant. "Come here, Jim," he said. I went up to him. He was as pale as a ghost. He said, "Say, Jim, that was Fred Gilbert on the line and he saw me. You know what he said about discharging anyone he caught listening on the line. I am going to beat him to it. Give me my time." It took me five minutes to convince him that Mr. Gilbert had not seen him, and that although the telephone was a wonderful thing, it had not advanced to the point that a man at Rip Dam could see another man at Sourdnahunk Falls, eight miles distant.

We all had a good laugh at Dave's expense. He worked with me for a long time after that but you could never get him to have anything to do with a telephone again.

The West Branch has a tributary called Pollywog Stream. A. G. Hempstead calls it "one of the most beautiful and terrible of waterways." It is a mean stream, steep, rapid, rock-strewn, narrow, cliff-bound. The drive was coming down it in the spring of 1907 and logs were being sluiced through a dam just above the head of the gorge. Down in the gorge, tending out to see that no jams formed, were John Hutt and J. P. Brown. Brown was a young fellow, twenty-four years old, from Edmundston, New Brunswick. He was half Irish and half French and a good riverman. The story of his death is told by John Morrison in *The Northern* of May, 1928.

On that day the logs came rushing down from the sluice, faster and faster, and at last, in spite of the tenders' best efforts, a jam was formed. Dynamite was tried, but it didn't work; the dam gates were closed and sluicing stopped until after much labor with axe and peavey the jam hauled. Or rather it didn't break, but was merely straightened out, while the closed gates made the water lower so the men could work. Then the gates were hoisted again, with the exception that the rush of water would float the straightened-out mass of logs downstream. But they didn't budge. Brownie and Hutt, contrary to the foreman's orders, took some more dynamite and descended onto the jam. The blast went off successfully, too successfully, for the momentum of the logs, in addition to the pressure of the rushing water behind, was swifter than the two men had counted on. They darted for the bank, but they didn't make it. Brownie grabbed a jill-poked log (a log stuck in the bank of the stream) that hadn't moved, and seemed to be safe. Hutt was swept under the rushing logs for twenty rods, but the water flung him up onto a shelf of the gorge and he came out unscratched. But Brownie's jill-poke was knocked loose and he went under. Those on the shore realized the danger, and the instant the jam hauled, a black flag was displayed, and the water was shut off at the dam.

They found Brownie's body, badly crushed, the clothes torn from it, a mile below the jam. The men nailed his spiked boots to a maple tree beside the trail, and they stayed there for more than twenty years.

23

River-Driving in New Hampshire

IN THE spring, all the brooks and streams in Coos County, that is, in the whole northern end of New Hampshire, were driven. When the ice went out and the melting snows furnished plenty of water, brooks one could step across in mid-summer became foaming streams down which long logs could be guided. It took a lot of know-how, but the know-how was there.

We have spoken of driving on the Diamonds and on the Androscoggin. Among other notable driving streams were Phillips Brook, Clear Stream, the Upper Ammonoosuc, Nash Stream, Indian Stream, Perry Stream, and Cedar Stream.

The Nash Stream drive was something special because the whole Nash Stream valley is something unusual. Its headwaters are three lakes (or ponds, as they are called in that region), each of which lies high above the next, and each of which is surrounded by unusually steep mountains—Sugarloaf, Whitcomb, Lightning are only a few. The valley was owned by the Odell Manufacturing Company, which had a big paper mill at Groveton, on the Upper Ammonoosuc, a few miles below the point where Nash Stream falls into that river. For many years the walking-boss, in charge of drives, was Mushrat Hayes, who earned his nickname from his habit of never seeking a bridge across a stream, but plunging right in and swimming across like a muskrat.

There wasn't much log-driving south of Mount Washington after Colonial times except on the Connecticut and the upper Saco. Nicholas Norcross did drive the Merrimack from 1846 to 1860, but after he died nobody else came along who could do it. Four-foot wood has been driven on the Mad River in Campton for years, and on Beebe River; and the Wild Ammonoosuc, flowing through Easton, Wildwood, Benton, and Swiftwater, was driven from 1891 to 1911 by the Champlain Realty Company, which became the International Paper Company in 1897. From that region they took out 130,000,000 feet of long spruce logs that were converted into paper pulp.

These logs were driven down the Wild Ammonoosuc into the Connecticut, at Woodsville. It is of interest to note that there are three rivers in New Hampshire bearing the musical name of Ammonoosuc. The Ammonoosuc proper rises near Mount Washington and enters the Connecticut at Woodsville. The Wild Ammonoosuc rises in Bunga Jar and flows into the Ammonoosuc proper at Bath. The Upper Ammonoosuc, into which empty Phillips Brook and Nash Stream, winds around from the eastern flank of the Kilkenny Mountains and falls into the Connecticut at Groveton.

The main river, the Ammonoosuc proper, is said to have got its name as follows: A white hunter came onto the stream at a small Indian camp, where a squaw was nursing her refractory child, whose name was Ammon. The hunter asked what the name of the stream was. The mother addressed her child loudly, "Ammon, you suck!" And the white man thought she had told him the name of the river. The story sounds reasonable, but does not explain how the other rivers got the same name.

The International Paper (I.P.) drive averaged about seven million feet each spring. In some years it was so far ahead of the Connecticut Valley Lumber Company's drive, which came from farther north, that it was let out of the Ammonoosuc and preceded the C.V.L. logs to its destination at Bellows Falls, but usually it was held behind a boom just above the dam across the Ammonoosuc at Woodsville until the much larger C.V.L. drive had passed. The reason for the waiting was one of practicality rather than politeness: If the I.P. wood was lying in the river at Bellows Falls when the C.V.L. logs came along, it was a difficult and acrimonious task to sluice the bigger drive through.

Vermont was chronically a "dry" state, but New Hampshire towns along the Connecticut often voted "wet." North Stratford, Woodsville, North Walpole, and other communities were notable havens for thirsty rivermen. North Stratford, where Ed Daley ran a boarding house and saloon for lumberjacks, was a very rollicking place indeed. Ed, who had worked on the river himself, knew his customers and how to handle them. Also, he had a sense of humor.

One day a fierce lumberjack from the Black River country in the Adirondacks strode in, looked around, and bellowed at Ed: "They tell me you're the man who sells the stuff! All right, give me some!"

As Ed looked him over and made no haste to answer, the man went on: "I'm a son of a bitch from Carthage, and I want service!"

Said Ed: "I could tell you were a son of a bitch the minute you opened your mouth, but I didn't know you were from Carthage."

Lewis Marshall, who became postmaster of North Stratford, recalls that one night when he was a boy there was a crew of Bangor Tigers camped across the Connecticut waiting for the Nulhegan drive to begin, and they came over to Ed's place and asked for rum. Ed had closed up, but obligingly answered the door. He told them to go away, since he was closed. They insisted on coming in.

"It was like a scene from a Grade B Western movie," says Lewis, "except it was real. They kept crowding up the steps and Ed kept knocking them down, one after another, until at last they were convinced."

Ed Bateman, who began scaling for the C.V.L. in 1890, has told me he once counted nine separate fist-fights going on at the same time on the crooked hill leading north out of Stratford. That must constitute some sort of record, and at least shows the rugged quality of the inhabitants.

Some sixty miles below Stratford, and having passed the difficult Fifteen-Mile Falls and the Twenty-Six Islands, the drive down the Connecticut arrived at the Narrows, just above Woodsville, where it was the custom to hold it in a boom for a few days. It is a pity that touring motorists seldom go up the east side of the river, for they miss the imposing Narrows.

Since Woodsville was not only the focus of two different log drives, but also a railroad center with shops and a roundhouse, and the Grafton County jail, known as Horse Meadow, was only a mile away, the local police-court judge was kept pretty busy. The dry observations of the editor of the weekly Woodsville *News* over the years are revealing:

On May 12, 1899, "Judge Dow is doing a very good business at his stand. Two more cases of drunkenness and one of assault were brought before him Saturday. But this is the unusually busy season anyway."

On May 4, 1906, the *News* recorded the death of four river-drivers who were killed by the explosion of a large quantity of dynamite which they were thawing over a fire.

On June 5, 1906, the *News* told its readers that "there has been the regular batch of drunks before the police court the past week, increased somewhat by the fact that the log drive of the CVL Company has not yet passed Woodsville. They were all sent down the river for the usual stay with jailor Phillips."

On July 3, 1908, "It took Judge Dow two sessions of his police court to find out whether one Edward Potter, familiarly known as 'Scotty,' was drunk when taken in by the officers Tuesday afternoon. Scotty declared he was not, and put up through his counsel, S. B. Page, a defense elaborate as well as forceful. Attorney F. B. Lang, who represented the State, introduced testimony to show that he was both drunk and promoting a brawl, he being charged with both offenses. The court dismissed the latter charge, but after due consideration held that while Scotty was not so very drunk, he was still drunk enough to merit 60 days retirement for reflection etc., and he therefore went down the river."

A famous story that has persisted through the years is about a riverman who was drunk and feeling his oats in Woodsville one day, and seeing the wax figure of a half-nude woman in a store window, uttered a

great logger's rutting-whoop and leaped through the plate-glass spiked
boots first, grabbed the female figure, and tried to ravish it. No dates are
given for this tour de force, and when the riverman's name is mentioned
he is usually called Ed Smith.

The facts underlying this story were modestly reported in the *News*
on March 11, 1910:

James F. McCormick struck town last Friday, and shortly after he struck town
he proceeded in the evening to strike the large plate glass window in Sargent's
store. The result was the destruction of the window, and wonderful to relate,
although James went through it head first, and was surrounded by splintered
glass, he was not destroyed but came out unscathed. He was gathered in by
Officer Davis assisted by two efficient citizens, John P. Battis and C. L. Bailey,
and on Saturday morning after the fight was over, and he had medical attend-
ance, he owned up before Judge Dow to the soft impeachment of being drunk.
He had not the wherewithal to pay his fine, and so as an inmate of the House
of Correction is assisting Superintendent Phillips in carrying on the county
farm. But what is quite an important question who is to reimburse the owner
of the block for the destruction of a valuable window?

Yes, the *News* was full of detailed reports on murders, drownings,
tar-and-feather parties, and other local diversions. An interesting item
that takes us back to northern Maine was printed on March 6, 1914: "Joe
Knowles, the alleged Dr. Cook of the Maine woods, was in Woodsville
Monday en route north and was gazed at by the curious while waiting for
his train." Somebody ought to resurrect Joe, who died only a few years
ago, and give him his just due. He won fame in the summer of 1913 when
the Boston *Post* hired him to go into the Maine woods stark naked, with
neither knife nor matches, to live a month or two "off the country." Each
day he wrote his adventures on a piece of birch bark and left it in a hollow tree. Most people don't know that besides being a licensed Maine
guide, a veritable Tarzan, and a mighty tippler, Joe was also a first-class
artist and did many cover pictures for the *Saturday Evening Post*.

When the I.P. drive on the Wild Ammonoosuc was ready to start,
most anyone who claimed to be able to use a cant-dog could get a job
breaking out rollways. Now breaking out rollways is a delicate and
perilous job, and just working around them in any capacity is dangerous.
In the winter of 1906, George McKellips, of Groveton, eighty-one years
old, was scaling for the Percy Lumber Company when he was struck by a
log which rolled from the top of the landing and went over him, breaking
his left arm and elbow, his collar-bone on the right side, and three ribs
on the same side, and cutting his left ear open and badly bruising his left
cheek. It was necessary to send ten miles for a physician. But men were
men in those days. Without Medicare they died and without Medicare
they lived. The *News*, which chronicled the mishap, terminates its report,

"Mr. McKellips is expected to be about in a few weeks."

Rivermen breaking out rollways never knew whether their pullings and pryings would bring out one log or a whole avalanche. Sometimes only two or three would rattle down; at other times the whole deck would suddenly bulge outward, hover for a moment, and hit the stream like grain swarming from an elevator. Often the logs would be frozen together and if one was started, they would all come. Often the loggers had driven a couple of stakes in front of the rollway to stop the first logs when they were being piled. These had to be knocked or cut loose. A sawlog was a heavy, inert thing, but it could lash out like greased lightning when those stakes were knocked out.

Leonard Dodge, who died in 1965, worked for a livery stable in Woodsville some sixty years ago. One day he was ordered to hitch up a pair of horses and take half a dozen men out to Swiftwater, where they would be employed in breaking out rollways on the Wild Ammonoosuc. He delivered the men, and without delay the boss handed out peavies and put them to work. Leonard lingered a few minutes to watch the exciting activity. Two of the men stepped up to a landing and attacked it with their peavies. The whole rollway collapsed, swarming over them as lava swarmed over Herculaneum, only a good deal faster. One man's head was cut completely off. Two hours from the time he had departed, Leonard returned to Woodsville bringing the two dead bodies and the head.

But the largest log drive in New Hampshire, and at the same time the longest drive in the world, was the one on the Connecticut River. The Connecticut is 345 miles long, and logs were driven from the headwaters, up against the Canadian border, clear down into Long Island Sound. Of course rafting and loose-log driving had been common on the lower part of the river since 1760, and many of those logs were cut in New Hampshire, but except for the 1851 raft of pine logs from North Stratford mentioned in the *History of Coos County*, I find no mention of any driving above the Fifteen-Mile Falls before 1868.

That year twenty million feet were cut by Fred Hanson at the lower end of Indian Stream and were driven to Brattleboro. The drive boss was Charles Weeks, and two young men working on it were George Van Dyke and Albert (Kirk) Patrick. They were friends, and twenty years later, in 1887, when Van Dyke dominated the river he hired Al and put him in charge of the logs at the Holyoke end. In those days the drive might cover a hundred miles from van to rear. This particular drive ended at Shephard's Island, below the Hadley bridges. The last camp of the rivermen was in a beautiful shady grove on the Hadley side, immediately below the present Coolidge bridge. The men were paid off in the office of the Mt. Tom plant. Through the seventies and early eighties the drivers were paid in gold rather than in greenbacks. This was evidently due to a skepticism that wasn't confined only to rivermen.

Al Patrick was one of those men you read about but don't often see: a thorough riverman who understood all the vagaries of water and of logs—and of men. He could handle the two-fisted loggers without exhibitionism, without shouting or any sign of tension, in any critical situation. He died in Hartford in 1939, aged ninety three. He was present at Turners Falls in August, 1909, when his old friend Van Dyke died, and he continued with the company until the last long-log drive on the Connecticut in 1915. When they boomed it in at the Great Oxbow, a turn in the river that surrounded the company's sawmill on the point of land locally called the "island," it was Al Patrick who closed the boom, as cameras clicked and cheers went up from the rivermen and the spectators. Among the rivermen was old Rube Leonard, of Colebrook, New Hampshire, who had gone down with every drive since 1868.

Probably Al's greatest moment was one day in 1904. Below Turners Falls, at the Hadley banks, three bridges crossed (the Coolidge bridge now replaces two of them). Here one Sunday twenty million feet of logs jammed against the northernmost of the three, the Sunderland bridge, which was a railroad bridge. When there came a freshet and a quick rise of water, and the boom at Turners Falls broke, Al and his men rushed up from Mt. Tom. He took his stand at the middle pier of the railroad bridge. The two piers on either side were connected by heavy booms to the two other bridges, making two passageways for the logs to go through on their way to the piers at Shephard's Island.

The van of the twenty million feet appeared. The logs collected on the middle support of the railroad bridge, and just at the right moment Al directed his men to throw their strength to one side or the other, and the great mass moved to the right or the left. This was done again and again, with not too large a crew, from 6 P.M. until midnight. After an exhausting and ceaseless effort the task was done, and a fearful jam at those three bridges was averted. It was the greatest number of logs to pass through such a narrow space in that length of time in logging history.

Al used to say that he had seen thirteen men killed on one Connecticut River drive, but that each death was due to carelessness, even though rivermen as a matter of course walked into places no ordinary man would even think of entering.

In 1869, Warren Hilliard, of West Stewartstown, New Hampshire, was part-owner of a drive that came down to a new mill at McIndoes Falls. He was a stout young man, thirty years old, but with George Christie, of Canaan, Vermont, he foolishly tried to run a bateau over Mulliken's Pitch, at the foot of the Fifteen-Mile Falls. Both men were drowned. Christie's body was taken out of the water at Wells River, ten miles below, on May 25. Hilliard's was found by two fishermen just below the Pitch on June 9.

Mulliken's Pitch was known as the most dangerous place on the whole river, and rivermen always carried their bateaux around it. Yet Hilliard was only the first of many rivermen who met their death there. They used to bury them in empty pork-barrels. When the New England Power Company built the great dam precisely at the Pitch in 1930, it excavated half a dozen of those makeshift coffins, the old spiked boots still intact.

Fred Gilmore bossed the 1882 drive. At that time Asa Smith was in charge of the company. Al Patrick claimed that 120,000,000 feet came down the river that spring, and I have heard the same story from other old C.V.L. men, but I am inclined to doubt it. The St. Johnsbury (Vermont) Caledonian of April 24, 1882, reports that "Van Dyke has between 15 and 16 millions of lumber ready up the river, and his men are all ready to start the mills (at McIndoes) as soon as the river opens."

And on June 20 the same paper stated, "The Connecticut River Lumber Co. have been obliged to leave the rear section of their drive in the fifteen mile falls. There are some twelve millions in this section left."

The Windsor (Vermont) *Journal* of May 20, 1882, tells us, "A drive of 65 million feet of lumber has been started in the upper waters of the Connecticut River, near McIndoes Falls. It will be driven down to the Connecticut River company's mills at Turners Falls. The company employs 500 men at an expense of about $1300 per diem. The advance guard of drivers reached Windsor on Tuesday."

On June 17, 1882, "The log drive on the Connecticut River has now reached the Falls at McIndoes, in part, and one gang of the drivers, numbering 150 men is now encamped there and engaged in running the 'fifteen mile falls.' The high water resulting from the recent rains has so increased the current as to produce a formidable jam which will be likely to employ the drivers in its release for some weeks. Another gang of 250 men are at work at some point above, and the total drive is said to comprise some 65 million feet. The season has been an unfortunate one in the loss of men, eleven lives having already been lost in the work during the season."

On July 8, 1882, "The Connecticut River Lumber Company drive for this season passed Windsor Tuesday last."

The Connecticut drive was not only the longest in New England, it was one of the toughest. Everything to bother a riverman was there: falls, rapids, dams to be sluiced past, mill-owners to fight with, dry ledges to break a horse's legs on, freshets, droughts, ox-bows, bridges built on piers, . . . God! how the rivermen hated those bridges! They would skillfully build jams against them, hoping to carry them away and never see them rebuilt. Sometimes they succeeded, as on May 7, 1890, when there was a tremendous jam of ice and sixty-foot logs that took away the old covered bridge at Upper Waterford, Vermont. It was a sight to behold—the great logs shot straight up into the air their full length, as the pressure built up, and the jam extended upstream nearly two miles. The bridge went out, and the next day the one at Lower Waterford was carried away. The latter was never rebuilt, but a one-span steel bridge with no piers replaced the Upper Waterford structure and lasted until the great flood of 1927. The old covered Ledyard bridge at Hanover, beloved by so many Dartmouth students, sturdily withstood all the attacks of the rivermen, though many great jams piled up behind it. The Windsor railroad bridge went out in 1897, but the Boston and Maine rebuilt it.

Passing Bellows Falls could take from three to six weeks. In 1904 Van Dyke blasted a channel out of the solid rock on the New Hampshire side of the falls and for the first time in history logs were sluiced down on that side of the river. A good head wind could stop operations for days, when the logs refused to enter the sluice, and the becalmed rivermen would go over to the hell-holes of North Walpole to drown their sorrows in the Demon Rum. Still another real danger the rivermen gladly tackled was the wild women who frequented said dives. But the river-hog had great confidence in the efficacy of tobacco-juice or raw whiskey applied to the parts, to ward off the fiery darts of Venus.

Another exhausting task was sorting logs at various points— McIndoes, Wilder, Bellows Falls. The sorter, standing in the water, would shout instructions about where the different logs should go. His job was so exhausting, mentally and physically, that the sorter had to be relieved every hour.

Piers and booms were, of course, necessary in sorting. A device used a good deal on the lower part of the Connecticut was the fin-boom. This was a refinement of the sheer-boom (one log, or several joined end to end, fastened at strategic points along the stream to "sheer" the floating logs past obstructions or coves). The fin-boom, which was used on every navigable logging stream in the country, was not the invention of a Yankee, however. In 1861 two Wisconsin rivermen discovered how the force of the current could be utilized both to hold a sheer-boom across the channel and to remove it when a boat or raft passed by. Their device, one end of which was anchored to shore, consisted of a rigid chain of timbers upon the lower (downstream) sides which were fastened a series of collapsible rudders, or fins. When the fins were extended to an angle of 30 degrees or more on the lower side of the boom, the current pushed against them with such force that the boom was held obliquely across the channel. One man on the bank could easily pull the fins into a position parallel with the boom, whereupon the current would immediately push the boom aside to permit the passage of river craft. This type of boom was useful in Massachusetts, where the law prohibited blocking the channel of a navigable river with floating logs. It was used in northern Maine a good deal, for there pulpwood was driven at points where the wood might float off into a deadwater.

In 1910 the drive was at Plainfield, New Hampshire, when two young men came along in a canoe. The canoe overturned among the logs and the boys would have drowned if the rivermen had not pulled them out. Joe Roby, the boss, told a young riverman named Bill James to take them up to the cook tent, and have them take off their clothes and dry them at the fire and get something hot to drink from the cook. Having thus saved their lives, Joe gave them some profane advice about keeping away from log drives in canoes, and left them. Fifty years later the *Valley News* in Lebanon printed a big bi-centennial edition and asked Bill, now living at Windsor, Vermont, for some reminiscences, and he told that story. Three days later he got a letter from an old man in Bellows Falls, saying he was one of the boys.

Bill, in his old age, became Windsor's gravedigger. He first developed an interest in that profession while on drive. A Windsor undertaker named Lyman Cabot sometimes took a snort in a notorious bar-room across the river in Plainfield. This time Ed Hilliard and Bill and some of the boys were there, smoothing the brows of care, and Lyman was discoursing on his profession. He had been called that morning to lay out a corpse. An old man had died, and his widow called Lyman in. He looked at the deceased and remarked to the widow that her husband looked bald-headed. It seems that the old boy had worn a wig and it had slid so far back on his head that it showed a good part of his shining dome. Lyman asked the widow if she had any glue. She said she didn't think so but she would look. She was gone quite a while, but came back at last with some mucilage and asked if it would do. "Heck," said the undertaker, "never mind, I got it fixed. I used a nail."

It was at Lebanon the year before this incident that Joe Burke, a well-known riverman, suddenly threw down his peavey and said to his mates, "What in hell am I doing this kind of work for, anyway? I'm going to quit!"

"You quit now," they warned him, "and old George won't pay you."

"I'm quitting just the same," said the life-long river-hog, and quit he did.

Years went by. Nobody ever heard from him. Bill, seeking novelty, teamed up with another young fellow and went on the bum. One morning the two hoboes found themselves somewhere in Ohio, dead-broke and hungry. Off the road stood a handsome set of farm buildings, and they went over to ask for a hand-out. The woman who answered their knock said she'd have to ask the mister. The mister came to the door. He was Joe Burke! What a reunion took place! Not only meat but also drink was set out, and a good time was had by all.

Six miles above Windsor, at Hartland, Vermont, is a part of the Connecticut known as Summer's Falls. A rough cart track goes down through the woods to the river from the main road to the falls, and here the curious will perceive a mound of earth, six feet long, covered with flat stones.

On June 21, 1895, one of Van Dyke's rivermen, nineteen-year-old Charles A. Barber, from Cherryfield, Maine, lost his life there. He fell off the log he was riding into the swift water of the falls and was drowned. The drivers recovered the body, took it up into the woods, and covered it with a blanket. The paymaster who accompanied the drive sent a telegram to the boy's father, who came through from Cherryfield with a pair of driving horses.

The dead youth had about three hundred dollars coming to him. When the father received the money he put it into his pocket, jumped into the buggy, and took off for Cherryfield as fast as he could go. He left the body right there. The drivers then took it and buried it beside the woods road. Then those rough and mostly uncouth men took time to pick a slab of stone and scratch on it the boy's name, age, and hometown, and put it on the grave. I visited it on April 9, 1966. The headstone is still on the mound, but the inscription is getting faint.

After Van Dyke died in 1909 the C.V.L. jolted along for a few years on the momentum supplied by the old lumber king, but in 1913 it was acquired by Stone and Webster. This firm wanted to control the water-power on the river by acquiring ownership of the headwaters. But they continued to drive logs for three years, and then cut four-foot pulpwood and drove it down to Lancaster, Bellows Falls, and other points until 1921. In 1927 they sold out their lumber interests to the St. Regis Paper Company; which as late as 1948 ran a pulpwood drive down to Lancaster. Since that date no wood has been driven on the Connecticut.

The C.V.L. was in its glory when Stone and Webster owned it. It was a compact little subsidiary of the corporation, and they liked to come up to their "northern office" (the main office was in Boston) on weekend trips to fish and hunt. They owned maybe half a million acres of land up there, but it was only a drop in their bucket.

They fixed up old Camp Idlewild on Second Connecticut Lake, built a decent road to it, and put a man and his wife in charge. They bought a big new motorboat for the camp, and a big new flag. Nothing was too good for "our northern office."

They put two genuine foresters on the staff, and they put in as general manager a former major of the Corps of Engineers of the United

States Army, Earle Philbrook; still another Engineers officer, Orton Newhall, was appointed resident engineer, and he went around surveying for dam-sites and logging railroads and the like. Many of the old woodsmen who had worked all their lives for the company and maybe lost a leg or an arm in service, so to speak, were given pensions. So everyone was happy.

Then the blow fell. In 1927 Stone & Webster sold the C.V.L. for about twice what it was worth to the St. Regis, while the New England Power Company acquired the water-power rights. The power Company finally got around to building dams across the Connecticut, including one at Wilder and two on the Fifteen-Mile Falls, and the St. Regis is still cutting pulp, though it does it all through jobbers, under the able management of young Fred Cowan. In September, 1965, he inaugurated the largest tree farm in the East,—171,000 acres in Pittsburg, New Hampshire.

The last of the old C.V.L. men, Tom Cozzie, retired in 1958 after forty-five years of unbroken service, during which he rose from cook and cant-dog man to woods manager of the company. I worked with Tom more than forty years ago, and since then I've received medals and ribbons and letters of commendation, but I do not esteem any of them so highly as a remark Tom made to me in those days: "Well, Pikey, one thing can be said for you, you ain't lazy!"

The Connecticut River drive ended in a burst of glory. In the winter of 1914–1915 the C.V.L. had more than two thousand men in the woods, and the word went out that the long-log drive the next spring would be the last. It was the most exciting news that had hit the North Country since the Indian Stream War in 1835. Men talked about it in saloons and on street corners; they argued about it and fought about it; they said that it just couldn't be true. Many of them swore that logs would be driven down the Connecticut until the end of time. But before the ice went out, the rumor received official confirmation. The C.V.L. said that there would never be another saw-log rolled into the upper Connecticut.

Then everybody wanted to get onto the drive. It was the last chance for the young men to carve their names on the North Country totem pole of glory, so to speak, while the old-timers wanted to give it one more whirl. There were men in the border towns then who had gone down with every drive since 1868.

The C.V.L. did it up in style—more than five hundred men on drive, the greatest crew of rivermen who ever went down the Connecticut. Dan Bosse abandoned the Brown Company that spring, attracted by the lure of the last drive and the princely wage of four dollars a day. Bangor Tigers came all the way from Old Town, and some of the old ones among them had been with John Ross in 1876.

One night in April, 1915, the ice went out, and the next day the drive was under way. Forty million feet of logs massed at Second Connecticut Lake shot down the roaring river and in no time were spreading themselves quietly in the booms set to catch them on the choppy waters of First Connecticut Lake. There, fifteen million more came out of South Bay, and all of them were towed across the lake at night, when the wind was quiet, and sluiced through the dam into the channel below. Three million more came out of Perry Stream, and six from Deadwater Brook. And so, like a snowball, the drive grew and grew until, when it hit North Stratford, there were sixty-five million feet of logs in the river.

Two men were killed at Perry Falls that spring. "I saw one of them die," 'Phonse Roby told me. "There was a wing jam on both sides, and he was walking across the stream on a log wedged about a foot under water. He held his peavey dangling from his hand, on the up-stream side, and the current hit it just enough to throw him off balance. He fell into the stream, where the water was fast as a mill-race. He could swim some, and a log came along and he grabbed it by the middle and tried to hoist himself on top.

"If he'd only used his head and taken the log at one end, he could have held himself up until we pulled him out; but I suppose he was too scared to think, and he kept trying to wrestle that log, and it kept rolling out of his hands.

"The jam struck out into the stream a few rods below, and the current set in against it. I ran to beat hell over those logs and got out on the point and was all ready to pull him in when the cold water and the shock were too much for him, and he let go the log and went under. One of his hands came up as if he was waving good-bye—and that was the last of him."

But after a couple of men were lost at Perry Falls, the drive went merry as a wedding bell until it reached North Stratford. There the river was blocked by an ice jam, and the logs jammed behind it, rearing in huge piles, twenty and thirty feet high; the worst log jam ever seen, said Rube Leonard, who could remember them all, even the first one.* For there were thirty-five million feet of logs in one bunch, sticking straight up and sideways, and every other way, a diabolical and inextricable mass.

They kept piling up, and the water backed up and flooded houses and barns and tore up the Grand Trunk Railroad tracks, and the Grand Trunk started a lawsuit, and there was hell to pay.

'Phonse Roby had charge of the drive that year, and Win Schoppe, one of the great names in the North Country, bossed the rear. They got all the men down at the great jam, and they worked day and night.

---

* The author has known and worked with many participants of both the 1914 and 1915 (the last one) long-log drives on the Connecticut, but even forty-five years ago they were prone to confuse the two. Although there was a jam in 1915 at North Stratford, the "great" jam took place in April, 1914.

Finally, after many days, they had picked and dynamited the jam to pieces and set the logs floating off down the black, sullen river.

"I saw a funny thing while we were breaking that jam," John Locke, who was later general manager of the C.V.L., told me. "The dynamite had frozen, so they built a fire to thaw it out. They shoveled up a bank of earth all around the fire, a foot or two away, and stood the sticks of powder up against the inside of the bank. They left a young fellow in charge of it who didn't know much about the vagaries of dynamite. One of the sticks happened to slip and fall toward the fire, and he had reached over to pull it out. Probably someone had told him that dynamite wouldn't explode unless it was jarred. At that precise moment old Win came striding up to see if the powder was ready, and just as the youngster reached over the embankment, Win reached one paw and wrapped it around his short ribs and flattened him on the ground like you would a doll.

"Boom! And that stick of dynamite exploded all over the adjacent territory. But nobody was hurt. Win got up and brushed himself and says to the lad, 'G'acious! G'acious, sonny, you must learn to be more careful.'

"Dan Bosse was doing the shooting. He was a good man with powder. I saw him put in one blast that didn't do any good. He'd tied two sticks of powder onto the end of a pole and swum out with a lighted fuse and stuck it into a hole of the jam. When it didn't go off correctly, he was a little bothered. He wrapped some more dynamite around the end of a pole about fifteen feet long and skipped out onto the jam and pushed it into a hole he'd selected, and stood there watching to see what would happen. It happened all right. The whole front of the jam came loose, and I'll swear it looked as if Dan went up in the air more than ten feet. But when he came down he was standing with both feet on a log and headed downstream."

The drive got down to Fitzdale (today they call it Gilman), and the owner of the mill and the dam there wouldn't let them sluice through the dam. The Stone and Webster people were first-rate engineers but didn't know much about logging, so they had brought in a man from down country named D. J. MacDonald to be general manager. MacDonald, who accompanied the drive in a Buick touring car, advised waiting. Big 'Phonse, who had been brought up under Van Dyke, saw the water dropping every day, scowled, and said nothing, but he took it upon himself to go and call on the millman.

The tall, slim walking-boss strode into the office, his spiked boots gouging little triangular holes in the polished hardwood floor.

"You open up those sluices," he said, "or God have mercy on you when I turn these rivermen loose. There'll be nothing left of you, your mill, or your dam."

He meant what he said, and the other man knew he meant it. The drive went through.

Just below Fitzdale began the "Horse-Race," a quarter of a mile of rock-toothed rapids that were the start of the Fifteen-Mile Falls. Sam Martin, one of the rivermen, had managed to get drunk, and now, full of bravado and Old Grand-Dad, he got into a bateau all alone and started down through the Horse-Race. A hundred yards down, the boat hit a rock and turned over, leaving Sam out in the middle of the rapids, clinging to a boulder and sober as a preacher.

No man had ever ridden a log through the Horse-Race, and eventually a bateau would have been procured to rescue Sam, but some playful riverman bet Bill Bacon ten dollars he couldn't ride a log down past Sam and pick him off that rock. Bill ran out over the surging logs, picked a big spruce, and stayed on it through the white water. As the log drove past the rock, barely missing it, he grabbed Sam by the collar, hauled him clear, and brought him safely through.

Down the drive went, down and down. The wangan transported in high-wheeled wagons drawn by eight horses each, kept up with it. It's quite a trick to drive eight horses. Next to rivermen, teamsters were the most highly paid men in the woods. In the early days, selecting a campsite was a rather hit-and miss affair, but as drives got better organized, the custom was for the cook to pitch his tent handy to the river and to the most rivermen. John Pattee, a North Stratford storekeeper, was charged by the company with sending a man on ahead to choose good sites and to buy milk, eggs, and other fresh food for the rivermen, and hay for the horses.

Wherever they camped, near the little country villages, all the kids would come down and help dig the beanhole, and then they'd stand around the cook tent and watch the cook mix his biscuits in a pan as big as a bushel basket, and he would give them immense great sugar cookies and gingersnaps to eat, and they would fairly worship him. They watched the rivermen tramp down the board sidewalks with their fine, free gait, gouging out splinters at every step, and while other kids might want to grow up and become locomotive engineers or join a circus, all those lads firmly determined to grow up and be rivermen some day.

I was a boy myself then, living with my uncle on the Fifteen-Mile Falls. He was a farmer, but in his younger days he had worked for the C.V.L. in the great north woods, and he too had "gone down the river." The river-drivers always put up their wangan on his meadow, beside the old toll-bridge, over which "only rivermen and dogs" went free, and if the water was low they would camp there for three weeks while they were picking the log jams off the rocks.

That spring the wangan did not come until some days after the logs had begun to run past beneath the bridge. A man who happened to drive by the schoolhouse at afternoon recess told us the drive was coming. The teacher knew that no more work would be done that day, so she dismissed the pupils, and we went racing down to the bridge. Sure enough, the logs were coming, not many yet, but steadily growing thicker and thicker, rubbing and nosing softly against each other as the swift current urged them on.

We stayed there until suppertime, fascinated by that vast, silent army of marching wood, and after supper we went back again, accompanied by our elders. The bridge was lined with people who had come to see.

Presently, as we stood there leaning on the plank railing, with the cool breeze rising from the river and the sun setting behind us, from upstream around a bend a solitary riverman came straight into the red beams of the dying sun. His peavey point was stuck into the big log on which he rode, and both his hands were clasped around the top of the heavy handle. Seemingly oblivious to the slippery, unstable quality of his steed, poised in a splendid attitude of indifference to the many admiring eyes he knew were fixed upon him, he came whirling down the river, the twenty-foot spruce surging and lunging through the white water. By a miracle of good luck the log avoided all the rocks and the upright riverman swept grandly beneath us, so that we got a good view of him.

His sweaty suspenders were crossed over a red woolen shirt; his heavy black trousers were stagged off about the tops of his spiked boots. A torn, gray felt hat, its tattered brim turned up in front, revealed his eyes, watchful as any cat's, and by the look in his eyes and by the little bend in his knees we knew that while he appeared so nonchalant as he leaned there upon his peavey-handle, he was tensely alert. We almost wished that his log would strike a rock, so we might see what he would do, but really we were glad that it did not. So he went on, the vanguard of the drive, and disappeared in the fading light.

After all the timber had surged past us and on down the river and the wangan had departed southward, the walking-boss, a tall, slim man with keen black eyes and a graceful way of carrying his body (half a dozen years later he gave me a job and I went to work for the company myself) came and paid my uncle for milk and hay the rivermen had bought. They talked a little of the old days in the woods and on the river, and of how this was the last drive. After the boss had gone away, my uncle took a spotted red handkerchief from his hip pocket and blew his nose very loudly. Then he looked at me. His eyes were very bright and I remember I asked him why he was crying, and he said:

"I guess the wind makes my old eyes water, Bobbie."

The drive went down, over Mulliken's Pitch and past the Twenty-

Six Islands, and came at last to the Narrows at Woodsville, opposite the
Vermont town of Wells River. There was always much rivalry between
the two communities. A Woodsville bard once composed a poem of
which the refrain goes:

> *Oh Woodsville is the doughnut,*
> *Wells River is the hole* . . .

which did not help promote friendship.

It was the last time they ever put the old *Mary Ann*, the raft or scow
that carried the cook's equipment from Woodsville down, into the water.
There used to be a "little" *Mary Ann* that they launched below the rips at
West Stewartstown and ran over the Guildhall dam and broke up at Fitzdale, since it could not survive the Falls. It was also the last time they
built the horse rafts. There were several of these great affairs which, after
1900, were built on a scow, like the *Mary Ann*, with a hitching rack along
one side and a railing at each end. Before 1900 they carried eight horses
each, tied head to head. They were used to haul stranded logs into the
water. The work was dreadfully hard on the animals, who often had to
swim for their lives. Fresh replacements were constantly being walked
down from West Stewartstown, while the worn-out nags were taken
back up north and turned out to pasture.

Before 1900 the rafts were simply logs fastened together, as can be
seen in the extraordinarily clear accompanying photograph in the picture
section.

Win Schoppe was well over sixty years old that spring. For many
years he had been a woods boss and a dam-builder for the C.V.L. He was
an immensely powerful man, but he had never had a fight in his life. Indeed it was because he was always good-natured that his nickname was
Grinner. His strongest oath was "G'acious!"

Vern Davison, who worked on the drive, told me that there was one
man, a mean-tempered, red-headed bruiser working on the rear, who for
some reason had it in for the old man. He used to talk loudly to the others
about what he would do to Schoppe if the latter ever tried to ride him.

"This fellow came into the tent one night at Brattleboro, noisy and
drunk," Vern told me, "and Win told him to shut up, the men needed
their sleep. He called Win a son of a bitch, and proposed to give him a
licking. He made a pass at him, but Win reached out one hand and took
him by the throat and laid him on the ground and bore down. When the
fellow came to, Win said, 'G'acious, I hope I haven't hurt you. But really,
you shouldn't go around calling people sons of bitches.' The fellow took
his turkey and got out of there as fast as he could caper."

And so the drive went down and down. The old men showed the
young ones where the great jams of former years had piled up, where

men had been killed, and where some especially pleasant fight had taken place. Finally they came to Mt. Tom, and the last long-log drive on the Connecticut River, the longest drive in the whole United States, was over.

They kept the men in a hotel in Holyoke until they paid them off, and let them go. Vern Davison, who had at one time lived in Boston, had between six and seven hundred dollars coming to him.

"I gave half of it to Win," he told me, "and asked him to keep it for me. I took the rest and went to Boston. I had one great and glorious time. The first thing I did was to buy a ticket to North Stratford, and the next was to go over to the Adams House and get a room. Then I got all cleaned up—shave, shine, shower, shampoo, even a manicure. I bought a new suit of clothes at Filene's and then I started out to paint the town red.

"I'd lived in Boston some years, and I still knew my way around. I had a lot of friends there. It was wine, women, and song for two weeks. I never went on such a tear before, and I never will again. But I'll bet you there are still people in Boston who remember it! They had to lay new floors in some of their swankiest ballrooms after I led my Kitty out in the mazes of a waltz."

When Vern got back to North Stratford he met Black Bill Fuller, 'Phonse Roby, and Jigger Johnson, who had just returned from Holyoke. The four decided to go on a fishing trip over on the Diamonds. At a local livery stable they rented a two-horse, fringed-top surrey, and headed north. Vern sported a large handlebar moustache, Jigger was shaved clean, but both 'Phonse and Bill wore great black beards. At the Line House in Beecher Falls they stopped to buy two gallons of Canadian high wines, as pure alcohol is called along the border. A couple of miles above Beecher Falls, down below the road in the riverbank, is a fine spring known as Cold Spring.

The four friends stopped there to cut the alcohol. They tied the team to a tree, skittered down the bank, cut the liquor, and had a drink or two. It was warm, and they had all left their coats in the surrey. In his vest pocket Jigger had his whole winter's wages, more than five hundred dollars in bills. Because it was warm, he took off his vest and hung it on a limb.

"We sat there a while," said Vern, "and had a couple more drinks, and finally we started north again. We rolled along for more than fifteen miles, clear up to First Lake, before we noted Jigger didn't have his vest. 'Phonse and I wanted to go back and get it, but Jigger says, 'Oh, to hell with it! We're going fishing!" So we go over to the East Branch and stay ten days until our bait is all gone, and then we come back to the lake and get our team and start back to North Stratford.

"'When we come to the Spring,' Jigger says, 'just stop a minute while I go down and get my vest.' And so help me, there it was, still on the limb where he'd left it, and all the money still in the pocket."

Today the Fifteen-Mile Falls is buried under a hundred feet of water. 'Phonse and Vern and Jigger and Black Bill Fuller and Dan Bosse are gone where spiked boots aren't needed. It's just as well. Their era passed when the last log slid into the booms at Mt. Tom in the summer of 1915.

24

Sketch of a "Lumber King"

NEW ENGLAND can boast of several men justly known in their time as "lumber kings." Aside from William Bingham, who owned two million acres of forest in the state of Maine, from Messrs. Coe and Pingree, and from Abner Coburn, who became governor of the state (Abner operated on the Kennebec and had a remarkable reputation for generosity and square-dealing), one can take off one's hat and speak respectfully of General Samuel Veazie, of John Ross, of Milton Shaw, of Ed Lacroix, and of other flamboyant characters.

Vermont had George Fitzgerald, who made the biggest pile of sawdust in the state at Wenlock, while New Hampshire had such shining characters as Nicholas Norcross, Ave Henry, Ruth Parks, and George Van Dyke. There were indeed other great lumbermen, but they never attained the rank of royalty.

Perhaps Miss Parks, of Lyme, New Hampshire, a college graduate and still, in 1966, full of pep and ginger at the age of eighty-two, didn't, either, but she merits special attention because she was the only lady logger in the United States who swung an axe, handled a cant-dog, drove team, and ran her own camps. That well-known lumberjack Sherman Adams can testify that she was a hard woman to beat. I remember a song about her, the first line of which goes: "There's a lumbering lady in Lyme . . ."

But when we get right down to cases, I think anybody would have to choose between Ave Henry and George Van Dyke for the most picturesque king in the pack.

Henry was a railroad logger. Van Dyke was a river-driver. Henry put up a pulp mill at Lincoln, New Hampshire, foreseeing the end of sawn lumber. Van Dyke was contemplating doing the same thing at North Stratford when he was killed. Henry left an estate listed at ten million dollars. Van Dyke's obituary in the 1909 newspapers claimed he was the wealthiest lumberman in New England, "although the estimate of twenty million dollars is undoubtedly high." Both men started from nothing; both had genius and determination and no school education. Also, they were partners in many big deals. Which was the whicher?

I have chosen old George because I agree with Belcher that he was "beyond doubt the king of all the famed timber barons of his day in the Granite State."

George Van Dyke was born in a log cabin in 1846, and he died, appropriately, on a log jam in the Connecticut River in 1909. Long before his death the man was a legend. Every hair on his head and every drop of blood in his veins, and every ancestor back to the forty-fifth generation, was eloquently and heartily cursed in three languages and four states and two countries for more than thirty years. But at the same time he had many staunch friends, who knew him to be public-spirited and generous, while both foes and friends agreed that he was a born executive, possessed of a phenomenal memory, strong common-sense, and excellent practical judgment concerning men and things. Also, his private life was blameless. Even his worst enemies had little to say about his sexual mores. He never married and was devoted to his mother, who lived in his palatial home in Lancaster, New Hampshire, until she died in 1906 at the age of ninety-six.

He was born at Stanbridge, Quebec, on February 21, 1846. His father came from Highgate, Vermont, and before that the paternal ancestors were Dutchmen from Kinderhook, New York. His mother was Abigail Dixon, of good old Yankee stock.

The boy had but four years of schooling, and he never owned a pair of shoes until he was eleven years old. At that rather tender age he left home to shift for himself. He went to work as an axeman for David Beattie, the lumberman who owned Beattie's Gore in Maine, just over the line from Megantic. Later in life, George bought the whole township from Beattie and logged it off.

At the age of fourteen he was lugging a cant-dog on his shoulder on the Androscoggin drive, and for ten years he continued to work in the woods and on the river, doing everything from driving steers to breaking jams. There was nothing about logging and driving that he didn't know at first hand, and all his life he never hesitated to go out with his men and lead the way, to pick a key-log or to swing a boom, even after he was listed as a millionaire.

George was not a tall man, but he took a size-19½ collar and was very wide and thick. His powerful voice could be heard right across the Connecticut River from bank to bank. In his old age he began to acquire a corporation. That probably explains what happened one morning when one of his stable boys, Bill James, as he had been ordered, knocked at his door in the Willard House in North Stratford, to wake him up in time to drive to Lancaster and catch a train there. George hollered, "Come in!" Bill pushed the door open. The great man was dressed, even to his boots, but those were not laced. He ordered Bill to do that for him.

"I'll be damned if I will!" said the lad. "I'm a stable man, not a god-damned valet!"

"You're fired!" yelled George. Bill went out and sat on the steps. He was there when George appeared a few minutes later.

"Where are those black mares?" he asked. "Go hitch them up!"

"I'm not working for you any more," said Bill. "You fired me."

"Don't be a fool! You know I have to be in Lancaster at eight o'clock. Get moving!"

His health was of the best, and the strong constitution resulting from his youthful years of hard work alowed him to toil long hours in later life. No riverman overslept on the drive when George was around. If he did, he was roused from his peaceful snores in his soggy blankets by the old man's toe in his ribs, and a profane command to roll out.

Work George did. He could spot a money-making proposition a mile, or twenty miles, away; and his work on the river, where a man doesn't have time to call a committee-meeting to arrive at a conclusion—not if he wants to survive—cultivated in him the habit of swift decisions. A good example is the way he snapped up the option on the stumpage on the Dartmouth College Grant when the Brown Company hesitated, with the result that, as they had to have it, they finally paid Van Dyke for it—through the nose.

But a star in the ascendant often has luck, too, and George was not without his share. In 1872 he became a partner (and manager), along with Henry and Lewis Bowman, of a sawmill in Guildhall, Vermont. A couple of years later he bought a timber lot in Hereford, Quebec, for a hundred dollars. He put a crew into the woods, cut a million feet of logs off the lot—taking all the adjacent timber in the process—and drove them down the Connecticut to South Lancaster, New Hampshire, where he had agreed to deliver them to the man to whom he had sold them, a millman named John H. Locke. Locke was a good man, and years later Van Dyke made him manager of his enterprises in Zealand, but just now, as Van Dyke's drive was drifting into the booms, Locke went into bankruptcy, and George was left with a million feet of logs in the river. There he was, stuck. He hadn't paid his winter crew, but had hired them to bring down the drive, telling them he'd pay them when he got his own money. He'd done his winter's work on credit, and now his credit was all shot. But never say die! was George's motto.

The mill workers were on strike, so he arranged with the bank to take over the mill, put in enough of his rivermen to run it, and proceeded to saw out and sell his own lumber, the remainder of the men living mean-while at the wangan.

The price of lumber jumped three dollars a thousand, and Van Dyke cleared ten thousand dollars on the deal. With that to start on, he began to acquire timberland in the North Country.

In 1877, with Richard Peabody and Henry Merrill, he went to Mc-Indoes Falls, Vermont, at the foot of the Fifteen-Mile Falls on the Connecticut River, and operated a sawmill there. Peabody sold out to the other two, and presently Van Dyke bought out the other partner. He enlarged his mill, put in modern machinery and built a box-shook mill with a capacity of one car a day, and began to do quite a business.

About this time—1879—the Connecticut River Lumber Company (C.R.L.) was chartered under the laws of the state of Connecticut. It started when a prominent New York banker named George S. Scott found himself unexpectedly in the lumber business. A man who owed him a considerable amount of money had no assets left except a sizable tract of timberland in New Hampshire near the Connecticut lakes. Scott took over this tract, and with two other bankers, Pearsall and Thorne, acquired an old stone building in Hartford, Connecticut, and equipped it with sawmill machinery. Before long this group had also bought a sawmill at Holyoke and one at Mt. Tom, in Massachusetts.

Thus the company dominated operations on the Connecticut below McIndoes Falls. It was soon reported to banker Scott that everything was going well on the river except that there was difficulty with a man named George Van Dyke and his mill at McIndoes Falls. Scott, a very vigorous and strong man himself, replied, "Go back and kill him off." Scott's representatives went, but reported back to Scott that they couldn't kill him off. Instantly, the banker said, "Then he's the man we want." In 1884 Van Dyke was made general manager of the company, and two years later, perceiving the benefits of consolidation, he persuaded them to buy out his holdings for half a million dollars, and make him president of the company.

By 1902 he owned three-quarters of the company stock, and that year the name was changed to Connecticut Valley Lumber Company.

George was more than a riverman. He wanted a railroad up north, to save toting all his logging-camp supplies from North Stratford to the border. So he built the Upper Coos Railroad of New Hampshire, 21.45 miles long, along the Connecticut river from North Stratford to West Stewartstown, and became its president. This road was opened on December 26, 1887. It was leased to the Maine Central from May 1, 1890 to January 21, 1932, and then was purchased by the Maine Central. George also constructed the Upper Coos Railroad of Vermont, running a distance of 1.56 miles from West Stewartstown to Beecher Falls, Vermont. He was president of this road, too. It was opened in September, 1888, was leased to the Upper Coos of New Hampshire from November, 1888 to March, 1890, and then was leased to the Maine Central, which purchased it on January 21, 1932.

A railroad president had certain fringe benefits. For instance, George got free passes for all the other roads in the country to whose head men he sent courtesy cards, for such was the custom in those good old days. Ave Henry, with his East Branch and Lincoln Railroad down in Lincoln, did the same thing, and it is recorded that one or two main-line moguls were somewhat astonished when, vacationing in the White Mountains, they thought to avail themselves of a free ride on President Henry's road.

But meanwhile Van Dyke was busy building still another extension of his Upper Coos Railroad, northward from Beecher Falls into Canada. This was known as the Hereford Railroad, and he was president of that, too. As a canny lumber king who owned not only the whole north end of New Hampshire, but also much good timberland in adjacent Hereford, Quebec, he persuaded Canadian interests to build a new line south to join his Hereford road. This eventually saved him many miles of difficult toting when he built his great depot camp on Indian Stream, for he used Malvina, Quebec, on the railroad, as his jumping-off place. Ed LaCroix did the same thing thirty-five years later.

Being in the railroad business earned for Van Dyke the distinction of being the first, and probably the only, private individual in the United States to call out the militia. Furthermore, with a fine disregard of protocol and international law, he marched them into a foreign country and had them put down a riot. It happened this way: He had hired a New York City contractor to build the right-of-way for his Hereford Railroad. The contractor assembled from New York and Montreal a gang of five hundred Italians whom he paid a dollar a day along with beer and pizza to come and live in tents and fight mosquitoes as they plied their picks and shovels.

September 22, 1888, the contractor absconded with the pay-roll. The irate section-hands tore up two miles of track already laid, dilapidated company property, and threatened President Van Dyke, who had dropped by just to see that nobody was loafing, with great bodily harm.

George waved his arms and promised them justice would be done, and then, muttering great oaths in his walrus moustache, he hastened to Beecher Falls, whence he dispatched a telegram to the head man of the state guard in Lancaster, New Hampshire, ordering him to open up the armory there, summon his men and distribute rifles and ammunition, and proceed north to the scene of the disturbance.

It speaks volumes for the old pirate's authority that nobody questioned his right to issue such an order. The *Vermont Journal* of September 29, 1888, reports the incident as follows:

The 500 Italian laborers employed on the extension of the Upper Coos railroad between West Stewartstown, N. H., and the Canada line, went on strike Tuesday, on account, it is reported, of not receiving some two months' back pay through the failure or absconding of the contractor. At daylight Wednesday morning, the strikers had about two miles of roadbed torn up, and were fast making their way toward Canaan, Vermont. President George Van Dyke telegraphed to Lancaster Wednesday afternoon for Grand Army Post's rifles which were sent with plenty of ammunition by special train. The outcome of the affair is awaited with anxiety, as it is an unusual thing for private citizens to arm and equip a force of men to put down an insurrection.

Most of the papers didn't even bother to report it. A little incident like that in the lively career of George Van Dyke was just too commonplace, apparently.

At any rate, the war went on for some time, the Dominion of Canada mobilized several battalions to quell the predatory strikers, pitched battles involving firearms and bloodshed took place, two Italians were severely wounded, and then the rioters quailed. Like rabbits they took to the woods, and never stopped until they reached Coaticook, sixteen miles away.

One thing could be said for old George: it was never "Go, boys!" with him, but always "Come on, boys!" He was right in there leading his men. Of course, he claimed that the railroad company was in no sense responsible for the acts of the sub-contractors, whose failure to meet their obligations was the cause of the trouble.

J. Roy Lewis, of Holyoke, whose uncle was treasurer of the C.V.L., recalls sitting on the bank of the river at French King rock, a great boulder in the river near Turners Falls, where bad jams were wont to form. With him were his uncle and Van Dyke, watching one of the foremen vainly trying to break a jam out in the stream. Van Dyke, says Lewis, watched for a few minutes, and then started out onto the jam himself. "In an unbelievably short time the jam was on its way down the river."

After he reached maturity, George became friendly with an old-maid schoolteacher in Colebrook, who took an interest in him, and it is said, gave him a good deal of valuable advice in the choice and conduct of his enterprises. The great lumber king of New England, besides being president of the C.V.L., a railroad president, and a bank president, was also president of the Moose River Lumber Company in Lowellton, Maine, and of the Brompton Paper Company, in Quebec, and was a director or trustee of various other banks and enterprises. He was too busy to go into politics, although he was a presidential elector in 1888. In politics he was a Democrat, and in religion a Universalist. His greatest weakness was stock-market gambling. They say he went broke twice from indulging in that pastime, but the North Country forests were always there to help him recoup his losses.

For many years the headquarters of the C.R.L. was at Bloomfield, Vermont, where the Nulhegan joins the Connecticut, just across the river from North Stratford. From this vantage point, Van Dyke slashed off the pine and spruce on the many branches of the Nulhegan and the vast basin drained by Paul Stream, though at the same time he was constantly logging all over the country farther north on both sides of the Connecticut and even over on the Diamonds. Some of this logging he did on C.R.L. lands, some of it in partnership with characters as rusty as himself, old Hub Hall, for instance, and some of it by himself.

He had two brothers, Tom and Philo, whom he took under his wing and made his partners, so to speak. Tom lived in Hereford, where he was a power among the Canucks, while Philo dwelt at McIndoes and managed the big mill there. All the brothers blithely engaged in private undertakings, often at company expense—and sometimes even at each others'. Here is a typical incident:

There were some scattered timber lots on the Connecticut watershed, up near the Nash Stream height-of-land. Some belonged to George and some to Tom. In the winter of 1907, Al Jordan was cutting and landing logs on the Connecticut. George, who passed by there very frequently in his cutter, saw the operation and became curious at once. He had his driver turn right up Al's two-sled road, and when he saw where those logs were coming from, he proceeded to give Jordan hell. It turned out that Tom had hired Jordan to cut and land the logs, but the lot from which they were cut belonged to George.

By the time Jordan had got through explaining the kind of deal he had made with Tom, George had cooled down, and his foxy mind perceived a chance to make a dollar. He told Jordan to go ahead and finish his cutting, but to have Tom pay him each week as fast as the logs were landed, and to keep his mouth shut until it was all settled.

The skulduggery went along well until one day Tom telephoned in to Will Fuller, who had charge at the company office, to send a scaler upriver to scale those logs (which Tom expected to sell to the C.V.L.), for Tom had heard that the rivermen were going up to break out the landings the next day. Naturally, Tom wanted a better scale than his own scaler had given Al Jordan. But George, who was the big boss, had told Fuller the story, and now the latter refused to send up a scaler.

Bill Smart was walking-boss on the drive that spring, and he got a call from Fuller to get those logs afloat on the jump. When Tom got the word, he came down from Hereford, a-snorting and a-puffing, but brother George appeared at the same time. The rivermen kept on breaking out the landings, and the two brothers, after loud arguments, went away. George kept saying, "They're my logs!" while Tom's argument was, "Why didn't you have your lot staked out so a man could tell it was yours?" But George had a good answer: when he had questioned Al Jordan in the winter, Al had told him that Tom had given him a blueprint with the lot marked upon which he was to cut, and George had had Will Fuller check the lot number. The last word the rivermen heard between them was George threatening to sue Tom for cutting on his (George's) land.

Al Jordan claimed he was paid by Tom, and it was an evident fact that George got all the logs. Afterward, Will Fuller asserted that no record of Tom's being paid for cutting and landing the logs ever showed up at the office.

In 1902 the company moved its head office to First Connecticut Lake, where a big sawmill had been erected. That year the firm changed its name to the Connecticut Valley Lumber Company, and the name of the C.V.L. still dwells nostalgically in the memories of the old people of the region.

In 1908 the brokerage firm of Hornblower & Weeks floated a three-million-dollar bond issue for the C.V.L., two-thirds of which was bought by Van Dyke himself. In the prospectus that the brokers put out to encourage buyers it was stated that the company owned merchantable timber on the upper Connecticut worth twenty million dollars.

In the years after Van Dyke was killed in 1909, the ownership of the C.V.L. changed, but the old name was retained until 1927.

George was a forthright, violent man, a tremendous worker, an awful swearer, and a lover of good horse-flesh. He kept sixty blooded steeds in his private stable in Canaan, Vermont, across the river from the company office, and he had a private race track behind the old Canaan House. Some of his horses were consistent money-winners and were well known all over New England. One was a pacer named Frank Bogash. Another was a trotter, Early Bird, while another, Early Bird, Jr., had a mark of 2:10.

Van Dyke was well known to traveling men and horsemen in Boston, where he lived after 1902, and was popular among wool and leather men. The tragedy of his death cast a gloom over a host of friends.

But before everything else, George Van Dyke was a logger and a riverman. His motto was, Get out the logs! no matter what the cost, and he got 'em out. High water won't wait for protocol, and George didn't care a damn about the rights of other people when it came to driving logs, to say nothing of cutting them. He was involved in countless lawsuits for timber trespass (cutting on other people's land) and for the destruction of other people's property along the whole four hundred miles of the Connecticut River. Usually he won; sometimes he lost; often he was instituting lawsuits of his own, like the one in 1903 for $300,000 against the Grand Trunk. As his obituary in the Coos County *Democrat* modestly put it, "His business methods have not always been commended. . . ." Attorney Irving Drew was his close friend and his lawyer, and Drew earned his pay. What a pity that all the Van Dyke files were thrown out some years ago by the firm that succeeded Drew and Company!

George won many suits against him by using delaying tactics. His lawyer would use every trick in the book to keep a case from coming to trial, and if the judgment was adverse, would often appeal it. These tactics wore out numerous farmers whose damages were less costly than their expenses as litigants. But delays didn't always work to Van Dyke's advantage. In 1897 his log drive took out the Boston and Maine railroad bridge across the Connecticut at Windsor, Vermont. The railroad sued, but it was not until nine years later that the case was finally settled in its favor.

Bill James, of Windsor, recollects that when he was a very young man he went to work for the C.V.L. A salesman had inveigled George into buying a new snub-nosed type of motorboat, telling him it was just the thing for the drive, and the great man was showing it off to a couple of friends on the Connecticut, just below the mouth of the Nulhegan. The boat, however, could not make headway against the strong current of the Nulhegan as it poured into the main river, and George lost his temper.

He put the two passengers ashore and ordered James, who was standing on the bank, to jump into the boat with him. Then he pushed off into the river. He ordered the lad to start the motor, but he couldn't. Swearing impatiently, George made his way aft and bent over the motor. But he slipped and broke two ribs. He had not bothered to provide himself with oars, and now neither of them could start the damned thing. They drifted rapidly downstream until they came to the so-called Diamond Bridge and brought up against a pier.

A farmer was spreading manure in a field beside the bridge. He saw the frantic gestures of the marooned men, and came over. He got a rope and lowered it from the bridge. James tied it under the lumber king's arms and around his chest, and the stricken man was pulled aloft like a bag of beans. They laid him flat in the manure-spreader and away they went, jolting across the field at full gallop. George went to the hospital, but in less than a week he was out again, his ribs taped up, taking charge as usual.

The average size of Van Dyke's spring drive on the Connecticut was about fifty million feet. Low water could, and sometimes did, hang it up for two years. High water could, and often did, hurl hundreds of great logs up onto farmers' meadows, whence the rivermen, with teams of horses, hauled them back into the current. This damaged the meadows.

Van Dyke, of course, promised to pay, but never did. So the next season the enraged farmers would meet the rivermen, ready to fight. Nothing pleased the rivermen more. While some of them engaged the rustics in battle, other members of the crew would quickly rustle the stranded logs back into the water.

Sometimes the angry farmers would come out armed with shotguns. On such occasions, Van Dyke usually paid. Sometimes, a farmer would arrive with a sheriff. This is what happened in the famous Craggie case in Groveton, New Hampshire. A sudden freshet had washed a great number of logs onto Craggie's meadow, where of course they could not legally be touched without the farmer's consent. It was a time for speed. Some fifty rivermen with cant-dogs and teams of horses quickly began dragging the logs into the river. At this point appeared the farmer with a sheriff, and Van Dyke noticed that the men had stopped work and were waiting to see what would happen. He shouted to them, "Why are you standing around there like Stoughton bottles? Roll those logs in, and if those two say anything, roll them in, too!"

And in they went! As the lumber king once remarked, a good part of his time was consumed in throwing sheriffs into the river, and the remark contained more truth than poetry.

In the spring of 1897 the drive headed down to the mill at Mt. Tom. In June there came a sudden rise of six feet of water over the dam at Holyoke, just below Mt. Tom, and with the river swollen clear to the north the van of the drive came tearing down the Connecticut. The logs were not expected at that early date, and there was no boom swung except at Holyoke. This boom held for a considerable time, but the wild rush of logs piled up on it and it gave way in one or two places. Before the breaks occurred, Van Dyke, who had been notified at his Boston office, came on. The logs were sweeping over the dam, and it looked as if they all might go down into Long Island Sound—as, indeed, a lot of them did. As a large number of rivermen and interested spectators stood on the railroad track above the dam watching the turbulent scene, suddenly a bateau manned by six oarsmen shoved its nose through the bushes below the "island," the point of land on which the company's sawmill stood.

Standing in the back of the bateau, balancing with all the skill of the old river-hog, stood Van Dyke himself, his arms outstretched, directing the battle of the boom. The boat drew so close to the dam that it seemed they must go over—but not those men, not with that pilot! They swung just at the right time and came around the island and headed for the shore. The spectators stood open-mouthed. Van Dyke was always a distinguished-looking pirate, and when he was in action he was completely oblivious to appearances.

There were about a hundred log-drivers on the Boston and Maine

tracks, "bulling," as the expression went, and announcing in loud and profane language that they would be damned if they would go out onto that
break, and that Van Dyke could do various things with his old drive.
Floating at the shore was a frail, box-like boat full of boys. It was nothing
but a collection of boards nailed together. The bateau got as close to the
shore as it could, and George stepped out of it into the floating box.
When his large and massive frame hopped aboard, the boat looked as if it
would surely capsize, but he jumped from it to the shore in one agile leap
and came tearing up the bank.

In blistering language he bade the unwilling rivermen follow him,
and practically without knowing what they did, they went up the track
like sheep. Out into the water he went, up to his waist, followed by the
men, and in a miraculous hour of time they closed the boom. From then
on not a log passed the Holyoke dam.

Reporting the foregoing incident on Friday, June 18, 1897, the
Brattleboro (Vermont) *Phoenix* described what happened next: "Three
boats with 18 men [rivermen from Holyoke] were on their way to build
a boom in Hartford, and the second boat was capsized in attempting to
'shoot' the fishway at the Enfield dam and two logmen were drowned.
Three others clung to the boat and were rescued [on the preceding Sat-
urday]." But they swung a boom across the river before the logs reached
Hartford. To take care of the logs, the company set up a large portable
mill at Hartford, and C. H. Schuster, who had been plant manager of the
Mt. Tom mill since 1892, went weekly to Hartford to pay to loggers and
millmen.

This boom broke, too, and many logs drifted down into Long Island
Sound. Van Dyke offered a dime per log for all logs salvaged and landed
on the shore of the Sound near the mouth of the river, and the fishing
schooners did salvage a great many. They were eventually all towed back
up the river to the mill at Hartford.

But while the fishing boats and other craft were collecting the logs,
it was necessary for drivers to work with them and help them make tem-
porary booms in which to tow the logs they picked up. The salvaged
logs were then held in a boom at the mouth of the river. This meant that
the drivers had to get out onto logs in water to which they were not
accustomed.

The long river drive had left their boot calks pretty well worn down
and the boots in rather poor shape to make carding a log very comfortable. This brought on an argument with Van Dyke. He maintained that
they didn't need new boots, and at first refused to send for and pay for
them, but as Bill Daley (one of the drivers) put it in his unpolished but
expressive way, "We had old George by the nuts, and we applied the
pressure."

It was also necessary to have Will Fuller send down some rafting rigging with which to build small "plug" booms for towing the small bunches of logs into the main boom; this could by done only by rivermen. And in the water around the sound it took damn good men to do it.

When it came time to settle up, George claimed that it was up to the rivermen to provide their own boots, but the rivermen retorted that they hadn't planned on taking the drive to Europe, and they threatened to get a lawyer. George couldn't bulldoze labor in Connecticut the way he could in Vermont, and he finally paid.

That Van Dyke cheated his men flagrantly is a fact; that he yowled like a cut tom-cat when he had to spend a few unexpected dollars is a fact; that he ran rough-shod over the farmers is likewise true. But it is also true that when a former employee showed up in Boston, sick or broke, and needed funds to get back to North Stratford, he knew that George was always good for a touch.

But there are also quite different stories about the old lumber king. When Bill James was sixteen years old, he came down on the drive, and like the other men he was paid off at Mt. Tom—$335. Instead of taking the train back to North Stratford, he returned by road, bringing back some of the horses. The temptations at North Stratford were various, and in no time he was broke, without even enough money to buy himself clothes to get back into the woods for the summer. The episode made an impression on him, and he swore, as rivermen often did, that it would not happen again.

The next year Van Dyke was present at Mt. Tom when the men were being paid off, and told the paymaster not to pay young James. He told him to return to North Stratford just as he had the year before, back over the road with the horses. Bill did so, but when he arrived up north he went into the paymaster's office and demanded his pay, which again amounted to $335. By that time Van Dyke had returned to that end of the country, and again was present. He told the paymaster to give Bill $35, and have him sign a receipt for it, and he told Bill to go to Berlin and have his fling and then come back and go to work for the summer in the woods.

Bill didn't have much education, and didn't know what to do, but he refused to sign the receipt and went to see J. C. Hutchins, North Stratford's most considerable businessman, for advice. Hutchins told him to sign the paper for the $35, and to come back and see him if any trouble resulted, and he would take care of it. Bill went back to the paymaster again and had some more arguments, as he wanted the entire amount, but Van Dyke was adamant, would give him only $35 for the Berlin fling. He again went to Hutchins, and again back to Van Dyke, and finally signed the receipt for the $35.

When they handed him the money they also handed him a bankbook showing an entry for $300. Van Dyke said, "Now look here, young fellow, here is a bankbook with your money in it; if you are sick or need money you have some in the bank to pay with, but under no circumstances ever draw out the last dollar. To get a crop of potatoes you have to have seed to put in the ground to start with, so listen to me."

From that time on, Bill never did draw out the last dollar, and in later years asserted that whatever he had was based on the old lumber king's advice. Incidentally, although Bill after his retirement became the Windsor cemetery caretaker and grave digger, he did that only to have something to do, since by then he owned several apartment houses in Windsor, supplying a comfortable income.

Dorothy Hall Leavitt, of Norwich, Vermont, also tells a revealing story about Van Dyke:

"My mother's name was Sally Drew and her grandfather was Irving W. Drew, a lawyer. George Van Dyke was a client and also a close friend and neighbor of my grandfather's. They lived on the same street in Lancaster, New Hampshire.

"When my mother was a small child she was very fond of Mr. Van Dyke and one day she climbed up in his lap, put her arms around his neck, and said, 'Mr. Van Dyke, when I'm fifteen, I'm going to marry you.'

"The old gentleman was very pleased and said, 'Sally, when you are fifteen, you will have a diamond ring for that.'

"When mother was fifteen and was in Boston with her parents, Mr. Van Dyke sent for her to come to his office. On his desk were two solitaire rings and she was asked to choose the one she liked best. She chose the smaller, more perfect stone (both were large diamonds), and he gave it to her then and there. Her parents naturally wouldn't let her wear the ring until she was older, when she used to flash it to her friends and pretend she was engaged. Later, she had the stone set in a pin."

Illustrative of Van Dyke's suavity, fast thinking, and ready wit, is another episode. He was planning to log the spruce off a mountain in Lemington, Vermont, and to land it on the Connecticut, and the best place for his two-sled road was right across an old, abandoned farm—that is, it *had* been abandoned. He sent a crew down to build camps, and to swamp roads; and the boss laid out the main road right across the fields of that farm, breaking down fences regardless.

The next day Van Dyke was sitting in his private office when a tall, lean, raw-boned gent with a handlebar moustache came busting in, herding the bookkeeper in front of him by the persuasion of a double-barreled shotgun.

"I t-t-told him not to come in, Mr. Van Dyke," stuttered the bookkeeper, whose name was Wayne Nichols, "but he—he's bloodthirsty. He said he'd blow a h-hole through me I c-could jump a goat through!"

"What in hell do you mean by such actions!" roared the lumber king, jumping up from his chair, but the stranger reached around the bookkeeper and poked his shotgun into George's belly, and the great man sat down again.

"I'm running this show!" said the man with the moustache, and the cocked hammers on that weapon of his were mightily convincing. "Now you shut up and listen to me. My name's Higgins, and I live down on the old Nugent farm in Lemington. I came up from Maine and bought that place a week ago, and it's mine! Yesterday your damn foreman came there and broke down my fences and laid out a road right across my fields! I told him to quit, and he said to come to you. Here I am! My neighbors told me what kind of a crooked old skinflint you are, but you won't put over any guff on me, Mr. Van Dyke! I came prepared!"

And with that he shook that old blunderbuss, both barrels of it cocked, in George's face.

But George didn't scare very easy. He said to him, "Why, Mr. Higgins, I'm sure we can fix this up all right. I didn't know you were living on the old Nugent place. My foreman didn't, either. If he had, I'm sure he wouldn't have acted that way."

"The hell he wouldn't!" growled Higgins, his eye never wavering.

"Have a cigar, Mr. Higgins," said Van Dyke, shoving up a boxful, "and sit down and we'll talk this over like gentlemen. Now, I don't want any trouble with you," he said, after Higgins had finally decided to take a cigar and sit down. "As you can see, it was a mistake, and I shall not only speak to my foreman [who was a moose of a man named Dave Dillman] but I'll make it right with you, Mr. Higgins. Nobody could do more than that, could they?"

By then the raw-boned gent from Maine was beginning to think he'd been barking up the wrong tree. He still kept the shotgun cocked, but he'd turned the muzzle away and was sitting there opposite Van Dyke puffing away on the best cigar he'd ever had in his mouth.

"So you've just bought that old Nugent place," said George, "and there, I supposed it was abandoned. I suppose the fences aren't in very good condition?"

"No," said Higgins, "they ain't. Next spring I figure I'll have to lay out a hundred dollars on fenceposts.

"H'm," said George, "that's quite a lot of money. Look here, Mr. Higgins," he said all at once, as if struck by a bright idea—as indeed he was—"you know I've got a cedar swamp up back of that mountain. Now you need fenceposts and I need a road. I'll tell you what—you let me use that road this winter and I'll *give* you all the cedar in that swamp. It isn't worth anything to me. I only want the spruce. What you don't need yourself, you can sell. How's that?"

Well, Higgins thought that was just dandy. He took another cigar and went home, thinking what a good, kind man Van Dyke was. He thought so until the next spring, when he went up to get his posts. He found a swamp all right—but there wasn't a cedar tree in it.

So for years George Van Dyke was the most potent force in the North Country, and the most potent force the whole length of the Connecticut. He accompanied the drive behind a pair of high-stepping matched black horses for years, but in 1904 he bought a Stanley Steamer automobile. To drive it he hired a likable young fellow named Fred "Shorty" Hodgdon, of North Stratford. Shorty was a mechanic and an electrician by trade, and in the next five years he drove Van Dyke sixty thousand miles in his red devil-wagon.

Very early one quiet Sunday morning, August 8, 1909, he drove him to his death, which was as dramatic as his life, and entirely fitting.

After Van Dyke became president of the C.R.L. he had an office in Boston, at 89 State Street, and he lived at Young's Hotel in Boston until 1908. Then he moved to the Lenox, though he still spent much time around Young's, which was handy to his State Street office and where he met many of his business associates. His summers he spent in Lancaster. In the year 1908 he was seriously ill with water on the brain, and was unconscious for nearly three months, but his robust constitution and his will power brought him through and he regained his old-time vigor. He told his friends with great glee that he "had fooled them," but he also complained, for the first time in memory, that he got no fun out of life with all his money, and that there was nothing in it for him but his work.

He loved the drive, and the drive of 1909, with 53,000,000 feet, was the biggest of his entire career. It was his last and biggest piece of work, and for two weeks he accompanied it, seeing that it went as it should. Often he was up from three in the morning until ten at night. When the drive should be finished, he said, he was going to take a rest. He never got to do it.

On this fateful Sunday morning, having spent the night at a hotel in Greenfield, Massachusetts, he got up at four o'clock and had Shorty drive him to the edge of a seventy-five-foot cliff overlooking the dam at Turners Falls, where his rivermen were sluicing the logs through. This high bank is at a place called Riverside, opposite Turners Falls, and is clearly visible today from the bridge across the Connecticut. It had always been a favorite place for Van Dyke, and for others, to watch the rivermen sluicing through the dam, being about fifty feet off the highway, and a few rods farther down the river than the dam.

George had sprained his ankle badly the week before while walking in the rocky river-bed at Bellows Falls, where the Russell Company had built a new dam, but he got out of the car and walked around, looking at the toiling men below, who looked up and saw their boss and his chauffeur and his red automobile, outlined boldly on the cliff edge, in the first rays of the rising sun.

For two hours they stayed there, and then Van Dyke got back into the car. What happened next, nobody will ever know, though there were spectators close by and the men down on the jam saw the whole thing. Some say he spoke sharply to the chauffeur, bidding him drive closer to the edge, and that Shorty, angry, deliberately drove over the brink. Others say that the chauffeur mistakenly put the car into forward gear instead of reverse (it was headed toward the river). Still others say (which sounds the most reasonable) that the accident was due to a mechanical defect in the car, which went forward when the gear-shift was moved into reverse. ("This defect," said one of the obituaries, "was found in safer localities in other early cars of the same make.")

At any rate, both the early-morning onlookers and the rivermen down below saw the car when it plunged. Van Dyke's famous cry when a riverman working on a jam fell into the water—"To hell with the man! Save the cant-dog!"—came back at him that quiet Sunday morning, for when the sluicers looked up and saw him bouncing down the rocks they cried, "To hell with the man! Save the matches!" Yet, just like the old man himself, who would rush forward to help the struggling riverman, so did they now rush forward to aid their stricken chief.

George had seen the danger as soon as the car started forward, and jumped out. He cleared the machine and his hat lodged in the bushes at the top of the cliff, but he struck so near the edge that he fell over after the automobile. The bank drops sheer for about forty-five feet and then there is a farther drop of about thirty feet at an angle of 45 degrees. The machine struck this rocky river-channel wall and then crashed down nose first onto the rocks on the dry river bottom. It then tipped bottom up, pinning the chauffeur under it so that he had to be pried out. Van Dyke struck the ground near the machine.

The chauffeur was badly hurt in the lower abdomen, his pelvis being crushed in. Shorty was so terribly injured that he seemed to feel no pain. "I'm as good as three men, yet," he told the men who picked him up. He died two hours later. He was a universal favorite with the loggers, and his last words were, "Tell the boys I said good-bye to them."

Van Dyke's injuries consisted of fractures of the right arm, left shoulder, and several ribs on the left side, a punctured lung from one of the broken ribs, two large scalp wounds, and dangerous internal injuries. Yet he stood up and gave directions to those who came to his aid, though he was in agony.

A doctor came immediately and administered stimulants and a potion to ease the pain, and both men were taken to the Farren Hospital in an ambulance. No manure-spreader this time. It seemed ironic that Van Dyke should die in the Farren Hospital. Barney Farren, who owned the water-power at Turner Falls, was outraged if some of the mills had to close when the drive came through, but the drive had the right of water wherever they sluiced logs, and in time of low water the mills had to shut down. Farren had fought the drive (in vain), and he and Van Dyke used to have terrific word battles.

It took an hour before the men were in the hospital. The doctors did all they could, but it wasn't much. Several times George told the people around him that whatever happened to him, the accident wasn't the chauffeur's fault. "Don't blame Shorty," he said.

"What do you think of my chances, Doc?" he asked Dr. P. F. Leary. The physician, who knew he had no chance at all, answered evasively, "Well, Mr. Van Dyke, it depends a good deal on your courage."

"Hell!" said the old pirate, "I've always had too much of that!"

At five-thirty that afternoon he died.

25

Pulpwood and Paper

THE old way of lumbering was passing by 1900, driven out by the demand for pulpwood and by power companies wanting to control watersheds. Steamboats, motorboats, railroads, and gravel trucking roads turned the formerly inaccessible places in the woods into public highways and swept away the old industry with all its tools and retainers.

It didn't happen all at once. The last saw-log was rolled into the upper Connecticut in 1915, but there were log drives on the Kennebec and the Androscoggin until 1930, and on the Penobscot until 1933. Even in 1966 there is still one spring drive of long logs left—by the St. Regis Paper Company on the East Machias river, in Maine—while the Irving Pulp and Paper Company frequently has quite a large drive on the St. John. In 1964 it consisted of 25,00,000 feet.

But today even the four foot pulpwood drives are mostly a thing of the past. The Brown Company had their last one on the Androscoggin in 1963, and if you want to buy a bateau or a tow-boat cheap, just apply to that firm. The International Paper Company, the biggest paper company in the world, once operated mills all over New England, but it has got rid of all but three of them and moved south, where trees grow faster and labor is cheaper. The Great Northern still drives some of its wood down the West Branch of the Penobscot, but taken all together in the Northeast, only 13 per cent of the pulpwood volume is transported to the mills by river drive. Trucks and railroads account for the rest.

At first, pulpwood was cut and driven to the mills in the form of long logs. It was on the Kennebec that, for the first time, some of it was cut into four-foot bolts at the landings and driven down mixed with the long logs. This practice caused the rivermen to swear most sulphurously, for they were always, without thinking, stepping onto a four-foot stick, and of course they then promptly fell into the river. But by 1918 all the pulpwood cut in New England was being driven in four-foot lengths.

Many old-time rivermen hated the small stuff, and retired in low dudgeon to other kinds of labor, asserting contemptuously that it was all right for "Polacks" to bear-hug wood out of the brush, but no self-respecting riverman was a shitpoke to go wading into the bushes hunting for stovewood.

In this connection it is interesting to note that, though long-log drives are mostly a thing of the past, yet on December 6, 1965, the St. Croix Paper Company commenced hauling tree-length logs to their mill by truck, and they intend to convert gradually but completely from the four-foot to long logs.

For many years after 1912, when pulpwood first outstripped saw-logs in annual cut, there wasn't much difference in the lumberjack's life and methods of production except that the axe gave way to the bucksaw, and the sweating, fly-plagued pulpwood-cutter would often spend his summers peeling bark with a spud. Peeled wood is cleaner, lighter, drier, and therefore easier to transport than wood with the bark on it. So it is worth about ten dollars a cord more than rough wood.

Until about 1897 all the falling of trees in the lumber woods of northern New England was done with an axe. At that time the two-man cross-cut saw was greatly improved by the addition of the raker tooth, which cleans out sawdust. From then until about 1915, practically all woodsmen used the raker-tooth cross-cut saw for falling and cutting up trees.

About that time, the raker tooth was added to the one-man bucksaw, enabling one man to cut as fast as two with a cross-cut. From 1915 to about 1945 practically all pulpwood sawing was done with a one-man bucksaw. Then the two-man power chain-saw was put into use, but it never became very popular. This was followed shortly by the one-man power chain-saw, which is now used almost entirely.

So the trees were cut down, the trees were cut up, they were driven in the spring down the rivers to the mills, they were hauled out of the water by "pulp-haulers" into mountains twenty or thirty thousand cords high, where they might stay a year, be covered with ice and snow and freeze solid, and have to be blown apart by dynamite when needed at the mill.

The old whine and snarl of the saws gave way to the stink of sulphur, smellable seven miles away on a clear night, and thousands of acres of softwood were cut every year to provide the American people with their Sunday funnies.

This situation in the lumber business lasted until the 1920's, when someone discovered how to make paper pulp out of hardwood. Until then, in New England, the demand for hardwood had been limited to a few furniture mills, toothpick factories, and other not very voracious enterprises; the hardwood forests had been fairly safe from the lumberman's axe ever since the potash industry had abandoned wood for chemicals.

The early lumbermen went into the woods and cut, but they cut only pine, later spruce, and they cut only down to a certain diameter—say, a twelve-inch top. That left plenty of trees a-growing, and the loggers could go back thirty years later and make another season's cut.

The pulpwood people, whatever their theory, took the softwood down to a much smaller diameter, but even they left the hardwood—first, because they didn't know it would make paper, and second, because hardwood will sink unless buoyed up by softwood floaters, and river-driving was the only means of gettitng it out of the woods.

But along with the discovery that hardwood makes splendid paper, came the era of the gasoline truck and the diesel log-hauler; then World War II came along, making the government mighty prodigal in handing out money to build "necessary" truck roads; and then, finally, came the chain-saw.

This remarkable tool—in effect a one-man cross-cut saw run by a gasoline motor—had been used as early as 1924, but at first it did not catch on. However, constant improvements were made, and after 1940 it entirely replaced the old cross-cut saw and the bucksaw. It operates on gasoline; it is noisier than a circus calliope; it cuts off fingers and feet quite handily; like the old Lombard log-hauler it tends to break down, so that at least two are needed on hand to keep one going; but you arm a good man with one and he can mow down more acres of timber in a season than you would willingly believe. And he *does* mow them down, literally.

When lumberjacks, previously working for day-wages, shifted to "piece" work—i.e., payment by the cord for cutting four-foot pulpwood—they earned about $1.25 per day. In the week of September 12, 1965, a Canuck woodsman named Marc Larochelle, working for the Great Northern near Moosehead Lake, put up 36.91 cords in forty-five hours and earned $243.46. But after he had paid his social-security tax, his dog tax, his cigarette tax, his gasoline tax (state and federal), his excise tax, his union dues, his board bill, and a few dozen other deductions, one wonders if he had much more left than did the underpaid wage-slave of 1898.

For years the companies established the camps and hired and paid the men. Nowadays they "job" out the season's cut: they hire various men in whom they have confidence to cut and "land" the number of cords they figure they will need. Such men may contract to cut from a thousand to a hundred thousand cords of wood, and they prefer the more grandiloquent title of "contractor" to that of "jobber," just as today a janitor is yclept a "custodian" and an elevator boy is a "building engineer." These contractors in turn let out parts of their contract to lesser jobbers. It is a curious fact that a jobber can cut and land wood, and drive it, too, more cheaply than a big company can. The company of course helps the contractors and jobbers with equipment or even loans.

An interesting example of jobbing was Ed Lacroix's operation on Indian Stream, in Pittsburg, New Hampshire between 1924 and 1929. Up there, A. N. Blandin, an enterprising lumberman from Bath, New Hampshire, bought 200,000 cords of softwod stumpage from the C.V.L. for $6 a cord, and sold part of it to the International Paper Company and part of it to the Mt. Tom Sulphite Company, for $20 a cord.

Lacroix cut for three years, and then his brother-in-law, Beloni Poulin, cut the last two. Lacroix also drove the wood the first year, though after that Blandin did the driving, with Roaring Bert Ingersoll as drive boss.

Blandin paid Lacroix $6 a cord for cutting and landing on the Stream, and $1 a cord for driving. If figures don't lie, as middleman he must have cleared a right tidy sum on the deal.

The International Paper Company took out their wood at South Lancaster (Mount Orne), New Hampshire, and at Wilder, Vermont. The Mt. Tom wood was taken out at McIndoes Falls, Vermont, and loaded on cars.

Just in passing, it is noteworthy that other people mentioned in this book participated in this undertaking. The C.V.L. had scalers under 'Phonse Roby; the International Paper Company had check scalers under Charles Langley; and Blandin had as checkers Wayne Nichols, formerly George Van Dyke's bookkeeper, who died in Florida in 1964, and 'Phonse's brother Charles, who had bossed the Nulhegan drive in 1908.

As might be expected with all those expert and zealous scalers there was considerable friction. Especially over the proper way to scale saprotten wood.

The stumpage was paid on the scale made by the C.V.L. scalers on the banks of the streams. The selling scale to the International Paper Company was made by the count of the sticks taken from the river. The amount was arrived at by measuring four test cords daily, piled on a cord rack, the quality of the wood determining how many logs were needed to make a cord of sound lumber. The settling scale to Mt. Tom was a car scale made at the mill.

Those were the last drives taken down the Connecticut River below South Lancaster. The next year the New England Power Company built a big dam at Mulliken's Pitch at the foot of the Fifteen-Mile Falls and forgot to put in a log sluice. . . .

One change the four-foot logs brought about was in the construction of sleds, for such wood was loaded transversely and therefore required a different kind of sled for hauling. The Canadian jobbers were fond of using a one-horse rig. Two-horse drays and two-horse double-sleds were also used. Some fantastic loads were drawn from Lyman Brook, New Hampshire, by the Odell Manufacturing Company, but the biggest load of pulpwood ever brought out of the woods by two horses was drawn from Venture Brook, near Dennysville, Maine, to Great Works Landing, in March, 1923.

The record load was the result of a bet between two camps at the Venture Brook operation. Two rigs were specially built for the contest, with Jim Lyons the driver of one, and Willard Jones of the other. It developed that Lyons was the better teamster. The other load, though larger and drawn by a better pair of horses, tipped over going around a curve, which proved to all those present that Jones was not so good a teamster as Lyons. The sled was thirty-two feet, or four cords long, inside of twelve-foot stakes. The scaler of the Warren Paper Company at Cumberland Mills measured the load and found that owing to a spreading of the stakes the load consisted of twelve cords and three feet, or twenty-three tons. At any rate, it was a notable feat of loading and teaming.

Many new inventions in the paper-making and pulpwood industries are constantly appearing, all aimed at reducing work and increasing production. In the old days everything was done by main strength and ignorance, but at least, as in the case of the rival teamsters, there was always a chance for individual effort and excellence.

Mechanical gadgets have taken most of the work out of pulping, but they have also made it pretty humdrum. Today, instead of picaroons and pulp-hooks and elbow grease, motorized cranes are used to load wood onto trucks, and bulldozers push it from where it is piled on a riverbank into the stream. In 1935, two men threw 139 cords of wood into the Musquacook River in one working day. In 1966 one can hardly hire two men to throw (by hand) one cord into any river.

The old spud is being replaced by a chemical debarker, and as a matter of sober fact it is hard to find men who are willing to peel bark at any price.

The price of pulpwood varies according to supply and demand. In 1966 it is about $23 delivered at the mill. It may vary from $15 to $25 a cord, according to quality, with $10 added for peeled wood. The cutter himself gets about $6.50 a cord, cut and "yarded," that is, drawn to a road that can be reached by a truck. For "stumpwood," that is, wood merely cut and piled but not yarded, he gets $1 less.

The nefarious custom of paying by time slips (which the woodsman short of money was often willing to cash at a discount) was formerly used by smart but immoral camp clerks to fatten their own pocketbooks. And dishonest small jobbers used to cheat their men in numerous small ways. But of later years, with government doles, unions, and other factors, woods help has become scarcer and harder to get, and jobbers have become more honest.

The whole system of employing French-Canadian woodsmen from

across the border merits a book by itself. Suffice it here to say that the
sages in Washington in 1966 passed a decree making it much more difficult for Canadians to come into the United States, and various lumber
company managers and jobbers tell me that they cannot currently get
enough help to cut the wood they need.

An interesting note in the Bangor (Maine) *News* of October 30,
1935, shows that the problem is not new. It seems that two weeks earlier a
band of ten immigration-service agents had been beaten up and off by
husky woodsmen they had attempted to arrest as illegal entrants. Mad as
hornets, the band of ten made strong representations to their district
supervisor, who carried their story right up to headquarters.

Evidently the prestige of the department was at stake. In great se-
crecy the biggest band of immigration agents ever gathered at any one
spot, unless at a banquet, assembled from four states, and moved stealthily
against their foe. Fifty miles from the border town of Jackman, deep in
the woods, the intrepid agents "underwent great hardships"—walking fifteen miles to the logging camps—but their dander was up, and corns or no
corns, they walked. At two A.M. the solemn hoot of an owl, and glances
at well-synchronized watches, marked the time for attack. One hundred
and two strong they irrupted into the snory ram-pastures and in the
Name of the Law arrested forty sleepy criminals and brought them in triumph out to Jackman. Three trucks carted the outlaws away to stand
trial in Bangor.

Thus is justice attained and wisdom rewarded.

It is true that the old-time lumber barons often cheated their men
flagrantly on pay-day—which came only in the spring, when the men
came out of the woods just before the start of the spring drive, r'arin' to
go, and lined up at the company office to get their pay. Typical is a
famous story about J. E. Henry: A man came along in the line to the pay-
window. "Ten dollars deducted for tobacco you bought in the wangan
last winter," Ave told him.

"But Mr. Henry," protested the man, "I never use tobacco. Ask any
of the men. They'll tell you."

"Can't help it," retorted Ave. "It was there for you if you'd wanted
it. Next man!"

One laborer did get the better of J. E. He was a hard-hat man who
had been shipped up from Boston. When Ave interviewed him and
learned that he was inexpert in every kind of woods work, he grimly
bade him to "count the ties from here to Boston." Obediently the man
walked out and did literally what he had been ordered to do. In due time
he reported back, with the number of ties. Ave checked with the railroad
and found that the man was approximately right, so he paid him for his
time.

The Great Northern Paper Company has always had a fine reputation for paying its help. Perhaps that is because for its first thirty years the man in charge of woods operations was Fred Gilbert, himself a former woodsman. It was, I think, the first firm that ever paid the men in cash, rather than time slips—and whenever they wanted it. "Every night, cash on the barrel-head, if they ask for it," decreed Gilbert. And except for one exceptional moment on June 11, 1946, when a former employee went to Boston and shot Mr. Whitcomb, the president of the company, dead, in his palatial office on Devonshire Street, the company has always enjoyed the best of relations with its help.

Pulping is big business in New Hampshire; it is no small business in Vermont; it supports a great many mill workers in Massachusetts; and it is the primary business in Maine, where nearly every county in the state has either a pulp or a paper mill, or both. The reason for the multiplication of mills in Maine is of course the presence of ideal conditions—an abundance of accessible raw material, cheap ground pulp, low-cost transportation, enormous water-power, great networks of waterways, and good rail and tidewater shipping points.

The first paper mill in the United States was built in Philadelphia in 1690. The first one in Maine was built in 1735, at Portland, but of course it was operated entirely by hand and used only rags. There was a mill at Fair Haven, Vermont, making wrapping-paper from basswood bark as early as 1796. But by and large prior to 1840 the sources for paper manufacture were limited to rags and straw. The first mention of the possibility of making paper from wood was by a French naturalist in the eighteenth century (he got the idea from watching wasps make their nests from chewed wood), but not until about 1840 did a German inventor find a way of grinding wood pulp, which, a generation later, was to completely revolutionize the paper industry. It is interesting to note that before the Civil War, and for some years after it, most of the newsprint and book paper in this country was made from straw. Special inducements were offered to farmers to raise oats and rye to supply this straw.

Ground wood pulp made its first appearance in America in March, 1867, at Curtisville, near Stockbridge, Massachusetts. It was obtained by a process in which poplar logs were held against a grindstone. Today, almost any kind of wood is used, but the proportions in which the various kinds are mixed must be carefully controlled, and experience has shown that some are better suited to make certain sorts of paper (there are five thousand sorts of paper being manufactured) than others. The long-fibered spruce, for example, makes better high-grade bond paper than does poplar.

Incidentally, here is an unusual news item from the Woodsville (New Hampshire) *News* of May 3, 1901: "To see how quickly a spruce log in the wilds of Upper Magalloway River, in Maine, a short distance this side of Parmachenee Lake, could be made into paper and placed into the hands of newsboys in Boston and New York was recently tried in Berlin. The tree was cut and marked, carefully watched until it came to the pulp mill, and then to the paper mill and then was carefully marked and speedily placed on the rollers of the great dailies, and being sold on the street three days after it was cut by the chopper, fifty miles above Errol dam on the Androscoggin River. A most remarkable and unheard of transaction."

There exist four kinds of pulp processes: grinding or mechanical, sulphite, soda, and sulphate.

In the mechanical process of making pulp, a debarked piece of wood is held laterally under a plentiful supply of water against rapidly revolving grindstones. These stones tear apart the wood fibers and produce a finely divided mass of wood pulp which after screening is suitable largely for newsprint paper.

In the sulphite process, wood is mechanically chipped and then cooked in a "digester" for several hours by steam under pressure, in a liquor of bisulphite of lime and sulphurous acid. The chemicals dissolve out of the wood everything except the cellulose, which is the true wood fiber. After washing and screening there remains the sulphite pulp.

In the soda process, the wood is mechanically chipped and then cooked in digesters with a caustic-soda liquor.

The sulphate process is much the same as the soda process except that the cooking liquor is sodium sulphate instead of sodium carbonate.

Ground wood pulp commercially produced in Maine in 1868 sold for seven cents a pound. Sixty years later it was worth a cent a pound. In 1966 it is selling for twenty-five cents. It takes one cord of pulpwood to make one ton of ground wood, and newsprint sells today for about $140 a ton. In 1930 the price was $50 a ton, says Austin H. Wilkins, in whose useful little book *The Forests of Maine* much of the above information can be found.

The great newspaper combines and the great paper companies are pretty closely connected. From time to time the cartels are "investigated" by Congress, but nothing is ever done about them. When the Depression hit hard, back in the early 1930's, practically every paper company in Ontario went bankrupt, and practically every paper company in the United States was at least close to bankruptcy.

In Congressman Emanuel Celler's report *Monopoly Power* (p. 518) we read:

Exhibit N-217
Hearst Newsprint Creditors

By the latter part of 1939 the Hearst newsprint enterprises were in financial difficulties. Among their debts were amounts in the neighborhood of $10,000,000 owed to newsprint suppliers for newsprint purchased. These suppliers included International Paper Co., International Paper Sales Co. Inc., and from time to time one or more of the Canadian companies referred to in the final paragraph of your letter.

In order to protect their respective interests as creditors, these newsprint suppliers engaged Mr. Wilbert H. Howard, K.C., of Montreal, and P. S. Ross & Sons, chartered accountants, also of Montreal, to advise and assist them.

Frequent meetings of the creditors' group were held to consider the current and prospective financial condition of the Hearst companies and the obtaining of security for the suppliers' claims and, in general, to keep in close touch with the situation.

The one hope of ultimate payment was to keep the Hearst publications going, and this necessitated provision of, and payment of security for, current newsprint supplies. The Hearst companies looked for such supplies to the newsprint creditors and it was in the latter's interest to see that they were provided. The Hearst companies purchased their newsprint during this period on a month-to-month basis offering a percentage of the business in the first instance to each of the creditors. It is believed that these percentages were usually based on the respective amounts owed to the various suppliers from time to time.

The I.P. owes much of its pre-eminence to the recently retired chairman of its board of directors, John H. Hinman, an old logger from North Stratford, who got his start on the Nulhegan scrimmaging with George Van Dyke, a man-size antagonist.

Next to the tin can, probably nothing is so important and necessary to modern civilization as paper. What, I ask you, would we do without toilet paper, mail-order catalogs, trading-stamps, carboard cartons, newspapers, books, paper bags, paper plates, camera film—not to mention thousands of tons of telephone directories each year and an even larger tonnage of government forms to fill out?

Universities now offer four-year curricula of lectures, laboratory courses, and research on the making of pulp and paper, and graduates of such courses are eagerly employed by interested firms.

Probably the most important event in the history of paper-making, except for the introduction of wood pulp, was the invention in the first years of the nineteenth century of the Fourdrinier machine to make paper in an endless belt instead of in separate sheets. A modern Fourdrinier makes two thousand feet of paper a minute, but the older ones made only five hundred feet. Obsolescence of machinery is costly in this business.

But the possibilities for bright young men are limitless. A few years ago someone discovered a way of utilizing "chips," bits of wood about four inches square, which are now being manufactured by most debarking installations in New England. Sawmills find a constant market in paper mills for "chipped" slabs, at the rate of ten dollars a ton; a thousand board feet of softwood slabs produce a ton and a half.

There are other innovations too. Lighter-than-air balloons are being hooked onto great logs in inaccessible places; they lift them easily over the tree-tops and deposit them gently where directed. Trees are being planted by airplane, acres at a time; they are force-fed, and grow much faster than their grandmothers did. This is being done in British Columbia in 1966, and the practice will doubtless come to New England. Out in western Canada it takes an average of ninety years for firs or cedars to grow from seedlings to log size. So growth is being speeded up by having helicopters scatter urea nitrate in pellet form, to make the trees reach marketable size twenty years earlier than they otherwise would. The pellets have been dropped on stands of trees fifteen to fifty years old.

And just as the saw drove the axe into limbo as the traditional cutting tool for falling trees (in the years 1916–18 the Great Northern Paper Company manufactured its own axe-handles at the Kineo Machine Shop and for the three years the total was 43,498 handles, while in the 1964–65 period there were not two hundred handles used in all their operations), so today the saw is grinding its last teeth in despair. It is going to be replaced by laser (*l*ight *a*mplifiaction *s*timulated *e*mission *o*f *r*adiation). This is an optical electronic device providing beams of extremely high-energy light. It has already been tried out. Talk of a half-inch kerf! The laser doesn't make any kerf at all! In addition to sawing timber, it could also be used to prune high branches easily from the ground, for it produces an intensely hot, needle-pointed beam in excess of a million watts per square centimeters—a sufficient concentration to vaporize all materials.

But one shudders to think of the probable mortality rate among lasermen. I used to know an internationally famous chemist at the Burgess Sulphite Mill in Berlin. His name was Hugh Moore. One day he was explaining a new machine to a visitor. "Now here," he said, "you must be careful not to put in your finger, or it will be cut off." A couple of years later, showing another visitor the plant, he said, "Now here, as you can see by my hand, you must not put in your finger, or it will be cut off," and putting in another finger, he lost that one, too.

But Hugh was a good chemist just the same. I think he was the man who found that if you mixed pine logs with spruce in a digester, the pine simply disappeared. The process suitable for spruce was just too severe for pine.

Another possible substitute for the saw, which is being tried out, consists of powerful jets of water traveling at three times the speed of sound. To obtain this velocity, water (passed through an aperture as small as .01 inch in diameter) is compressed under pressure up to fifty thousand pounds per square inch. The water jets could be used to remove tree limbs quickly when logs were prepared for the mills, while smaller jets could machine furniture parts.

Another, more conventional, invention is just as important because it is immediately available and needs no more experimentation. It is a new saw blade that is said to increase the amount of valuable lumber obtainable from a log, reduce sawdust by more than 70 per cent, produce a smoother cut, and increase the speed of sawing.

Called a Griffsaw, the saw with this new blade will make a kerf only two-thirds as wide as that made by a normal saw. And instead of sawdust, it produces long, fibrous chips usable for making high-quality paper.

Recently a "safety saw" was developed by two professors at the University of Florida. This is a circular power saw with a cutting edge on both sides of the blade, which does not rotate, but oscillates back and forth in a tiny arc. The safety factor lies in the change from rotation to oscillation. The saw cuts by rapid vibration against rigid surfaces only, like wood or plaster. Soft substances, like flesh or clothing, are not rigid enough to produce the vibrations necessary for cutting. Thus the danger of serious injury is eliminated.

As there are more than thirty thousand sawmills in the country, the thing has a likely future.

The latest invention that I know of which is actually in use was described in the Littleton (New Hampshire) *Courier* in February, 1966:

A breakthrough is being undertaken in this area on the problem of utilization and salvage of hardwood timber that will never grow to merchantable quality for saw logs.

As the demand increased, it has become more and more apparent that much good growing timberland is being taken over by poor trees that can never develop, and by inferior species.

Now the Connecticut Valley Chipping Mill, Inc., has invested over $30,000 in equipment designed to utilize this material. A debarker to handle eight foot logs and a sawmill to cut this to usable dimensions has been installed at their plant on the plain below Woodsville. The material will be moved directly to their modern chipping plant where it will be converted into chips suitable for chemical pulp mills.

Logs should be delivered to them on weekdays in eight foot lengths loaded on trucks in a manner so that it can be unloaded by a fork lift truck. Diameters 5″ and up will be accepted.

On March 24, 1966, the same newspaper had a big spread, with pictures, about the Groveton Papers Company (the old Odell Manufacturing Company, which was about to spend seven and a half million dollars to increase the capacity of the paper mill at Groveton, New Hamsphire, "to utilize the generous supply of hardwood available in the region."

The expansion will certainly be a big boost for the economy of the region. I hope and pray that the hardwood will grow fast enough to keep the boost permanent.

L'Envoi

IN some parts of the United States the epic of history has been the filling up of vast spaces, but in New England it has been the long struggle with the wilderness. For generations the forest was the settler's friend and foe—it furnished him with his home and his fuel, but it was an obstacle to his plow and frequently the cause of his death, as is attested on numerous gravestones. I think of two in East Poultney, Vermont. One is for twelve-year-old Paul Marshel, who died in the woods when a sled loaded with wood ran over him. Two years later his father, Ichabod, died when a wagon "wheal" ran over him. There was another pioneer who went out to cut down trees, a log rolled onto his leg, he saw he could not get loose, so he took his sheath-knife and sawed off his foot, bound his shirt around his leg, and hobbled home.

Yet, for all their hazards the forests were from the beginning a source of wealth—at first from furs, then from lumber, and in the last sixty years from pulpwood.

The gloom and mystery of the woods formerly caused them to be regarded as the abiding place of the powers of the unseen, and there is no doubt that the forest has exercised a subtle and profound influence on many generations of New Englanders. The constant danger and stillness made both red men and white men taciturn and helped to develop the fatalism that has often been remarked among Yankee yeomen and that is noticeable among woodsmen everywhere. Many of the distinctive qualities of the Yankee temperament can be accounted for only by the proximity of the forest—of a feeling, unconscious but deep, of the presence of nature.

In short, the woods and the rivers played a large role in the lives of those people and in their contribution to an ever more complex and wealthy civilization. The woodsman was brought up as a child on a farm at the edge of the great forest areas. Almost as soon as he could walk he would get started on his future career by filling the kitchen woodbox and splitting kindling with which to light the morning fire. He learned to build brush and pole fences, he split fence rails, he split shakes with a froe and shaved them with a draw-knife. He learned to make axe-handles, whiffletrees, neck-yokes and crude sleds.

His first actual lumbering experience would be in logging from the family land whatever merchantable timber it contained, and in providing the immense amount of firewood that was required for cooking and for heating a house that was usually not wind-proof.

These activities and many others formed the basic training of the future woodsman. By the time he was sixteen years old he was already becoming a good axeman and was often quite capable of filling a man's place with a cant-dog. Ralph Gould asserts that when he was nine years old (he was born in 1870) he was given a man's axe and ordered to use it. Some people think that is an exaggeration. Nothing of the sort. My own father and grandfather did the same thing, and so did I. Abraham Lincoln in his autobiography states that he was born in 1809 and in 1816 was handed an axe and put to work.

Each year the boy's elder brothers and neighbors would return from the lumber camps, after five months' work, with as much as seventy-five or even a hundred dollars in their pockets, and of course they painted a romantic picture of working and living in the camp, and the sixteen-year-olds would long for the coming fall, when they would join the reckless, generous, and social confrerie.

I think I have shown in these pages why a youth would choose to follow the woods and the river. But what is it that makes the difference between the men who are still cutting down trees today for two or three hundred dollars a week, and the old-time woodsman?

The answer is gasoline and the internal-combustion engine, chain-saws, bulldozers, log-hoists, and huge trucks. Woods work is merely incidental, to today's lumberjack. He could operate just as appropriately digging a canal, building a highway, or demolishing a slum. He's merely using a piece of machinery of which he really knows nothing and cares less. He acquired his training and qualification by playing with a motor-cycle and tinkering with a hot-rod.

So the old-fashioned, red-shirted, two-fisted, calked-booted woodsman of former eras has disappeared, and the tar-paper flaps forlornly on the roofs of the old log camps. Thus

> *The old order changeth, yielding place to new,*
> *And God fulfills himself in many ways,*
> *Lest one good custom should corrupt the world.*

I know that the present-day woods-laborer is economically far better off than the impoverished woodsmen who worked for Van Dyke sixty years ago, and I am glad of it, but as Ernest Martin Hopkins, the late president of Dartmouth College, wrote to me shortly before he died, "I know too that he is a damned sight less interesting!"

Glossary

alligator. A flat-bottomed scow used as a warping-tug. It is provided with a capstan and is run by steam or by gasoline.

bar-room, or *ram-pasture.* Not a saloon, but the bunk-room, or sleeping quarters, of the lumberjacks.

bateau. The double-ended boat (both ends alike) used by rivermen on log drives.

boom. A line of logs connected at the ends and used to confine saw-logs, pulpwood, and the like in the water; also, the enclosed area.

bridle-chain. A chain wrapped around a sled-runner to serve as a brake.

bunkhouse, or *bunk-room.* Sleeping quarters *and* living quarters of the lumberjacks.

calks, or *corks.* Spikes set in the soles of shoes.

cant-dog, or *cant-hook.* About the same as a peavey (*q.v.*) save that it has a blunt tip provided with a "toe," and with an iron ring around it, instead of a steel pike. The term is used in the North Country to designate a peavey.

chance. A working area in the woods. A "good chance" is one that is easy and profitable to log; a "poor chance" is difficult and costly.

cookee. A cook's assistant.

cook-room. The kitchen and dining-room of a camp.

cribber. A horse who gnaws his feeding crib—or anything made of wood.

cruiser. A man who estimates standing timber.

dry-kye, spelled in various ways. Driftwood and dead trees in the water at the edge of a pond or lake.

to fall. To "fall" a tree is to cut it down. Lexicographers and some woodsmen from regions other than New England prefer to use the verb *to fell in* this sense, but in the New England woods *to fall* is a transitive verb, always used instead. The past tense of *to fall* is *fell,* and the past tense of *to fell* is *felled.* The past participle of both verbs is the same, *felled.*

falling-wedge. A flat steel wedge about six inches long and three inches wide, inserted into a saw-kerf to keep the saw from binding, and tapped in farther and farther as the saw continues to penetrate. It also aids in throwing the tree in the desired direction.

flash dam. See *squirt dam.*

to haul. To draw or pull; also, a log jam or a rollway "hauls" when it starts to give way.

heaves. An equine lung malady.

height-of-land line. A height-of-land is the top, crest, or highest point of land between two watersheds. Logs could not be hauled uphill, so the height-of-land where a lumbering operation was going on was marked by a spotted line (i.e., a blazed trail) to help the loggers avoid cutting over the top. To distinguish it from other spotted lines, the spots were often painted red.

holding ground. The place in a pond or lake, or even a river, where logs or pulpwood are "held" in a boom and released as needed.

jill-poke. In a stream, a log with one end stuck in the bank, where it may cause a jam; also, an awkward person.

kennebecker. Any sort of knapsack.

kerf. The cut in a tree or log made by a saw.

killig pole. A pole that every axeman took along when he went out to fall trees. With it he could push against a tree to make it fall in the direction he wished.

landing. The place where logs are assembled for loading or to be rolled into the river. Also, the logs assembled there.

notch. See *undercut.*

peavey. A stout wooden lever about five or six feet long, with a strong steel spike at the end, and an adjustable steel hook. Used for turning logs. Named after the inventor—Joseph Peavey, a Maine blacksmith.

picaroon. A steel hook provided at its butt-end with a thirty-inch handle. Employed to draw pulpwood toward the user.

pike-pole. A long pole with a sharp spike at one end, used to control logs floating free in the water, and especially to guide them through dam-sluices.

plug-boom. A boom the logs of which are connected by ropes passed through holes bored in the ends of the logs, with wooden plugs driven into the holes to wedge the ropes.

pole. See *tongue.*

powder. Dynamite.

pulp, or *pulpwood.* Four-foot bolts of wood, formerly only softwood, used to make pulp paper.

pulp-hook. A short, curved, steel hook with a handle grasped like the bail of a bucket. Used with one hand to draw a stick of pulpwood. Formerly much used in loading pulpwood.

raker tooth. The teeth on a cross-cut saw are arranged in sets of two, three, or four, each set being separated from the next by a cleaner, or raker, for removing the sawdust. The cutting teeth constitute a series of knives which strike the fibers at right angles and sever them on either side of the cut. The cleaners, or rakers, free the severed fibers, which are then carried out in the form of sawdust occupying about six times as much space as the fibers did previous to cutting.

ram-pasture. See *bar-room.*

rear. The tail-end of a log drive. The main drive goes on as fast as possible, leaving to the crew on the rear, perhaps as much as a hundred miles behind, the job of picking up all the stranded logs.

road monkey. A man with the job of keeping a two-sled road clean.

rollway. About the same as a landing (*q.v.*), but the latter may be right on top of the river ice, whence it goes downstream when the ice breaks up in the spring, whereas the rollway is on the bank, whence the logs have to be rolled into the water.

run dam. Tiers of hewn logs built into the bank at the curve of a driving stream. The logs hit it and run past instead of jamming.

scaler. Man who measures ("scales") logs or pulpwood.

scarf. Surface of the undercut (*q.v.*).

sheer-boom. A boom (*q.v.*) strung so as to keep floating logs sheered away from obstructions in the river.

sky-hooker. A top-loader, or cant-dog man, with the job of loading logs onto a two-sled rig.

sluiced. Upset. Said of a team that has accidentally gone off the road and piled up.

to snake. See *to twitch.*

splash dam. See *squirt dam.*

spot. An axe-blaze on a tree. Also, to make such a blaze.

squirt dam, or *splash dam.* Usually built on a small brook tributary to the driving stream and opened to give a "squirt" at strategic moments.

stumpage-inspector. Having sold "stumpage" (i.e., standing timber), the lumber company has an inspector to see that the buyer does not cut trees of the wrong size.

sweenied. Said of a horse whose shoulder muscles are atrophied.

to tend out. The drive boss stations men at places along a stream where he thinks jams may form, to "attend" to keeping the logs moving. The work is called "tending out."

ton timber. In Colonial days it was preferred to ship logs which had been squared or hewn so that they would take up less space. It was estimated that forty cubic feet of such timber made one ton.

Hence, it was commonly called "ton" timber.

tongue, or *pole.* The shaft connected with the front wheels or front runners of a sled or wagon, while the other end is connected by means of a neck-yoke to the harness of the two "wheel" horses (the pair of horses nearest the rig). They are hitched on each side of the shaft. Its purpose is to enable the team to steer the rig.

tote-road. The road going into the woods to a logging camp along which supplies are hauled ("toted") from outside.

to twitch, or *to snake.* A horse drags ("twitches") a log along the ground to its destination without having to be loaded onto a sled.

two-sled road. Not a road where two sleds could pass, but a main logging road down which logs were drawn from the woods on a "two-sled" rig—in effect, two yarding-sleds, one behind the other, connected by an adjustable piece of timber called a reach.

turkey. The meal-sack or handkerchief containing the personal belongings of the lumberjack or riverman; also, the belongings themselves.

turn-and-a-half road. The round trip by a two-sled rig from yard (that is, from camp) to landing was a "turn." A "turn-and-a-half road" was one that the teamster traversed three times in one day, between yard and landing. It required a separate camp at the landing in which he and his horses spent the night. To elaborate: when new territory was to be lumbered, first the cutting area was marked out. Then the landing area was selected. If these were so far apart that the teamsters couldn't make two (or three, or whatever) complete round trips in one day, the main camp was built as near the yard(s) as possible and a small horse-hovel was built at the landing, with a comfortable bunk for the teamster, a stove, and an alarm clock. A tote-team brought in hay and grain for the horses, and the teamster who was to spend the night brought along food in pails and a wooden lunch bucket. He had to do a little cooking, such as making tea, warming up the beans, and the like. There might be half a dozen teams hauling from the main camp, but they took turns at this night-away-from home vigil: while one was doing a turn-and-a-half, the others were making only one trip.

turn-out. It was not feasible to make two parallel two-sled roads (*q.v.*), but sometimes portions of such a road had to be used by other rigs, for instance, tote-teams. Since the loaded two-sleds always had precedence, short semi-circular "turn-outs" were made at strategic spots onto which the other traffic could turn out to avoid the two-sleds.

undercut, or *notch*.   The incision made with an axe into a standing tree, to fall it. It has a horizontal face and a sloping face.

walking-boss.   A lumber company's head man in the woods, theoretically "walking" from one camp to another.

wangan, also spelled *wanigan*, and other ways.   The word is of Indian origin and refers to the outfit—wagons, tents, blankets, cooking equipment—of rivermen on drive; also, the company store at a logging camp.

yard.   The place for assembling newly cut logs, brought by yarding-sleds, before their transportation to the river.

yarding-sled.   A short, heavy sled used to haul logs from the stump to the yard, or sometimes, from the stump to the landing. The butt-ends of the logs were placed on the bunk (the connecting portion between the two runners), while the tips of the logs dragged behind on the ground. Sometimes this position was reversed.

Index